RADICALIZATION TO TERRORISM

WHAT EVERYONE NEEDS TO KNOW®

RADICALIZATION TO TERRORISM

WHAT EVERYONE NEEDS TO KNOW®

SOPHIA MOSKALENKO
CLARK McCAULEY

OXFORD
UNIVERSITY PRESS

OXFORD
UNIVERSITY PRESS

Oxford University Press is a department of the University of Oxford. It furthers
the University's objective of excellence in research, scholarship, and education
by publishing worldwide. Oxford is a registered trade mark of Oxford University
Press in the UK and certain other countries.

"What Everyone Needs to Know" is a registered trademark of
Oxford University Press.

Published in the United States of America by Oxford University Press
198 Madison Avenue, New York, NY 10016, United States of America.

© Oxford University Press 2020

Library of Congress Cataloging-in-Publication Data
Names: Moskalenko, Sophia and McCauley, Clark, authors.
Title: Radicalization to terrorism : what everyone needs to know® /
Sophia Moskalenko and Clark McCauley.
Description: New York, NY : Oxford University Press, [2020] |
Includes bibliographical references and index. |
Identifiers: LCCN 2019032299 (print) | LCCN 2019032300 (ebook) |
ISBN 9780190862596 (hbk) | ISBN 9780190862589 (pbk) |
ISBN 9780190862619 (epub) | ISBN 9780190862602
Subjects: LCSH: Radicalism. | Radicalization. | Terrorism.
Classification: LCC HN49.R33 .M675 2020 (print) | LCC HN49.R33 (ebook) |
DDC 303.48/4—dc23
LC record available at https://lccn.loc.gov/2019032299
LC ebook record available at https://lccn.loc.gov/2019032300s

1 3 5 7 9 8 6 4 2

Paperback printed by LSC Communications, United States of America
Hardback printed by Bridgeport National Bindery, Inc., United States of America

CONTENTS

3. How Are Individuals Radicalized to Join a Terrorist Group?   36

4. How Are Small Groups Radicalized to Use Terrorism as a Tactic?   55

5. How Are Mass Publics Radicalized to Support Terrorism? **62**

6. What Is the Relation Between Radical Ideas and Radical Action? **74**

1

WHAT IS RADICALIZATION?

Who are we to talk about radicalization and terrorism?

In recent years, terrorism and radicalization have (unfortunately) become something of a regular topic in the news, in movies and TV shows, and even in dinnertime conversations. It seems like everyone knows something and has a theory or two to explain the growing number of terrorist attacks around the world. Some blame it on Muslims, some on the news media and the internet, and some on the Central Intelligence Agency and the US government. It has become difficult to judge the quality of all this information. Thus, it makes sense to ask for credentials of the messengers.

We are social psychologists who have dedicated our careers to studying the psychological processes that underlie transitions to radicalism and terrorism. Clark McCauley was among the first psychologists to focus on terrorism, publishing and lecturing on the psychology of terrorism since the 1980s. Sophia Moskalenko became interested in the topic when she was a student of McCauley's at Bryn Mawr College in the 1990s.

Together we have authored a number of articles and books on the psychology of terrorism and radicalization, including the most cited article in the history of the main academic journal that focuses on terrorism, *Terrorism and Political Violence*.[1] As terrorism experts, we are regularly consulted by the media, including radio shows, television news shows, and newspapers, as well as by the US Department of Homeland Security, the US Department of Defense, and other government agencies.

What kind of bias do we bring to the book?

Academics don't like to admit to biases. We like to think we are led only by the facts before us. However, being an academic creates a bias of its own. We approach social problems with the assumption that there is an explanation for what we are seeing—an explanation that is testable and falsifiable, one that can be confirmed by other researchers looking at the same problem.

For those who study terrorism, this bias means that we do not accept explanations of terrorism that border on mystical ("terrorists are evil") or that are too vague to be tested ("terrorists are crazy").

Another bias of academics is to try not to reinvent the wheel. It has been said that the goal of science is to explain as many phenomena as possible with as few ideas as possible. We like to draw upon the body of knowledge already accumulated by social science rather than trying to invent new explanations that relate only to the facts of radicalization and terrorism. In other words, we aim to integrate terrorism research inquiry into the more established branches of social science.

There are good and bad consequences of this scientific approach. The good is that there is an economy of terminology and concepts. If an aspect of terrorism is like something already found in the vast library of social sciences (e.g., violence and aggression), we can take the terms and results of studies that were already done and use these to understand terrorism. The bad consequence is that existing social science may miss something important about how individuals and groups move to political violence. That is, concepts and results from existing social science may miss something unique about the psychology of terrorists. We are willing to accept the possibility of missing something unique in order to obtain the value of applying knowledge already available.

Our bottom line is that the concepts and results of social science are our best tools for understanding terrorism. Even if the data are limited and the theories are still evolving, scientific inquiry continues to refine them, independent of public opinion and political climate. The alternative is to rely on pundits' opinions, on journalists' sensationalist headlines, and on politicians' self-serving interpretations of terrorism. These are not likely to be sufficient to understand the complexities of how normal people are moved to abnormal violence.

What are some of the issues related to radicalization that this book will not cover?

We are not theologians and cannot speculate on whether or how certain sacred texts justify radicalization and terrorism. For psychologists, the more interesting question has to do with what is happening to people who decide to take up radical activity, whether they pledge allegiance to Islam, Buddhism, communism, anarchy, or white supremacy.

Psychology has demonstrated again and again that people tend to justify and intellectualize choices and actions they take for reasons that have little to do with their justifications. When we say we do something for a particular reason, very often we are wrong.

For example, we are more likely to like a stranger we meet while we are holding a warm cup of coffee than a stranger we meet while holding a cold cup of coffee. But, if asked why we liked the stranger, we are not going to mention the cup of coffee, offering instead explanations that have to do with the stranger or with our own character.[2] Violence (riots, violent crimes, and aggression in competitive sports) is more likely on hot days than on cool days, though people who act violently hardly ever notice how the heat affects their behavior.

Similarly, radicals and terrorists sometimes use ideology to justify choices they make for reasons that have little to do with religion or politics.

Because we are not politicians, we have the luxury to leave aside moral questions related to radicalization: Who is right and who is wrong? Who started the violence? Who has the right to escalate violence? Who should be responsible for ending violence? Questions like these are beyond the scope of this book. Both terrorists and states have moral arguments for violence. "Collateral damage" of drone attacks is justified by governments that wage wars in terrorists' homelands; "collateral damage" of suicide bombing is justified by terrorists who wage wars in Western cities. Violence is gruesome and not easy for an average person to undertake. As psychologists, we are drawn to the mystery of how and why people cross over the threshold that makes violence acceptable.

What does radicalization mean?

Radicalization is a process by which individuals, groups, or even large publics become increasingly accepting of violence for a cause. Terrorism is an end point; radicalization is the road that leads to that end point.

Radicalization may begin with thinking about destroying property of, or hurting or even killing someone who represents a group or a cause that the individual finds objectionable. This is the mildest form of radicalization. At one time or another, many of us may have experienced something like radicalization of opinion.

For example, some get so emotionally involved in US presidential elections that they entertain violent thoughts about representatives of the candidate or party they oppose. These thoughts are a symptom of radicalization: radicalization of opinion. These thoughts are just thoughts: Most people will never form a plan for carrying out their violent fantasies, much less act on them.

A small minority, however, will go beyond radical thoughts to engage in radical actions. These individuals might break windows of campaign headquarters, destroy campaign signs, or even physically attack those who express support for a candidate they oppose. Behaviors like these are evidence of radicalization of action.

To understand radicalization to terrorism, both radicalization of opinion and radicalization of action are important to consider. For the purposes of terrorism policing and prevention, however, radicalization of action is more important than radicalization of opinion. We have more to say about the distinction between radicalization of opinion and radicalization of action, and their relationship with terrorism, in Chapter 6.

What is the difference between activists and radicals?

Activists are people who are engaged in nonviolent and legal political action. Radicals are people who participate in actions that are illegal, including violent actions.

Participating in political protests, circulating petitions, carrying political slogans, or speaking one's political mind in public forums are all examples of activism. By contrast, staging illegal sit-ins, clashing with police or security forces, and burning or breaking property are examples of radicalism. Planting explosives and shooting or throwing Molotov cocktails are even more radical actions.

At times, the transition from activism to radicalism is a matter of being at the wrong place at the wrong time. For example, a protest that starts out peacefully is attacked by security forces, and activists who see their friends being battered must choose: to remain nonviolent or to engage in violence to protect their friends. Some might become radical in that moment, reciprocating violence directed against those they care about.

Most activists never become radicals, remaining committed to accomplishing their political goals through socially and legally acceptable means. When asked about activist and radical intentions, people in the United States and other countries generally show a negative relationship between the two. The more one is inclined to engage in activist action, the less likely one is to engage in radical action and vice versa. This inverse relation suggests that activist action may act as a buffer against radicalization, or perhaps that activists believe that legal protest can make a difference but radicals do not believe this.

Does radicalization always lead to terrorism?

No.

Sometimes, instead of leading to terrorism, radicalization leads to a life of crime, where smaller infractions become more and more serious, culminating in violent crime. Perhaps, in the process of radicalization, an individual might join a criminal organization—a street gang or a drug cartel. At the apex of this trajectory is a hardened criminal who uses violence to get money and status, not to achieve political goals.

Radicalization is a term mostly used in the context of terrorism, but the process is general and can be observed in other contexts in which newcomers must habituate to violence. An individual joining the military learns a code of conduct and a value system that justifies a certain kind of violence—that commanded by a military superior. Even in the context of terrorism, radicalization does not necessarily progress to terrorism. Many people become radicalized in thoughts, justifying violence in their minds yet never doing anything about it.

For example, studies show that about 10 percent of US Muslims believe that suicide bombing is "sometimes" or "often" justified in defense of Islam. From the total of about 1 million adult Muslims living in the United States, that percentage corresponds to about 100,000 people. Fewer than 1 percent of these "radicalized in opinion" among the US Muslims have been implicated in any kind of terrorist plot or action.[3]

Thus, 99 percent never move from radicalization of opinion to the more extreme radicalization of action.

Some people might progress from thoughts to small actions in support of terrorism—for example supplying terrorists with money, shelter, or giving them other material support—but draw the line at committing terrorist actions themselves. These individuals have moved past radical opinion to radical action––illegal support for terrorists—but not to terrorist action.

Only a small minority will ever directly engage in terrorist action. For example, in the United States between 2011 and 2015, a total of 11 terrorist attacks were carried out by jihadist Muslims. (For comparison, 78 terrorist attacks were carried out in the United States by non-Muslims in the same time period.)[4]

As atrocious as the idea of justifying suicide bombing is, for the overwhelming majority of those who entertain it, it is just an idea. Only a tiny proportion of those with radical thoughts will engage in radical actions.

Is radicalization always bad?

Not always.

Radicalization is a rite of passage for those who want to serve the nation in the military, police, or security forces.[5] Training for these professions includes building up one's tolerance for violence and willingness to engage in it—for the right reasons. We all benefit from these brave men and women's radicalization in service of our freedom and safety.

Every revolution in history has been a result of radicalization, including the American Revolution. Even today, the US government would classify the Founding Fathers as an extremist movement.[6] Radicalization is what created the American nation.

The revolutions of the Arab Spring that toppled dictatorial regimes, the Georgian, Ukrainian, and Armenian revolutions that toppled Russian-installed puppet governments—all resulted from radicalization of citizens who marched in the streets, facing police weapons, throwing Molotov cocktails, and engaging in combat with pro-government forces. When peaceful democratic processes are compromised, radicalization can offer the only path to freedom.

While radicalization is not always bad, it is always dangerous. Like a weapon, it can defend or protect, but it can easily be misused. The powerful force of radicalization can be manipulated by cunning and calculating powers. Hitler's government included a ministry of propaganda, headed by Joseph Goebbels, whose goal was to radicalize the German populace. It succeeded first in radicalizing Germans against Jews and other minorities within Germany and then against other nations that Germany fought in World War II.

In Chapter 11 on mass identity manipulations (MIMs), we lay out some tools for mass radicalization, many of which were successfully utilized by Goebbels. The unprecedented interconnectedness through the social media that we experience today makes a fertile ground for radicalization through MIMs (e.g., the targeted ads designed by Cambridge Analytica to influence US politics). In Chapter 12 on modern US radicalization, we showcase evidence for radicalization among US citizens and illuminate some of the MIMs and mechanisms responsible for this mass radicalization.

Do people at the extreme of radicalization, like Osama bin Laden or Ayman al-Zawahiri, share the same path of radicalization?

As with many human experiences, radicalization is not the same for every person. Identical events affect different people differently, depending on their genetics, upbringing, and situational factors. Being robbed at gunpoint in a dark alley will cause one person to develop anxiety disorder, another to stock up on ammunition and never leave home without a gun, a third to become obsessed with revenge against the criminal, and a fourth to shake off the incident and move on with their life.

Not only do identical events affect people differently, radicalization may result from different events. While one individual needs to be robbed at gunpoint in order to become a vigilante, for someone else, only hearing about someone being robbed at gunpoint would be enough to set them off on a radical trajectory. So, too, no two radicalization histories are exactly alike.

Understanding radicalization that leads one to become the leader of a terrorist organization, such as Osama bin Laden's trajectory, means considering not just the events that precipitated transition to terrorism but also the individual's character and personality. Terrorists are rare, but terrorist leaders are rarer still. Not only do they themselves radicalize to violent action, they also inspire others to do the same.

Osama bin Laden was shy and religious as a youth, a son of a multimillionaire businessman. Many in his position would have chosen to live an easy life of inherited money, leaving all politics aside. Instead, bin Laden chose to use his money to fight what he saw as a holy war against the apostate governments of Muslim countries and against the United States, which he saw as their backer. His unwavering devotion to his cause, coupled with his considerable wealth, won him admiration of jihadis worldwide and made him the leader of al-Qaeda.

The pivotal moments in bin Laden's radicalization are shared by many other terrorists. Like other terrorists, bin Laden was personally moved by what he saw as victimization of Palestinians by Israel and, more generally, by victimization of Muslims around the world. Like others, his radicalization was fueled by his love for an already radicalized individual— in his case, Dr. Abdullah Azzam, who became his mentor. Like others, bin Laden's radicalization was affected by attraction to the thrill and status of combat: He personally engaged in combat against the Soviets in Afghanistan and became something of a Saudi war hero as a result. Slippery slope, or a gradual progression of increasing commitment to the cause, where each previous action justifies the next, marked his as well as other terrorists' radicalization. The dynamics of the close-knit group of fighters that bin Laden led in Afghanistan and, later, those who made up the kernel of al-Qaeda contributed to bin Laden's radicalization.

What made bin Laden a terrorist is not unique. What made him unique among terrorists is another question. A part of the answer lies within bin Laden's own character—his piety, his willingness to live his beliefs to the fullest no matter the cost, and his steadfastness and devotion to the cause. These may be inborn personality traits. The other part of the answer is perhaps the special way bin Laden was treated by his enemies— first the Arab governments that he opposed, including his home-country government of Saudi Arabia, and then the United States. His provocations made him—one person—the target of powerful enemies. Withstanding attacks directed against him, he grew in the eyes of Muslims sympathetic to his cause. Bin Laden developed skills and persona to stand up to mighty enemies, in the process becoming the international symbol of Islamic terrorism.

Who studies radicalization?

We are psychologists who study radicalization. Along with our colleagues in the same field, we try to understand the mechanisms that move someone from peace to political violence. *Clinical psychologists* are interested in the psychopathologies that may contribute to radicalization. Clinical psychologists explore, among other things, what is psychologically atypical or abnormal about terrorists. *Social psychologists*, like us, are more interested in the circumstances that may result in individuals or groups becoming radical. Social psychologists ask questions such as What were the events or relationships that made thoughts, feelings, or behaviors more radical?

Sociologists consider radicalization in the context of the culture and society in which it arises. They try to uncover the tendencies that affect broader populations and make them more prone to radicalization. Sociologists ask questions such as How do poverty and marginalization affect radicalization rates across communities?

Political scientists view radicalization through the lens of political systems, government policies, and their impacts on populations affected by them. They seek answers to questions such as What are the conditions in which turning to terrorism is a rational choice?

Historians study radicalization as it developed over time, seeking informative patterns. They study, for example, how and why some terrorist groups deradicalized, moving away from political violence, sometimes becoming legitimized as political parties.

Criminologists study radicalization as a form of criminal behavior that may be related to gang violence, assassinations, and school shootings. They trace the dynamics of terrorist incidents and try to relate their occurrence to gun sales, age and education of offenders, rates of incarceration, and proliferation of radical rhetoric in print or internet in particular regions at particular times.

Since the attacks of September 11, 2001 (9/11), the US government has made a concerted effort to bring these different specialists together for collaboration and exchange of ideas. For many years, the authors of this book were part of the National Consortium for the Study of Terrorism and Responses to Terrorism (NC-START) that was created especially for the purpose of bridging disciplinary divides for better understanding of radicalization. Many important studies emerged as a result of the collaborative efforts of NC-START and other interdisciplinary centers.

What are some of the methods used to study radicalization?

Interviews

The most direct method of studying radicalization is to talk with radical individuals. Psychologists, sociologists, and political scientists sometimes conduct interviews with terrorists or their supporters. As you might imagine, this is a very labor-intensive, expensive, and elusive task. First, where can we find terrorists to talk with?

The easiest place to find them is prison. The problem is that, in the United States at least, access to imprisoned terrorists is restricted to those with high security clearance and permission from the relevant government agencies. What's more, the data from these interviews would likely be classified, meaning they would not be available to share with other researchers or the public. Other countries, including Israel, allow researchers access to terrorists in their prisons, and we have learned a great deal from interviews with terrorists conducted by psychologists such as Ariel Merari, who is based in Israel.

In addition, researchers have sought access to former terrorists who have become deradicalized. Researchers such as Donatella della Porta and John Horgan have explored what ex-terrorists report about their own experience of radicalization and deradicalization.

The advantage of interview studies is obvious: You gets answers from the radical individual on how and why they became radicalized, with no guesswork, no filters, and no interpretations. The disadvantage is, well, that people lie. Imprisoned terrorists may want to appear better for a possible parole hearing or an appeal; deradicalized terrorists may want to project a manicured image of themselves for their legacy.

Also, people often can't recall their own motives accurately. Suppose someone asked you how you ended up in a particular school or occupation. Can you really remember what was in your teenage mind?

Case studies

Second best to an actual interview with a living, breathing terrorist is a detailed study of a terrorist's "footprint"—their own blogs, posts, diaries, emails, and letters, as well as friends' and relatives' witness accounts. These data are put together in a case study, which is then analyzed for evidence of trends or characteristics that may explain radicalization. We are among the researchers who have used case studies to understand mechanisms of political radicalization.

One disadvantage of a case study is that it may not answer all the questions the researcher wants to ask. There may simply be nothing in the terrorist's own or her contemporaries' writing to explain why one day she transitioned from giving money to jihadists to becoming one herself. On the other hand, a case study may open unexpected directions for research, whereas an interview is limited by the questions asked and answered.

Surveys

The most frequently used method of social sciences is often used to study radicalization. Some researchers have traveled to areas where radicalization is prevalent, such as Palestine, Yemen, Iraq, or Syria, to administer surveys face to face. Others have used commercial polling agencies that are still present on the ground in those dangerous regions. Because radicalization is not limited to war-torn areas in the Middle East, researchers have solicited survey data from populations at risk in Western countries—for example, Muslims in the United States and Europe. We have used polling data from both Muslim and Western countries to try to learn where radical opinions come from.

One disadvantage of a survey is that the questions have to be very carefully phrased so that they are not threatening for the participant and yet are revealing to the researcher. Some clarity can be lost in framing the questions.

Another disadvantage is that terrorists are few and dangerous; security services would like to know how to spot them, not look at survey responses from people with violent fantasies that will never materialize. Thus, surveys usually provide answers to questions about lower level radicalization of opinion, not about radicalization of action. Advantages of surveys are that they are cheap, fast, and more objective than the qualitative data from interviews or case studies.

Databases

All kinds of data are collected and compiled into databases that can then be used to try to find connections between a variety of individual characteristics and terrorist acts. For example, the Extremist Crime Database (ECDB) compiles data on crimes committed by ideologically motivated extremists in the United States. Using ECDB, criminologists Josh Freilich and Todd Chermach were able to show that the greatest number of terrorist attacks in the United States are not by immigrants from Muslim countries and not even by US-born Muslims. Instead, it is far right extremists who have perpetrated the most terrorist attacks in the United States between 1990 and 2017, with more than twice as many victims as those of jihadist terrorists.[7]

If the far right extremists are more deadly than Islamic extremists, then why is public perception of their relative threat so mistaken? To answer this question, psychologist Erin Kearns and colleagues analyzed a different database, the Global Terrorism Database (GTD), looking at all terrorism attacks on US soil from 2011 to 2015. They then searched the internet for mentions in the news media of each one of the incidents in the GTD for those 5 years. What they found that there were about 4.5 times as many news media stories about Islamic terrorism incidents as there were about any other kind of terrorism. The general public gets the idea about the relative danger of terrorist attack from the amount of media coverage. It is not surprising that the public perception of the threat of

Islamic terrorism is far greater than it should be: It is informed by a disproportionate attention in the news.

Summary

Interviews, case studies, surveys, and database analyses are the most prevalent methods of studying radicalization. Researchers continue to develop new and different ways of researching terrorism and radicalization. For example, linguistic analysis of terrorists' writings and speeches, including internet postings, can identify particular words or phrases that correlate with radicalization. Network analysis can help identify social connections between terrorists and nonradicalized individuals, and trace the degrees of separation that affect radicalization. The organizational structure of terrorist groups is studied to try to understand how hierarchy and leadership affect radicalization of new members. Content and musical structure of songs popular among terrorists are analyzed for elements that make these songs appealing and emotionally mobilizing.

There will be more methods for studying radicalization. With the rapid development of the digital domain, new methods relying on an individual's digital footprint are yet to come. The field of radicalization research is young and growing.

How can researchers believe anything people say on surveys or interviews about radicalization?

It is a fair concern. People lie. When it comes to questions about radicalization, people may lie to avoid detection by security services, to minimize their responsibility for damaging and illegal behaviors, or to project a more socially acceptable persona to the researchers—or even to themselves.

One way that social scientists address the problem of lying is assuring anonymity of responses. Responses to interview questions or to survey questions are coded in a way that makes it impossible for the researchers themselves, not to mention any government officials, to connect participants' answers with their personal information. All participants are assured of anonymity before they agree to be part of the study.

Of course, it is possible that participants wouldn't believe assurances of anonymity. But then, they can always say no to the study—the fact that they agree to participation suggests that they feel safe in answering questions. Participation in itself is evidence of participants' willingness to contribute truthful information.

Second, social scientists who work with survey data have "tricks" they use to maximize truthful responses to sensitive subjects such as radicalization. For example, we often ask questions about radicalization in two formats: personally (i.e., "Do you believe the War on Terrorism is a war on Islam?") and also as *meta-opinion*, or opinion about opinions of others (i.e., "Thinking now not about yourself, but about other US Muslims, how many would you say agree that the War on Terrorism is a war on Islam?"). Meta-opinion questions allow participants to express their true feelings without risking being considered a radical. In places where many fear the operations of security forces (e.g., Palestine), we find a big difference between personal and meta-opinion questions about radical opinions: Meta-opinion responses tend to be more radical than personal responses. Where this is the case, we rely more on meta-opinion responses than on personal responses. On the other hand, in the United States, the difference between personal and meta-opinion responses is so small as to be negligible, suggesting that respondents are answering honestly to personally worded questions.

Third, in dealing with survey data on radicalization, researchers can anticipate the way in which participants would lie, if they were indeed lying. If anything, participants' responses would be minimizing their violent ideas and intentions, not maximizing them. So, to the degree that participants do report radical thoughts or intentions, we can be more confident that they are telling the truth. For instance, if someone reports that they believe suicide bombing is "often justified in defense of Islam," we can be fairly confident this participant is reporting their true feelings. We are therefore much more attuned to the "undesirable" responses on questions about radicalization than to the more "desirable" responses. Research aims at understanding relationships among these radical responses and between these responses and other opinions or personal characteristics. In other words, we try to identify factors that differentiate between those who give more radical responses and those who give less radical ones.

Finally, surveys and interviews are great methods of studying terrorism, but in social science different methods of research are used to triangulate—that is, to subject findings to cross-examination by different people and different methods. Triangulation produces increased confidence in research findings. In other words, data from surveys about radicalization need to be supported by data from interviews and case studies; data from one research team needs to be supported by findings from a different team. When survey data produce results similar to results from case studies or database research—methods that do not rely on self-report—we can be confident that participants' responses to the survey were largely truthful.

How can research on radicalization help the government fight terrorism?

The government needs research to know where best to invest in prevention, where to look for potential danger, how to identify terrorists from the pool of potential suspects, and how to apply deradicalization efforts. Researchers working on radicalization and terrorism are often funded by government grants, meaning that the government can request specific research questions to be investigated and gets the first look at any findings.

Radicalization researchers are interested in many of the same questions as security professionals who fight terrorism. How does someone progress from uninvolved bystander to become a supporter of terrorism? How does one progress from being a supporter on the sidelines to being an active participant in radical actions? If we know what moves someone to radicalization, perhaps we can stop them. Perhaps we can even move people already radicalized back to being less radical. That is the goal of research into radicalization: to identify milestones, situations, and sequences of events that lead people to terrorism so that security services can be alert for these markers and use them for identification of dangerous people and groups as well as for deradicalization efforts.

Some researchers study effects of government interventions on radicalization in populations at risk. For example, when the government implements a campaign such as "see something, say something," how do radical opinions and intentions change among populations at risk of radicalization after the campaign's implementation? Knowing the effectiveness of government efforts helps ensure that taxpayer dollars are wisely spent.

Other researchers identify spikes or drops in numbers of terrorist attacks and then try to understand what caused them. Were new antiterrorism policies implemented just before the drop in terrorist incidents? Have there been influxes of migration into or from the region just before the spikes? Are certain political events likely to inspire radical action? Since President Trump took office in 2017, right wing terrorist attacks have increased in the United States.[8] In Chapter 12, we consider some causes of this increase. Being able to predict terrorist attacks helps prepare for them and possibly prevent them.

Still other researchers look at cases of known terrorists for clues that could help identify individuals who pose a risk of becoming terrorists. Is there something like a profile of a terrorist? Knowing what marks a terrorist helps channel intelligence attention to the most dangerous individuals.

Social scientists around the globe are working in close co-operation with government officials tasked with fighting terrorism. Research findings are presented to government officials at conferences, through "white papers" (short versions of research papers) and briefings. Terrorism is a global threat. Researchers and governments work together to meet the threat.

2

WHAT IS TERRORISM AND WHO BECOMES A TERRORIST?

What kind of violence is called terrorism?

There is no one accepted definition of terrorism. There is, however, a general agreement among government definitions that terrorism is either violence or a threat of violence whose purpose is to coerce a government or citizens. Another common characteristic of government definitions is their emphasis on terrorists' intent to terrorize: scare, instill fear, or intimidate. Definitions of terrorists and terrorism used by the United Nations, the United Kingdom, and various US government agencies are below.

The proposed United Nations Comprehensive Convention on International Terrorism:

Any person commits an offence within the meaning of this Convention if that person, by any means, unlawfully and intentionally, causes:
   (a) Death or serious bodily injury to any person; or
   (b) Serious damage to public or private property, including a place of public use, a State or government facility, a public transportation system, an infrastructure facility or the environment; or
   (c) Damage to property, places, facilities, or systems referred to in paragraph 1 (b) of this article, resulting or likely to result in major economic loss,

> when the purpose of the conduct, by its nature or
> context, is to intimidate a population, or to compel
> a Government or an international organization to
> do or abstain from doing any act.[1]

Because of a disagreement about whether this definition would apply to government forces and government leaders, it has been under discussion at the United Nations since 2002.[2]

The United Kingdom's Terrorism Act 2000 defined terrorism as follows:

(1) In this Act "terrorism" means the use or threat of action where:
  (a) the action falls within subsection (2),
  (b) the use or threat is designed to influence the government or to intimidate the public or a section of the public, and
  (c) the use or threat is made for the purpose of advancing a political, religious or ideological cause.
(2) Action falls within this subsection if it:
  (a) involves serious violence against a person,
  (b) involves serious damage to property,
  (c) endangers a person's life, other than that of the person committing the action,
  (d) creates a serious risk to the health or safety of the public or a section of the public or
  (e) is designed seriously to interfere with or seriously to disrupt an electronic system.[3]

In the United States, Title 22 of the US Code of Federal Regulations, Section 2656f(d), defines terrorism as "premeditated, politically motivated violence perpetrated against noncombatant targets by subnational groups or clandestine agents, usually intended to influence an audience."[4] The US State Department uses this definition for its yearly reports on terrorist activity, and the Central Intelligence Agency likewise uses this definition. Note that this definition is the only one that does not assume an intent to coerce by fear.

The US Federal Bureau of Investigation defines terrorism as "the unlawful use of force or violence against persons or property to intimidate or coerce a government, the civilian population, or any segment thereof, in furtherance of political or social objectives."[5]

The US Department of Defense defines terrorism as "the unlawful use of violence or threat of violence to instill fear and coerce governments or societies. Terrorism is often motivated by religious, political, or other ideological beliefs and committed in the pursuit of goals that are usually political."[6]

Finally, the US Federal Emergency Management Agency defines terrorism as follows:

> Terrorism is the use of force or violence against persons or property in violation of the criminal laws of the United States for purposes of intimidation, coercion, or ransom. Terrorists often use threats to:
> Create fear among the public.
> Try to convince citizens that their government is powerless to prevent terrorism.
> Get immediate publicity for their causes.[7]

Most of definitions can be summarized by saying that terrorism is violence designed to terrorize!

Is terrorism something old or something new?

If we take the two common themes from current definitions of terrorism—violence (or its threat) and an intent to terrorize—we can find examples of terrorism reaching as far back as the Roman Empire. Roman emperors—Gaius Marius, Lucius Cornelius Cinna, and Mark Anthony— displayed severed heads of their political enemies, skewered on pikes, on the speaking platform from which they addressed the masses.

This tradition of terrorizing the public through display of heads of notorious individuals continued in the Western world until the late 1700s. Following an unsuccessful revolt by Bohemia against Austrian nobility, the Hapsburgs publicly executed leaders of the revolt and displayed the heads of 12 of them in iron cages hung on bridges. This act of terrorism was successful: No revolt against the Hapsburgs was attempted by Bohemians for another 300 years.

The term terrorism dates back to the French Revolution. The revolutionary government was threatened by a brewing civil war and by foreign armies on French borders. To suppress dissent, the government decided to make "terror" the order of the day (September 5 Decree, 1793), starting what has become known as "the Reign of Terror." It included harsh measures such as confiscation of property and imprisonment for anyone considered an enemy of the revolution, including priests, nobles, rich merchants, and peasants. With judicial process later simplified, enemies or critics of the government were executed without a trial.

Thus, the term terrorism was originally used to describe violence of the state against its citizens. Today, however, terrorism is usually used to describe non-state actors' violence against the state or its citizens.

Modern-day terrorism (non-state political violence) was pioneered in the 1870s by the Russian group People's Will: Russian students who wanted more than the political reforms czar Alexander II was promising. Especially, the young activists wanted more rights for Russian peasants. Over the course of its conflict with the Russian government, People's Will transformed from an activist protest group into a terrorist group. Its tactics included targeted assassination of government officials, planting of bombs, and suicide missions, one of which succeeded in killing Alexander II.

Terrorism, therefore, is not something new. Even in its modern use, terrorism and most of its tactics are over 100 years old.

What is the difference between terrorism "from above" and terrorism "from below"?

Terrorism from above is also called state terrorism. In terrorism from above, a government engages in campaigns of violence against its citizens with the intention to coerce them or intimidate them, as the French Revolutionary government did against French citizens.

Terrorism from below is also called non-state terrorism. In terrorism from below, non-state actors engage in violence against the state, or against some of its citizens, in order to change the government or government policies.

What are three big examples of state terrorism?

Communist China

The biggest example of state terrorism comes from Mao Zedung's post-revolution China. Mao killed an estimated 65 million people[8] in his effort to keep the population of China under control and in compliance with the communist government's agenda. Intellectuals presented the biggest threat, and Mao boasted of killing 46,000 academics.

But academics were not the only victims of Mao's state terrorism. In the Great Leap Forward, millions of peasants died from famine when bad agricultural practices were combined with misdistribution of food. The Cultural Revolution followed, and anyone who appeared not in compliance with the government's Marxist agenda, either by trade (artists) or by looks (dressed in a way that made them stand out), were beaten and sent to concentration camps. Millions died in the camps from starvation, harsh living conditions, and 14-hour workdays.

Soviet Union

Another example of state-based terrorism comes from the Soviet Union. In the years after the Bolshevik revolution, Vladimir Lenin's government instituted Red Terror—a practice of fighting dissent by relentless violence. An estimated 28,000 were executed without trials. Collectivization followed, and an estimated 10 million peasants who were considered too well-off were declared "kulaks" and sent to Gulag concentration camps in Siberia or killed.

The Great Purge that came after collectivization targeted anyone who was deemed an "ideological enemy" for their background (religious, ethnic, or educational), their expressed dissent, or their connection to another ideological enemy. "Enemies of the state" were imprisoned or killed. An estimated 2 million people died in the Great Purge. Genocides of whole nations within the Soviet borders were perpetrated through artificial famines, with the death toll estimated at 10 million people.[9]

Iraq

A more recent example of state terrorism comes from Saddam Hussein's Iraq. Notoriously, Hussein's Baathist government engaged in torture, persecution, and widespread murder of Kurds. Kurds were stripped of their Iraqi nationality and declared Iranians. Their ancestral lands were destroyed by the government—marshes turned into a desert—and they faced the choice of either dying of thirst or relocating to barb-wire surrounded "modern villages" without proper sanitation, water access, or prospects for employment. Systematic torture and executions led to deaths of an estimated 25,000 Kurds. Poison gas was used by Saddam's regime to attack the city of Halabja, populated mainly by Kurds. Chemical weapons, mass executions, extreme deprivation, and torture resulted in the deaths of thousands more Kurds in northern Iraq during the Anfal Campaign. Human Rights Watch estimates that about 100,000 Kurds died as a result of Baathist government terrorism against them,[10] which only ended when the United States invaded Iraq in 2003 and executed Saddam Hussein.

Kurds were not the only ones targeted by Hussein's government's terror campaign. Severe penalties, including branding, amputations, and death, were instituted for a large number of offenses, many of which were specified by Sharia law. Journalists, dissidents, and businessmen were disappeared, tortured, and killed.

Summary

State terrorism is designed to maintain control over citizens through violent and terrorizing means. The three examples above illustrate just how horrific, and how deadly, these means can be.

What are three examples of non-state terrorism?

Modern Jihadist Terrorism

One big example of non-state terrorism is, unfortunately, well known to those who lived through the attacks of 9/11: al-Qaeda. Headed by Osama bin Laden and Ayman al-Zawahiri, al-Qaeda got its start fighting Soviets who had invaded Afghanistan. After the Soviets left, bin Laden began to attack US military and diplomatic targets abroad, then moved to attack the US homeland. The attacks of 9/11 were the pinnacle of al-Qaeda's operations. Almost 3,000 people were killed and more than 6,000 wounded. In the wake of 9/11, concerted efforts of the United States and its allies effectively suppressed al-Qaeda's operations.

With al-Qaeda's leaders imprisoned, assassinated, or in hiding, jihadist terrorism found another representative: ISIS (Islamic State of Iraq and Syria) or IS (Islamic State). Unlike al-Qaeda, ISIS did not form around one leader and his agenda. Instead, it formed around disgruntled Baathists and military officers who lost their jobs after the US-led intervention removed Saddam Hussein. Paul Bremer, the US Viceroy in Iraq, banned members of the ruling Baathist party from all but the lowest government positions. He also disbanded the Iraqi army, putting about 250,000 armed men on the streets, unemployed. As a result of its origins in reactions to invasion and defeat, ISIS has a different structure than al-Qaeda, and different goals, too.

Where al-Qaeda wanted to fight against Western interference in Muslim countries, ISIS sought immediately to form a new Islamic state. It began as a terrorist group but captured broad areas and collected taxes, policed streets, and performed other functions usually performed by states. Like al-Qaeda, ISIS wants to establish Sharia law. Unlike al-Qaeda, ISIS does not shrink from attacking ordinary Muslims, executing Muslims who disagree with its rule, and shelling Muslim towns, hospitals, and schools. ISIS thereby combines elements of state terrorism and non-state terrorism.

As we write this in 2019, ISIS appears to be retreating from insurgency to an underground terrorist group.

Right-wing terrorism

Although the news media give the impression that Jihadist terrorism is the main terrorism threat, this does not reflect the facts. Journalists simply report stories about Islamic terrorism disproportionally more than they do stories about any other type of terrorism.[11]

In fact, since 9/11, right-wing terrorism attacks have been both more numerous and more deadly than Jihadist terrorism in the United States.[12] From 2008 to 2016, there were 115 right-wing terrorist plots in the United States, with one-third of them foiled through the efforts of law enforcement. Compare this to 63 cases of Islamic terrorism in the United States in the same period, with three-fourths of these plots foiled. Of all terrorist incidents that were carried out on US soil from 2008 to 2016, twice as many right-wing incidents produced fatalities as did Islamic terrorism incidents. In short, right-wing terrorism is the most prevalent and deadliest terrorist threat to the United States today.

Right-wing extremism has many faces and names. The most easily identifiable representatives are neo-Nazis, whose goal is to limit what they see as undue influence of minorities and Jews in the United States. Their attacks are usually directed against African Americans, as was, for example, the 2015 Charleston church shooting, in which White supremacist Dylan Roof shot and killed nine people, all African Americans.[13]

Right-wing terrorists also target other minorities. In 2017, in Charlottesville, Virginia, a White supremacist torch-lit rally with anti-Semitic chants ended in three fatalities when a car rammed into a crowd of people protesting the march.[14]

Between 2016 and 2018, right-wing attacks have increased in the United States. In Chapter 12, we have more to say about this trend and what might be responsible for it.

The Irish Republican Army

The Irish Republican Army (IRA) is a nationalist terrorist organization whose goal has been a united and independent Ireland. The IRA started at the beginning of the 20th century, when its members refused to be conscripted into the British Armed Forces to fight in World War I. Later, the IRA fought in the War of Independence against the United Kingdom, which resulted in an island divided between a free state of Ireland and a state of Northern Ireland that is still part of the United Kingdom. The IRA continued its fight against the United Kingdom in Northern Ireland using a variety of tactics, including targeted assassinations and planting bombs in buildings and cars.

Over time, the IRA fractionated into a number of terrorist groups, all claiming to fight for the same cause, even as they violently competed among themselves. Thus, the Provisional IRA, Continuity IRA, Official IRA, and Real IRA occasionally killed members of rival terrorist groups or their supporters in addition to their main targets: Royal Ulster Constabulary, the British Army, and British institutions and economic targets.

Beginning in the 1980s, various factions of the IRA were involved in peace talks among themselves and with the British government. These efforts came to fruition with the 1996 ceasefire agreement among the IRA factions. In turn, the ceasefire led to negotiations with the British government that resulted in the Good Friday Agreement, signed on April 10, 1998, in Belfast. The agreement included a multiparty agreement by most of Northern Ireland's political parties, and an international agreement between the Irish and UK governments. Among points agreed to were decommissioning of militants' weapons, cultural rights and civil rights, sovereignty, and release of prisoners. Two separate referendums showed support for the agreement among Northern Irish voters, and the agreement went into effect on December 2, 1999. The IRA was dropped from the international list of terrorist groups.

The IRA offers an example of how a terrorist group can turn away from violence. Other paths to deradicalization are discussed later in this book. For the IRA, negotiations with the government it fought resulted in its gaining legitimacy, allowing the tactics of violence to be replaced by open political competition for votes.

This success story is not without a caveat, however. After the implementation of the Good Friday Agreement, Real IRA issued a call to arms in 2000, and a number of bombings and bombing threats—as well as shootings of police officers and government officials—have since been carried out by Real IRA. Some began to refer to the new terrorist threat in Ireland as the New IRA.

Which is more dangerous, state or non-state terrorism?

State terrorism is much deadlier than non-state terrorism. The numbers of people murdered by the terrorist regimes of Mao,

Stalin, and Hussein are in the millions. Non-state terrorists claim perhaps thousands of victims.

Looking at only the 20th century, Rummel (1996) estimated that governments killed about 170 million people (not including about 34 million who died in battle). He contrasted these numbers with the estimated 500,000 killed by non-state groups: guerilla fighters, terrorists, and other non-state groups. This is a ratio of about 260 to 1, with states doing the vast majority of the killing.

As we discuss radicalization to terrorism, in its present-day meaning as violence by non-state actors against the state, it is important to keep in mind the scale of the problem. Terrorism is a serious threat. But it is a molehill on the mountain of mass political murders perpetrated by states.

Are terrorists just crazy?

No.

Researchers have used both qualitative and quantitative methods to answer this question. Qualitative studies have analyzed terrorists' detailed personal histories as well as data from interviews with terrorists. Quantitative studies have compiled medical histories, psychiatric evaluations, and responses to surveys from terrorists who have been captured and imprisoned.

Both qualitative and quantitative studies have concluded that terrorists do not have psychological problems (psychopathologies) any more than non-terrorists do. Terrorists are no more prone to depression, anxiety, bipolar disorder, schizophrenia, dissociative disorder than the rest of the population. For the most part, terrorists are "normal."

Especially among group-based terrorists (who are the majority of terrorists), participating in secretive social groups requires planfulness, responsibility, consistency, and reliability that would be impossible to maintain while suffering from a psychiatric illness. Terrorists like bin Laden or al-Zawahiri masterminded elaborate plots and controlled a large organization while under siege from powerful governments. Not a mark of psychopathology, rather effective terrorism suggests psychological stability and resiliency.

There are, however, notorious terrorists who have received psychiatric diagnoses (for example, Ted Kaczynski, the "Unabomber," was diagnosed with paranoid schizophrenia). Psychopathology seems to be more common among lone wolf terrorists such as the Unabomber. We discuss lone wolf terrorists in Chapter 7.

And yet the idea of terrorists being crazy persists in popular discourse, in the news media, and in some professional writings. Why?

One possibility is that insanity is an easy explanation for a complex and frightening problem. When we say someone is crazy, we don't need to try to understand their behavior or predict their actions. We add them to the list of unfortunate things beyond our control: earthquakes, tsunamis, hurricanes, and now terrorists—these are bad, we try to avoid them, we can only hope these perils do not strike us or our loved ones.

Another possibility is that labeling terrorists "crazy" separates us from them: They are crazy, and we are normal; we are nothing like them. It may seem irrational, but the desire to put barriers between ourselves and all things unpleasant and scary runs deep in human beings. We especially loathe to see our own capacity for violence that might make us like them.

Finally, labeling terrorists crazy means they and only they are the cause of their actions. As a result, we don't look for anything in their personal situations or in the political situation that may have contributed to terrorists' radicalization. We certainly don't think about how political interventions might change the situation to reduce radicalization and terrorism. If terrorists are *not* crazy, then perhaps we can do something toward deradicalizing them. Then again, whatever such action would be, it would require vastly more effort than merely saying "They are crazy."

The desire to chalk terrorism up to insanity is understandable. However, research has been clear: Terrorists are psychologically no different from us. This book offers a way of understanding radicalization and terrorism that does not include denial.

Are terrorists psychopaths?

Psychopathy, or antisocial personality disorder, is a psychiatric diagnosis. The section above considered the more general question about whether terrorists are crazy. This more specific question, whether terrorists are psychopaths, can be answered in the same way: No.

Psychopathy is a personality disorder that is marked by low impulse control, disregard for other people, low empathy, irritability, aggressiveness, irresponsibility, instability in home, work, and social life, deceitfulness, and lack of remorse. The diagnosis requires that at least some symptoms appear in childhood.

You can already see how this condition would make it impossible for someone to become a group-based terrorist. Psychopaths would be unable to maintain secrecy, be dependable, consistent, reliable, in tune with other group members, or respectful of the group's hierarchy and goals. This would make a psychopath a liability for any terrorist group, and subject to quick rejection.

Even to become a lone wolf terrorist, one must be passionate and consistent about some political issues; psychopaths are only consistent about their selfish desires in the moment. Terrorists give up many things for their radical beliefs: a "normal" life and life span, expectation of safety, social and family connections. Psychopaths don't put anything or anyone above themselves; giving up something they enjoy does not fit with their mindset.

Therefore, as with other psychological disorders, psychopathy, or antisocial personality disorder, is not more prevalent among terrorists than it is among the rest of us.

Do terrorists love hurting others?

Here, some qualification is needed. It is true that some terrorists seem to revel in the thrill of gruesome beheadings, killing of civilians, torture, and mutilation. Abu Musab al-Zarqawi, the butcher of Baghdad, seems to have been just this type of a terrorist. He did not care too much for political platforms or ideology, outsourcing these to his more bookish sidekicks. All he wanted was the thrill of violence and the power that violence gave him—terrorizing not only terrorist targets but also his subordinates in the terrorist group.

Blood-thirsty and power-hungry individuals such as Zarqawi exist, unfortunately, everywhere. In the United States, they may seek a life of crime, joining street gangs or criminal networks where their actions bring them rewards in the form of status and power. In war-torn countries such as Congo or Columbia, they may join guerilla armies or insurgencies. And in places like Iraq, they may join terrorist groups or militias.

Overall, however, terrorists are no more sadistic than soldiers. They see violence against civilians as the only means available to them (as they don't have the military power of a state) to force the powerful into acknowledging their claims. Violence to them is a means to an end.

Terrorists justify violence by pointing out that governments kill vastly more civilians than they do. In addition, terrorists argue that civilians they kill are not completely innocent: They voted for the politicians who ordered policies that victimized those the terrorists care about, and they funded these policies by their taxes.

Whether or not one agrees with these justifications, the fact is that terrorism is a tactic of the weak against the strong. However it may appear to those living in the relative safety and prosperity of the West, terrorists see themselves as fighting a war. In wars there are casualties, including civilian casualties. That's how they see it.

Are they doing it for money?

There has yet to be an individual who has made a fortune by terrorism. (Here, we set aside criminal gangs that can make big money by terrorizing business owners and competitors.) Terrorism is an expensive enterprise. Explosives and weapons cost money. Training camps cost money. Fake documents and safe houses cost money. Communications, including traveling for meetings, cost money. For individuals who dedicate themselves to terrorism full-time, these expenses can be staggering.

Terrorists must therefore care about money. Sometimes they depend on sponsors: Osama bin Laden used his considerable wealth to sponsor al-Qaeda, including the 9/11 attacks on the United States.

With governments cracking down on banking transactions that may benefit terrorism, donations have become sparser and more difficult to transfer. Wire transfers are easy for banks to red flag and report to security agencies; they are also easy to trace and use in court as evidence. Fewer individuals are willing to donate when donations are all but certain to result in quick convictions and severe sentences.

A strong source of terrorist funding is kidnapping to extract ransom from families and governments. The US government famously does not negotiate with terrorists, and if private citizens of the United States or US-based companies pay off a terrorist group, the US Justice Department is required by law to prosecute them for funding terrorism.

Other governments, however, including those of Germany, France, Italy, and Spain, do pay terrorists for release of their citizens. The United Kingdom's former Prime Minister David Cameron estimated that ISIS received "many tens of millions of dollars"[15] from ransom payments. *The New York Times* reported that ISIS collected $66 million in ransom payments in 2014 alone.[16] Citing US government official sources, the report concluded that ransom money is used to fund terrorism rather than to enrich individual terrorists.

Are terrorists in it for the money? It is difficult to learn how much terrorists spend on themselves—for fancy houses, fancy meals, or fancy women. But the costs of underground life, hiding from government power, are clearly high. It seems unlikely that terrorists are in it for the money when so much of what money can buy is out of reach. For ISIS, at least, the report is that they are creative about raising money but that the money goes to the cause rather than to individuals. Money, like violence, is a means to an end for terrorists.

What, then, is the end they seek? There is no one answer, as every individual terrorist might have his or her own reason. Some radicalize because they want revenge; others because they want power and status; and still others because they seek close-knit companionship that a terrorist group offers. We discuss 12 such reasons in Chapters 3–5.

3

HOW ARE INDIVIDUALS RADICALIZED TO JOIN A TERRORIST GROUP?

How can personal grievance radicalize an individual?

Imagine you have been wronged. Imagine the person or people who wronged you represent a superior power, like the government. Imagine that your pain is too great to just forget about it and continue living your life as if nothing has happened. Maybe the same power hurt you before. Maybe you have seen others suffer like you did. Maybe you have heard others fume about similar injustices, and now your own experience fits with the story you have heard. For some people, a personal grievance, a first-hand experience of injustice and suffering, can lead to radicalization.

This is what happened to Mohamed Bouazizi, a Tunisian street vendor who, on December 17, 2010, was insulted by a female police officer for not having a proper permit. Allegedly, the female officer confiscated his scales, slapped him in the face, spat on him, and made a slur against his dead father. According to Bouazizi's family, this was not the first time the government officials harassed him; on many prior occasions, they confiscated Bouazizi's fruit cart, produce, and money, demanding bribes that he could not afford. Corruption in Tunisia was a sad and common story.

For Bouazizi, the incident on December 17 was apparently the last drop that overfilled the cup of his patience. Bouazizi attempted to get his scales back from the city officials but was rebuffed. In response, he doused himself with gasoline in the middle of traffic in the busy city center and, with the words "How do you expect me to make a living?" set himself ablaze.

Bouazizi's personal grievance—his experience with the government officials who repeatedly harassed and humiliated him—turned into a radical action: public self-immolation in protest of the government's corruption and injustice. His action embodied the frustration and anger with the government that many in Tunisia shared. As a result, Bouazizi's death ignited a series of public protests, including self-immolations, throughout the Muslim world, and started what became known as the Arab Spring. In Tunisia, as in other Muslim countries, these protests culminated in revolutions.

Personal grievance is perhaps the mechanism of radicalization that is easiest to understand. Although few would go as far as setting themselves on fire, many can relate to the experience of anger and shame that comes with humiliation by those with power and impunity. In places where justice cannot be achieved through peaceful and legal means because the whole system is corrupt, personal grievance can lead to radicalization in action.

In their accounts of radicalization, many Chechen Black Widows recall the murders of their menfolk—husbands, brothers, and fathers—as pivotal points in their transition to terrorism. Unable to get justice from the Russian government responsible for the murders, they turned to terrorism for revenge.

How can political grievance radicalize an individual?

Political grievance is, at a first glance, more difficult to relate to than personal grievance. Individuals radicalized by political grievance suffer no injustices or pains themselves. They may be miles or continents away from where the injustices take place. Yet distance means nothing to someone who feels empathy for victims and anger at perpetrators. Individuals radicalized by political grievance become so moved by the plight of another that they take it upon themselves to do something about it.

Radicalization by political grievance is what moved a young Canadian Information-Technology specialist to terrorism despite having a loving family, a well-paying job, and a fiancé he hoped to marry. Momin Khawaja was the third of five children of Pakistani immigrants; his father was a professor, and his mother a homemaker. Khawaja's early years were spent in Arabic countries, where his father held academic appointments. The family settled in Ottawa when Khawaja was 14 years old.

His family life was happy. When arrested for terrorism at age 25, he was still living at his parents' house—not because he could not afford his own place (he made good money as a software developer) and not because he was not socially adept (he had friends and a fiancé) but because he loved his mother and siblings and enjoyed the perks of having the women of the house take care of him.

Khawaja became radicalized by watching news and internet videos that depicted Muslims around the world suffering at the hands of Western powers (we do not here vouch for the accuracy of these videos, but there are many to be found on the internet). Watching Muslim women being assaulted by Westerners, watching Muslim children suffer in wars that the West brought to their homelands, watching Muslims in Palestine humiliated at Israeli checkpoints, Khawaja felt their pain as his own.

Sure, he was safe and secure in Canada. But what did that matter when so many of his "brothers and sisters" were suffering overseas? Not only did Khawaja feel their pain, he felt guilty for not doing anything to help. Another kind of videos radicalized him to action.

Khawaja wrote to his fiancé and in his diary how much he enjoyed watching videos of Chechens brutally attacking Russian soldiers. Watching these Muslim fighters take their anger out on their enemies filled him with pride and a desire to do his part to avenge injustices against Muslims.

Khawaja started to act on his radical thoughts and feelings, first, by donating money to terrorist groups overseas. These financial transactions through a third party helped law enforcement zoom in on Khawaja. Although financial support of his ideological commitment was satisfying and gave his life new meaning, Khawaja realized he wanted to do more.

After the 9/11 attacks, the United States and its Western allies were at war with the Taliban in Afghanistan. Khawaja decided to travel to the conflict zone to join the fight on the Taliban's side. He arrived in Pakistan in 2002, too late to join the Taliban, who were retreating under US attacks in Afghanistan. However, on that journey he met some people who were part of a UK-based terrorist cell. Khawaja became part of a plan to detonate fertilizer bombs in several busy areas of London. Khawaja's role was to design and build detonators and remote controls that would activate the bombs.

The plan was never carried out. The terrorists were apprehended before they could act. Khawaja, convicted of terrorism, is serving a life sentence in a Canadian prison.

In theory, personal and political grievances are distinct paths to radicalization. In practice, it is often difficult to separate the personal from the political. Khawaja's reactions to videos he watched on the internet were intense and personal. He called the victims in the videos his brothers and sisters. He shared their pain and ached for revenge.

Although few of us move from empathy to radical action, most of us can relate to feeling intensely someone else's suffering and wanting to do something about it. Most humans have the capacity to care for others, empathize with others' pain, and identify with groups and individuals we don't know personally. Whether it is your country, your ethnic group, or your religious community, chances are there is a group that you would be willing to sacrifice for, to fight for, and even to die for. After the terrorist attacks of 9/11 against the United

States, there was a surge in men and women joining the US military. Many new recruits felt the suffering of the victims of the 9/11 attacks as their own, and wanted to do something to avenge it.

Among terrorists, political grievance is one of the most common mechanisms of radicalization. Even when the grievance is personal, some political framing usually takes place before radical action is possible. The phrase, "the personal becomes political, and the political becomes personal" is an accurate description of the blending of personal and political grievances that lead to radicalization to terrorism.

Political grievance is also another way of describing the role of ideology in radicalization. For Khawaja, the mobilizing force was the vivid images of suffering Muslims. These videos were not random. Someone recorded and edited these videos. Someone posted them online, likely with the intention of radicalizing those who would watch them. The Islamic State of Iraq and Syria (ISIS) is infamous for their clever use of internet videos to radicalize Muslims around the world, soliciting donations and leading some to leave their old lives behind to travel to Syria and Iraq to join ISIS.

Internet videos such as the ones produced by ISIS tell a story. The story is carefully constructed by those who record the video, edit it, overlay it with some inspiring music, and insert grabbing captions. This story is ideological: It frames individual suffering in terms of a larger political problem.

When one person's suffering is interpreted to exemplify the suffering of many others, a street vendor's squabble with a police officer can turn into a revolution. Political grievance is possible when a story of suffering becomes a symbol of a political problem and a call for action.

How can slippery slope radicalize an individual?

The idea of the psychological power of a slippery slope belongs to psychologist Stanley Milgram, who wanted to understand how millions of ordinary Germans could be complicit in the Holocaust. In laboratory experiments, Milgram exposed ordinary Americans to a situation that, for two out of three participants, led them to participate in torturing an innocent man. What was this situation, and what was so powerful about it?

Participants were asked to be part of a learning experiment. In a rigged drawing, they were assigned the role of the teacher, and the "other participant" (actually an accomplice of the experimenter) was given the role of the learner. The learner was strapped to an electric shock generator. In an adjacent room, the teacher had the controls for the electric shock generator. The job of the teacher was to deliver ever-increasing electric shocks to the learner for every mistake the learner made on a memory test.

The learner made lots of mistakes. Quickly the levels of shocks went up from the initially mild 15 volts. The learner grunted, moaned, and complained as the shocks escalated. At 300 volts, the learner screamed, complained of his heart aching, and demanded to be let out. After that, the learner made no more sounds, as the voltage of successive shocks went all the way up to 450 volts, past the "danger, severe shock" marker on the generator. (In reality, there were no shocks; it was a performance by the learner for the real subject of the experiment—the "teacher.") Two-thirds of all participants, regardless of gender, age, education level, or income, proceeded to the highest level of the generator: 450 volts. They only stopped shocking the victim when the experimenter told them to stop.

The results of the study were, well, shocking. Teaching college undergraduates about Milgram's research, we ask students how many think they would have gone all the way to the highest shock. Nobody does. Milgram asked psychology professionals unfamiliar with his results—psychologists, psychiatrists, and psychology graduate students—to estimate the proportion of the population who, being put in the study as "teachers," would go all the way to 450 volts. The estimates were about 1 percent: The psychology professionals estimated that was the proportion of psychopaths in the population.

Yet Milgram demonstrated that these estimates were wrong—that the experts discounted some important elements of the situation that Milgram constructed in his experiment. What then were these elements that can make "normal" people do radical things—inflict violence on a person who has done them no harm?

Milgram pointed out two culprits for his participants' behavior. First, there was an authority in the situation: an experimenter in a white lab coat who was dispassionate yet persistent in his demands that participants continue with the procedure no matter what. When asked, "Who is responsible for what happens here?" the experimenter always said, "I am." It seems that to some degree, participants in Milgram's experiment delegated their own agency and moral judgment to the authority: the experimenter.

This is not terribly satisfying for those of us who wish to understand human motivation. Yet it squares with observations of others who tried to account for Nazi radicalization: Hannah Arendt's account of Adolf Eichmann's testimony at his trial for war crimes was titled "The Banality of Evil." Eichmann, a major organizer of the Holocaust, testified that he did what he did because he was given orders. To his mind, following orders was reason enough.

The second powerful element of the Milgram's experiment was slippery slope. Recall the electric shock panel that the teachers operated by flipping switches to deliver shocks to the learner. The first shock was only 15 volts—not painful, not violent, and not radical. Each following shock was only 15 volts more than the previous one. Thus, the second shock would have been 30 volts—still mild. The third was 45 volts—unpleasant but not painful. At 300 volts, when the learner screams, complains of his heart aching, and demands to be let out, participants would have delivered 20 shocks. They now had a history of delivering lower intensity shocks. Twenty times they found a reason to press the lever and deliver a shock. The increment to 300 volts is only 15 volts from the last shock participants delivered. If 300 volts is too much to justify pressing the lever, 285 volts must have been wrong, too. If 285 volts was OK to deliver, 300 must be OK as well. This is a psychology of self-justification: If I stop at 300 volts, I must be guilty for administering 285 volts, but if there was nothing wrong with 285 volts, there must be nothing wrong with 300 volts.

Slippery slope is a series of steps in which every successive step is only minimally different from the previous one. Each previous step serves as a justification for the future one. There is never a clear line in the sand where one can stop and say, "This is going too far." The progression is too smooth, the escalation is too gradual, and, looking back, individuals can have a hard time figuring out how they got to where they are.

In terrorism, too, radicalization often follows a slippery slope oiled by terrorist groups intent on radicalizing new recruits. A new member of the group is brought into the operations gradually, not only for radicalization purposes, but also to test loyalty and character.

First, the newcomer may be asked for material support: money, the use of their car. Then they may be asked to deliver some insignificant piece of mail. Later, they may be trusted with some more important communications. Later still, they may be asked to serve as a lookout, then a getaway driver, and so on. Planting explosives one day, the person may not remember exactly when they made the choice to become a terrorist. Their radicalization to terrorism went smoothly down the slippery slope of self-justification, just as Milgram's participants went smoothly down the shock panel to 450 volts.

How can thrill-seeking and desire for status radicalize an individual?

Risk-taking and status can be powerful motivators, especially for young men. Calculations of risk and reward can be foggy when testosterone, a hormone associated with both aggression and status, is peaking in males in their late teens and early twenties. Testosterone affects the brain, making the appeal of a short-term gain in status much greater than the appeal of a long and healthy life.

Higher automobile insurance premiums for young men reflect the reality that young men are significantly more likely than anybody else to drive recklessly, especially when there are male passengers in the car. Young men are much more likely to play dangerous sports, join the army, and become involved in dangerous professions such as firefighting or police work than any other demographic category. Risk-taking and status-seeking are common among young males.

Especially among young men with poor prospects for education or a good job, risk-taking is about the only way to gain status. Sociologists Margo Wilson and Martin Daily analyzed all violent crimes that took place in 1 year in the city of Detroit. They found that most violent crimes were status related, with both victim and perpetrator being predominantly young males, unemployed, and single. The initial "showing off dispute" in these crimes escalated to violence; this was especially likely when there were witnesses to the conflict. When status among other males is one's only asset, guarding it to the death is the only thing to do.

For no-prospects young men in Detroit, bar fights are a way to assert their social standing. For a first-generation immigrant in Los Angeles, joining a street gang may fulfill the same need for status. And for many young men, the appeal of terrorist groups has to do less with ideology than it does with the weapons, power, danger, and thrill that terrorism promises.

Risk and status were what attracted Abu Musab al-Zarqawi to terrorism. Zarqawi was not a good student: He dropped out of school, refusing to take up a trade or vocational training. Instead, he preferred to hang out with a group of Palestinian refugees who were known as troublemakers in his hometown of Zarqa, Iraq. Zarqawi became their informal leader. Repeatedly, Zarqawi was arrested for shoplifting, drug dealing, attempted rape, and stabbing—every time causing his father the embarrassment of having to pick up his son at the police station.

He was not a good Muslim: He covered his body in tattoos (a practice forbidden by Islam), drank alcohol, and did not attend religious services. He was only interested in status and power.

He went to Afghanistan, where the war between the Soviets and the Taliban seemed to offer plenty of opportunities. Alas, he was too late for the war, but he decided to stay anyway: The region was in ruin, and Zarqawi saw possibilities for adventure. Here, he befriended several individuals steeped in radical Islamic ideology and began his career in terrorism, attending training camps; learning to use automatic weapons and rocket-propelled grenades; and absorbing the methods of wartime, including beheadings and rape.

Returning to his native Jordan, Zarqawi founded his own terrorist cell, funded in part by Osama bin Laden. Arrested and sent to a maximum-security prison, Zarqawi continued his strategy of gaining status by brute force, eventually becoming de facto ruler of one of the prison blocks, his authority there recognized even by the prison officials. When he was released on an amnesty after a 5-year imprisonment, Zarqawi sought a position of power within the largest terrorist organization of the world: al-Qaeda.

He succeeded, reigning over terror across Iraq, his name equated with the most brutal tactics of radical Islamists of his time. In pursuing power and thrill, Zarqawi defied even the al-Qaeda authorities: Ayman al-Zawahiri sent him letters, pleading with Zarqawi to limit his brutalization to infidels, sparing Muslims and al-Qaeda's good name. But Zarqawi was not one to be contained. When the United States finally hunted him down and killed him in an air raid, he was known to the world as "The butcher of Baghdad."

Status and thrill appeal to young men. Those with few socially acceptable opportunities to pursue thrill and status can look for such opportunities in terrorism.

Recently, ISIS made a concerted effort through online recruitment to mobilize Muslims in the West, calling on youth to leave the boring safety and routine of their lives for the thrill of the war in Syria and Iraq. Many of those who heeded this call were young second-generation immigrants who felt disenfranchised and discriminated against in their country of birth. For them, joining ISIS was a chance to establish themselves, feel powerful, and experience the thrill of weapons and explosives.

Hate groups in the United States have been using online recruiting tactics identical to those of ISIS to appeal to young Americans. They have succeeded: The number of unique monthly views on a racist and anti-Semitic website (The Daily Stormer) climbed from 140,000 in the summer of 2016 to 750,000 in August of 2017, just before the violent Right Wing rally in Charlottesville, Virginia.[1]

How can "unfreezing" and need for escape radicalize an individual?

For most of us, life is full of constraints—some pleasant, others not so pleasant. We have homes that need to be paid for and maintained; we have jobs that require our physical presence and attention; we have families and friends who have feelings to keep track of and opinions to contend with. Our lives are constrained by these pressures day after day; routines are easy and changes are difficult. In a way, we are "frozen" in our present selves, prisoners of our circumstances.

But sometimes life can change suddenly and dramatically. Perhaps war comes to a region, uprooting people, destroying property, disrupting industries, and tearing families apart. Or an individual suddenly loses a job, suffers the death of a family member or friend, or moves to a strange city. Suddenly, life that has been predictable and connected becomes uncertain and disconnected. The individual experiences what social scientists call disconnection or *unfreezing*.

Loss can make us reconsider what we hold as absolute truths. We may become open to new people—people we wouldn't have had anything to do with in our "old life." We may become open to ideas we hadn't contemplated before. We may even become open to actions that would not fit with our old life but, with old constraints lifted, now seem within reach. You may have heard of people who have survived cancer or a divorce, and how the trauma of that unfreezing experience liberated them to take up something they would not have dared to do before—a new profession, a new relationship, a new hobby.

In the same way, unfreezing can create an opening for radical ideas and actions. Terrorist groups (and religious cults) know about the power of unfreezing. They often recruit individuals who are going through some painful ordeal, feeling isolated and uncertain of their future. Offering someone in a vulnerable state a place to stay, a social connection, an acknowledgment of their humanity opens the unfrozen person to the group's ideas and goals. Before, one would have been critical and fearful of radical ideas, but now the people expressing these ideas are friends, and their ideas are important.

Unfreezing happens against one's will. Nobody wants to lose a job or a relationship; nobody wants to end up in a war-torn zone, separated from their home and loved ones. These things happen *to* a person, releasing them from prior commitments and making them open to new ones. A similar state of openness to new, at times radical, ideas and actions can also result from the person's own efforts to escape their life's circumstances.

When one's family life is troubled and painful, when there is no love to be found at home, a young person can become a runaway, willfully breaking ties with everything and everyone they have known, escaping their old life. When one's career is at a dead-end and friendships seem empty, one may leave the boring job and the uninspired friendships in search of an adventure. When one is a target of persecution by police or security services, facing risks of imprisonment, brutality, and torture, one may seek support and refuge with people who are used to evading the government.

The need to escape can make an individual break away from the routine that held them "on the straight and narrow." Unconstrained by social norms and commitments of "normal life," they can become open to radical groups, radical ideas, and radical actions.

Major Nidal Hasan, a lone wolf terrorist who shot and killed 13 and injured more than 30 at Fort Hood military base in Texas, appears to have gone through unfreezing, leading to his radicalization to terrorism. Hasan joined the military after graduating high school, and while serving, went through college and medical school. His father died in 1998, and his mother died in 2001.

Hasan became a military psychiatrist and began to see patients who, for the most part, were soldiers suffering with post-traumatic stress disorder after active tours of duty in Iraq and Afghanistan. Their accounts of the horrors of war deeply disturbed Hasan, a sensitive and religious man. Adding to his discontent was harassment by soldiers who learned he was a Muslim.

And then Hasan learned of his pending deployment to Afghanistan. The prospect of having to support soldiers who were killing fellow Muslims filled him with dread. On several occasions, he expressed to his relatives his desire to get out of the military. Hasan began to express radical opinions to his fellow soldiers, and connected online with radical Islamic cleric Anwar al-Awlaki.

Deeply unhappy with his life, Hasan found an escape in radical rhetoric and eventually in radical action. With deployment to Afghanistan only days away, Hasan gave away his prized possessions and planned his act of terrorism. On

November 5, 2009, Hasan walked into Fort Hood's Soldier Readiness Center, shouted "Allahu Akbar!" and opened fire.

How can love radicalize an individual?

Compared with all the things that have been done for love—going to war, abdicating the throne, losing fortunes and making fortunes—turning to terrorism may not be the most radical action. To researchers, the surprising fact is not that love can lead to terrorism but that love can lead to terrorism without any commitment to the terrorist's ideology. In fact, individuals who vocally opposed violence in support of the terrorist's cause can turn to terrorist violence for love.

This was the story of Sonia Perovskaya, a Russian activist who advocated for land reform and constitutional democracy in czarist Russia in the 19th century. Among other progressive young people, Perovskaya traveled to remote regions of Russia to try to help poor peasants. A daughter of a wealthy nobleman with royal connections, Perovskaya preferred plain clothes and a simple lifestyle, leaving her family for her work as a nurse.

Among fellow "Narodniki"—the name idealistic activist Russian youths gave themselves—Perovskaya gained authority for her unwavering dedication to the betterment of Russia. She wrote and delivered speeches at political meetings advocating nonviolent activism. When some Narodniki declared their intentions to pursue terrorism instead of what they saw as impotent attempts to convince the tyrannical government to give up some of its power, Perovskaya remained in the nonviolent activist camp.

One of the leaders of the terrorist breakaway faction was Andrei Zhelyabov—a handsome, charismatic, and brilliant peasant. An unlikely romance between a noble woman and a peasant grew into a deep bond. Suddenly, Perovskaya, the adamant advocate for activism and against terrorism, was planning bombings and assassination attempts alongside

Zhelyabov. Logic became irrelevant in the face of love; political allegiance mattered nothing in comparison to passion.

Italian Red Brigades and German Baader–Meinhoff members often recalled their initial contact with these terrorist groups as stemming from a love connection. Not necessarily a romantic relationship: Love for a brother or sister, for a father or mother can lead an individual to throw logic and caution aside and put themselves where their loved one is, hoping to protect them or, if not, to share the dangers with them.

The Boston Marathon bombers, Tamerlan and Dzhokhar Tsarnaev, were Chechen brothers who immigrated to the United States. Tamerlan, the older brother, never felt at home in the United States: He said that he did not understand Americans and had no American friends. His application for college admission rejected, he attended community college but dropped out to pursue a boxing career. Here, too, Tamerlan failed to progress; he was disqualified from the US Olympics because he was foreign-born. Tamerlan married and had a daughter, but his married life was marked by violent conflicts. He was unemployed and living off of state-funded welfare benefits.

Tamerlan became steeped in radical Islamic ideology on his visits to Chechnya, Russia. His radicalization in Chechnya became strengthened through radical internet websites he visited while in the United States. He attended a mosque in Cambridge, Massachusetts, but repeatedly interrupted sermons to spew radical Islamist ideology, and was finally kicked out for good.

The younger brother, Dzhokhar, was better integrated into the United States: He was not perceived as a foreigner and spoke with no accent. Dzhokhar was well-liked by his friends and was enrolled in college. Unlike Tamerlan, Dzhokhar did not show any signs of radicalization. For Chechen men, however, an older brother is an example and an authority to be taken seriously. Dzhokhar admired Tamerlan and his physical prowess.

His brother's authority led Dzhokhar down a trajectory of radicalization that culminated in the brothers planting and detonating pressure cooker bombs at the Boston Marathon. In the manhunt that ensued, Tamerlan was shot and killed. Dzhokhar was wounded and captured. His defense mounted a convincing argument that Dzhokhar was radicalized as a result of his attachment to and love for his older brother, who was the ideologue and the mastermind of the attacks. Although a satisfying psychological explanation, radicalization for love was not a good defense in the court of law. Dzhokhar was convicted of terrorism and on May 15, 2015, sentenced to death.

Is one mechanism enough to radicalize an individual?

Sometimes, one mechanism is all that it takes. Examples of radicalization for grievance, radicalization for thrill and status, and radicalization for love that were offered in this chapter provide cases of single-mechanism radicalization. But don't let our selection of examples fool you into thinking that most cases of radicalization are similarly clear-cut. We chose these cases to demonstrate mechanisms of radicalization most effectively. In reality, most individual paths of radicalization include more than one mechanism.

A hint of this complexity was already described in the sections on grievance. Personal grievance can sometimes lead to radicalization to terrorism. More often, however, personal grievance has to be reframed from an individual's personal problem into a more global problem—a political grievance—before a transition to radical action can take place. Sometimes, as with Perovskaya, radicalization can be the result of love and nothing else. More likely is a case in which one's love connection to a terrorist leads to an exposure to the radical ideology that asserts a political grievance, or leads to a slippery slope of introduction to the terrorist group's activities.

Mechanisms of radicalization can combine in many different ways. In addition to individual mechanisms of radicalization, there are also group and mass publics levels of mechanisms of radicalization, which are discussed in Chapters 4 and 5, respectively. In addition to combinations of individual mechanisms of radicalization, there can be combinations of individual mechanisms with group mechanisms and with mass mechanisms.

Social sciences are different from natural sciences like physics in that psychological events are multiply determined. In physics, a particular action will lead to a particular reaction every time. When an object drops, it will always drop with the same speed because the same force of gravity will affect it every time, every place, no matter who is watching it fall. In contrast, the same event can have drastically different effects on different people and even on the same person, depending on his or her mood, preceding events, and the situation at the time when the event occurs. The complexity of the human psyche can be both fascinating and frustrating. Psychologists work to identify mechanisms that lead to particular outcomes (e.g., radicalization), with the understanding that there is going to be some variation among different people, situations, and sequences of events.

Is there a profile of individuals who join a terrorist group?

As you might imagine, this question has interested security professionals and social scientists alike since the beginning of modern terrorism. Unfortunately, the answer is no. A profile of a group-based terrorist is not possible for several reasons.

First, as mentioned in the section above, mechanisms of radicalization are many and different, and can be combined in many different ways. Someone who seeks out a terrorist group because they want to kill and dominate, as Zarqawi did, is vastly different from someone who joins a terrorist group because they love someone already in it, as Perovskaya did. Someone who happens to run into a friendly terrorist in the midst of their unfreezing is vastly different from someone who, in their personal grievance, takes up a personal vendetta against the forces that made his or her life intolerable. No one profile could accommodate the variety of circumstances and personal qualities that can radicalize an individual to terrorism.

Second, a profile of a group-based terrorist is impossible because groups are different, even terrorist groups. People in a group are subject to social pressures that form inside that group. Social psychology is a branch of psychology that focuses on ways in which people influence each other. Thousands of studies, such as Milgram's obedience study, show that we can be influenced by others in unexpected, sometimes dramatic ways.

Members of a terrorist group, therefore, in addition to their unique background and individual radicalizing mechanism(s), are also influenced by the group. An individual profile cannot accommodate information about the group, and yet the group may be the main radicalizing influence in an individual's radicalization to violent action. In Chapter 4, we discuss group-based mechanisms of radicalization—ways in which groups can move people in them to more radical opinions and actions.

You may have already begun to wonder: If a group-based terrorist profile is not possible, what about a lone wolf terrorist profile? Indeed, in the absence of group influences, profiling becomes more feasible. In Chapter 7, we discuss two possible profiles of lone wolf terrorists.

The final reason profiling terrorists is impossible is that, as mentioned earlier, radicalization to terrorism is not so different from radicalization to join other violent groups—joining a gang, joining a militia, joining a revolution, or even joining a regular army. Had the Founding Fathers not succeeded against the British in the American Revolution, history would have put them down as traitors and terrorists. Their actions were radical and illegal, a fact recognized in the US Department of Defense's training manual, which states that the Founding Fathers were an extremist movement.[2] The leader of the Bolshevik revolution, Vladimir Lenin, openly advocated terrorism, sponsored it, and demanded it from his followers.

Although he is not known as a terrorist, his rhetoric and action make him a terrorist.

In other words, *terrorism* is a political term that describes not a criminal type but a tactic that is usually deployed by the weak against the strong. Trying to profile a terrorist is like trying to profile someone shooting a gun. Sure, not all people would own a gun or shoot it. But among those who would, a gun can be used for different purposes: armed robbery, murder, threat, but also self-defense, protection of others, and protection of property.

Terrorism is a weapon. Not everyone is capable of becoming a terrorist. But among those who are, the differences can be as great as those between the Founding Fathers and the Tsarnaev brothers.

4

HOW ARE SMALL GROUPS RADICALIZED TO USE TERRORISM AS A TACTIC?

How can interaction of like-minded people make them more extreme?

Imagine you got together with some friends for dinner, and in the course of the evening a politically charged topic came up—implementing prayer in school or making abortion illegal, for example. Because you are in a group of friends, it is likely that most of you will be on the same side of the issue: Most will be for prayers in schools, for example, or most will be for legal access to abortion. But because people in the group are all different, they are probably not going to feel equally strongly about their position. Supporting prayer in school, one person would be full of righteous conviction, while another would be somewhat ambivalent.

In a group discussion that would follow, the group as a whole is likely to become more extreme on the issue. This change in group opinion is explained by two forces that affect individuals in like-minded groups during group discussions. The first force has to do with information presented during discussions; the second force has to do with social relationships within the group.

Every member of the group had arrived at his or her pre-discussion political position because of some information—a fact, a logical argument, or an authority who endorsed the position. Ask yourself: Why are you for or against abortion? You are likely to come up with your reasons (let's call them A, B, and C). Another person who shares your position will come up with their reasons, not all of them identical to yours (let's call them A, B, and D). Discussing the issue together, you will share your reasons and hear theirs. You had three reasons before; now you have four reasons to support your position (A, B, C, and D). Your position on the issue is going to be strengthened: You now have a new reason in addition to the old ones to feel the way you do.

In a group discussion, like-minded groups (groups that start out favoring a particular side of an issue) discuss reasons for their position. Following these discussions, group members emerge enriched with new arguments for their initial position. Their support for the position is made stronger as a result.

The second force within group discussion is not intellectual but social. Some group members are more influential than others: Maybe a person has a dominant personality or has more information about the topic of interest. But one way to extraordinary influence is perhaps surprising: People who represent extreme positions on an issue—who advocate the most drastic measures in support of their position—are more admired by other group members than are more "middle-of-the-road" individuals.

When we admire someone, we listen to them; we even want to be like them. Those who advocate extreme positions on an issue inspire others in the group to move their opinions toward the extreme. As a result, the whole group's opinion shifts toward the extreme.

This paradigm, the tendency of like-minded groups to become more extreme because of group discussion, is called *group polarization*. The two forces that are believed to cause group polarization, the informational pressure and the social pressure within the group, are called *persuasive argument theory* and *social comparison theory*.

Radicalization of opinion is one kind of group polarization that can happen when like-minded people discuss political issues. In fact, some notorious terrorist groups have crystallized out of activist groups through intense discussions about the issues that moved them.

The Weather Underground, a US terrorist group that attacked the US government in the 1970s to protest the Vietnam War, broke off from a larger and nonviolent anti-war group— Students for a Democratic Society (SDS). Intense discussions among members of SDS converted some of them from activists to terrorists.

In 19th-century Russia, another activist student group, Narodnaya Volya, encouraged debates and forums among its members. The discussions were marked with persuasive arguments and social comparison that moved some activist members of Narodnaya Volya to become terrorists who formed People's Will, the first modern terrorist group.

How can competition with government and security forces radicalize an activist group?

The actions of the government are as important for understanding terrorism as the terrorists' own actions. Often, terrorists are made in a prolonged conflict with the government in which action and reaction radicalize both the government and its challengers.

To make a radical out of an activist, few experiences are as effective as unfair and brutal treatment by the government. An activist group organizes a protest; the government responds with rubber bullets, pepper spray, water cannons, and batons. In the aftermath of the protest, the activist group will view the government's overreaction as group grievance. Perhaps some members of the protest were arrested, perhaps some reciprocated the government's violence and were beaten and jailed; perhaps some were brutalized in police custody. These group members' experiences are likely to radicalize them against the government; their comrades are likely to feel indignation and outrage at their mistreatment, causing them to become radicalized as well.

Prison in itself has been shown to be a source of radicalization. In prison, many activists who would have never interacted with hardened radicals get a chance to meet them and spend time talking with them. The time they spend together serves to introduce activists to a radical ideology, to social connections in which radical actions and ideas are the norm, and to technologies and tactics of radical action against the government. Some have seen the exchanges among jailed radicals as a kind of "prison university."

Many jihadist terrorists have gotten their radical education in prison. These include Abu Musab al-Zarqawi, who became the head of al-Qaeda in Iraq, and Ayman al-Zawahiri, Osama bin Laden's second-in-command. In Europe, jihadist terrorists responsible for recent ISIS-inspired attacks in France, Belgium, and Germany have spent time behind bars, often for nonpolitical offenses, before they mounted their terrorist attacks. Social connections made in prison with like-minded prisoners strengthen radicalization.

The more the government cracks down on activists, the more likely it is that some of them will move on to radicalism. The majority will be deterred by the prospect of being brutalized, arrested, and imprisoned. But a minority will become hardened by such experiences, their radicalization boosted by their personal grievance. They are likely to break away from the larger activist group and go underground as a terrorist cell, as happened with the Weather Underground in the United States.

How can competition with other activist groups radicalize a group?

Psychologist Muzafer Sherif captured the effects of group competition in his 1954 naturalistic study, the Robbers Cave experiment. In Robbers Cave State Park in Oklahoma, Sherif set up a summer camp for boys. Two groups of 12-year-old boys camped separately and without knowledge of the other group for the first week of the study. During that week, each group developed its own norms of behavior (one forbade cursing; the other encouraged it), its own leadership, its own network of friendships, and each chose a name for itself (the Eagles and the Rattlers).

During the second week of the study, the two groups of boys were made to run into each other when each approached the baseball diamond. A weeklong tournament was organized, with competitions in baseball, tug-of-war, and other sports between the two groups. The winning group received trophies, and members of the winning group got individual prizes such as multiblade pocket knives.

The second week of the study, therefore, was all about competition. Sherif was interested in psychological changes that group competition would have on the boys. He found that the groups became more cohesive than before: They enforced a lot more subordination to group leaders and discouraged dissent. Furthermore, boys became aggressive toward the other group: Food fights broke out, each group raided the other's bunks, each burned the other's flag, and each came up with offensive names for the other group. In other words, competition created radicalization in both opinion (boys on the other team were "stinkers" or "smart alecks") and action (fighting). With the data from his study, Sherif formulated realistic group conflict theory, which states that when resources are limited, groups fighting for them will develop in-group cohesion and out-group hostility.

With adults, competition can lead to similar radicalization, often with much more drastic consequences than those of Sherif's summer camp for boys. Activist groups compete for funding from sponsors; they compete for airtime on the news; they compete for the base of sympathizers from which they recruit new members, draw resources, and seek political support. When more than one group claims to represent the same cause, conflict between them is inevitable. As with the boys in Sherif's experiment, group cohesion will increase, with increased respect for leaders, glorification of in-group values, and increased punishment for deviates. Also likely are hostility and aggression against the competing group.

This is what happened in competition between the Armenian Secret Army for the Liberation of Armenia (ASALA) and the Tashnaks, another activist group competing for resources and support from the Armenian diaspora. ASALA was first to attack Turks in retribution for the Armenian genocide of 1915–1917, when other Armenian activist groups were only talking about what to do. Not to be outdone, the Tashnaks established the Justice Commandos of the Armenian Genocide, their own terrorist group. Competition between activist groups led to their radicalization to terrorism.

Similarly, in the second intifada, the Palestinian Front for the Liberation of Palestine (PFLP) dropped in poll ratings among Palestinians to near zero as suicide bombings brought Hamas and Fatah to the forefront. PFLP scrambled to compete. Reneging on its own opposition to jihad, PFLP recruited its own *shaheeds* and carried out a number of martyrdom operations, restoring its standing in the polls.

Group influence is not easy for most Western-minded people to accept. Even students of psychology have a hard time accepting that Milgram's results would hold for them. We are raised to think for ourselves, to stand out from the crowd, to be unique. Nonetheless, experiments and naturalistic studies show that for all our cultural independence, we are still very much affected by groups, more than we are ready to admit. In radicalization, individual trajectories are affected by groups as well. Especially when the group is isolated and threatened, and becomes the only social world its members know, its power is greatly amplified. As with individuals who lose social ties and routines in unfreezing, isolated and threatened groups open themselves to radical ideas and actions.

Chapter 5 discusses an even subtler influence on radicalization—not individual, not group, but mass publics. We are imbedded in a culture, its influence on us constant and elusive at once. Radicalization can take place when this influence affects emotions toward particular groups of people: positive emotions toward "us" and negative emotions toward "them."

5

HOW ARE MASS PUBLICS RADICALIZED TO SUPPORT TERRORISM?

How can overreaction to a terror attack build support for terrorists (jujitsu politics)?

A group of nobodies get together and declare war against some massive entity like the cell phone industry, perhaps because they believe the radiation is harmful and the towers are a blight. Who cares? Nobody. Even if they topple a tower or two, the cell phone industry is swimming in money; it can reroute calls to other towers while it builds a new one where the old one stood. The wannabe anti-cell phone terrorists are still nobodies, except now they are facing criminal charges.

But what if the cell phone industry alerts its lobbyists in Washington, DC, and then every politician's speech mentions the "terrorists" who attack the cell phone towers, wreaking havoc on hard-working Americans' rights to stay connected? What if the government unleashes an army of FBI, police, and special investigative teams to search for the terrorists, breaking down their doors at the crack of dawn and dragging them, kicking and screaming slogans, through the streets to the police station? What if in the process of going after the terrorists, the government breaks a few rules and establishes new ones, causing an outcry in the media about restriction of freedom and front pages with sympathetic profiles of the terrorists in colorful detail?

In this case, the terrorists have received what they wanted. Instead of being nobodies with criminal records, they became celebrities with public figures opining for and against their cause and methods. They get sponsors who have a grudge of their own against cell phone companies or against the government that backed up the cell phone companies. The terrorists get recruits who heard their stories and want to be as famous, as pivotal, as powerful as they. In other words, by causing an overreaction from the powerful—the cell phone companies and the government—the terrorists manipulated them into creating publicity that would build a base of support for the terrorists and would provide them with resources and recruits.

Jujitsu works by using the strength of the opponents against them. For terrorists, the government they oppose is indeed strong, wielding the savvy of its security services coupled with the might of its military and police forces. Jujitsu allows terrorists to position themselves as a dangerous enemy of the government. That status helps the terrorists' fundraising and recruiting efforts.

The most famous example of a successful jujitsu strategy is al-Qaeda's 9/11 attack against the United States. According to al-Qaeda's second-in-command, Ayman al-Zawahiri, the attacks were designed to entice the United States into a protracted battle in Muslim countries that would drain the US treasury and create enough death and destruction to rouse even the most apathetic Muslims to jihad. With the United States in wars in Iraq and Afghanistan— wars we are still fighting more than a decade later—al-Qaeda's strategy has succeeded.

Jujitsu as a mechanism of mass radicalization is powerful because terrorist attacks incite strong emotions: anger, outrage, fear, and humiliation. These emotions make us want to do something to avenge the attacks, to feel protected and proactive, and to restore our shaken perception of power and control. Terrorists capitalize on both the emotions and the desire to act on them. Emotional decisions are rarely the best ones, especially policy decisions.

The masterminds of the 9/11 attacks counted on us to change our way of life and to prioritize wars that would put a dent in the US financial system, polarizing the population at home and compromising the country's image abroad. In many ways, we played into their plan.

Beyond the reaction in the United States and in the Western world, the 9/11 attackers counted on jujitsu to work in the Muslim world. Where al-Qaeda failed to radicalize mass publics in Muslim countries, they expected US missiles and drone attacks to do it for them.

A war is bound to create casualties. The wars in Iraq and Afghanistan are no different. Intelligence is never perfect, and mistakes led to attacks on weddings, funerals, and marketplaces; the West called these mistakes "collateral damage" but created outrage nonetheless. United States troops on the ground became convenient targets for ambush or improvised explosive devices. Radical Islamist rhetoric that may have seemed marginal before suddenly became popular. Indeed, the rise of ISIS was part of the fallout from the Iraq war. Al-Qaeda has largely disappeared from the news, but the legacy of its jujitsu politics still haunts us.

What emotions can push terrorists' targets toward overreaction?

As the section on jujitsu politics mentioned, terrorist attacks raise powerful emotions in those they target. The word "terrorism," and indeed most definitions of terrorism, suggest that fear (terror) is the most prominent emotion that terrorists aim to elicit. And yet fear may not be the most important emotional reaction when it comes to radicalization.

Fear is what psychologists call an "avoidance motivation" emotion. Fear makes those who experience it want to avoid the threat that produced it, if possible. If fear were the predominant emotion in response to terrorism, instead of wars and other retaliation tactics, denial and surrender would be the predominant responses. Instead, terrorists count on and routinely precipitate reactions of aggression, which is the natural response for a different emotion: anger.

To understand radicalization, an increased willingness to use violence for a cause, we are better off focusing on emotions that are "approach motivating," such as anger and outrage. Humiliation is another emotion that is common among targets of terrorism.

Anger, outrage, and humiliation are powerful motivations to action against terrorists or those seen as affiliated with them. Whether wars abroad, support for politicians using hawkish rhetoric, or attacks on people who share with terrorists their ethnicity, faith, or skin color, these reactions testify to the power of emotions in intergroup conflict. Emotional responses push both terrorists and their targets to violent action.

How does dehumanization of the enemy contribute to radicalization?

Humans are loath to kill other humans. All kinds of barriers—physiological (disgust at the sight of blood and guts), moral (prohibitions against murder are part of every religion), and social (social norms regulate and control violence within a group or community)—stand in the way of violence. But these barriers can be lowered.

One way to get past moral and social barriers to killing is to see the target as less than human. If the "other" is seen as not worthy of considerations extended to humans, moral and social barriers to violence no longer apply.

Dehumanization marks any prolonged conflict. Each side, in an effort to prevail over the other through violence, begins to create imagery and rhetoric that separate "us" from "them." When "they" are seen as less than human—as pests, vermin, or disease—killing them becomes not only easy but necessary.

In the years leading up to World War II, German propaganda created posters, slogans, stories, and films that depicted Jews as cockroaches, rats, and spiders sucking the blood out of the German nation, gorging themselves on the flesh of German youth. Visual depictions of Jews were caricatures that referenced genetic disorders. Metaphors used for Jews in Germany drove home the message that Jews were inferior to Germans in every way, and yet they were taking advantage of Germans.

The result of this dehumanization campaign was the greatest tragedy in modern history, with 6 million Jews dying in the Holocaust. The German extermination machine worked seamlessly, in part because any pangs of conscience, any doubts about the "ultimate solution," any sympathy had given way in most Germans to emotions usually directed toward pests. Mass radicalization against the Jews in 1930s Germany was immensely effective.

The cognitive foundation of dehumanization is the human proclivity for understanding natural kinds in terms of essence. Bluebirds differ from blackbirds because they are different animals. In layman's terms, we may think that, deep down inside, they have different essences. An essence—sometimes called nature or spirit—is invisible and enduring. No surgery or dyestuff can make a bluebird into a blackbird.

Human groups can be essentialized, too. What makes a New Yorker different from a Londoner is not just a style of English language but a character permanently stamped by being raised in New York rather than in London, by following football and basketball instead of soccer. Twenty years in London will not make a New Yorker into a Londoner. Essence is forever.

Prolonged conflict between groups produces essentialized stereotypes of the enemy: They are the way they are because, deep down, they share a corrupt and dangerous essence. We, on the other hand, are the way we are because we share a good and cooperative essence.

Mutual essentializing can usually be observed among groups in conflict, including even the boys who were part of Muzafer Sheriff's Robbers Cave experiment. Before the conflict, the other group was seen in more diverse and less negative terms; after the onset of the conflict, epithets like "pigs" and "stinkers" were used far more commonly to describe the enemy.

In a conflict between terrorists and their targets, each side begins to see the other as not worthy of compassion or consideration. Individual members of the enemy group are seen as largely similar, with the same corrupted essence that cannot be cured and therefore needs to be eradicated.

A member of the Weather Underground, Bernadine Dorn, applauded the brutal murder of pregnant Sharon Tate by calling it a "pig slaughter." To the Weather Underground, Tate was not a person worthy of compassion but a member of the elite they were fighting against—a pig to be slaughtered.

After the attacks of 9/11, a number of US Muslims were attacked, not because of evidence that they were responsible for 9/11 but because they were of the same religion as the terrorists. Non-Muslim Sikhs were also targeted because their darker skins made them look like they could be from an Arab Muslim country.

Essentializing the enemy makes it easier to kill them; they're not quite as human as we are. Collateral damage to Arabs and Muslims in the war on terrorism (mentioned in relation to jujitsu politics) does not weigh as heavy on us if they have a different essence.

In these examples we can see that dehumanization via essentializing takes place on both sides of the conflict. Terrorists see us as having a bad essence, and we see terrorists as having a bad essence. Both sides are radicalized in the back and forth of terrorist attacks and government responses. Essentializing supports escalation of violence on both sides.

How does a martyr draw new support for the martyr's cause?

A martyr is someone who peacefully accepts suffering and death for a cause. A martyr is a powerful force for radicalization on both sides of a conflict.

For the cause the martyr upholds, the sacrifice is a signal to others that someone valued the cause more than life. The worth of the cause is therefore lifted above everyday concerns for all who care about it. The supporters of the cause now have the martyr's sacrifice as a benchmark against which to measure their own dedication. When someone gives a life for the cause, excuses for not giving money, time, or effort become petty.

For the bystanders who are not yet committed to the martyr's cause, the sacrifice tells a story about the conflict that is simple and convincing. The martyr knew she would be attacked and maybe killed. She did nothing to provoke the attack. The fact that she was attacked nonetheless means those who attacked her were unjust. She did not reciprocate violence, raising her above most humans' morality. The fact that she was attacked or killed nonetheless paints her persecutors as cruel. She gave her life for something she believed in. This makes her cause important, measured in the scale of sacrifice.

Thus, martyrdom defines the conflict. On the one side are high morals, pure motives, and a worthy cause. On the other side are injustice, cruelty, and questionable motives. Many bystanders will be moved by a martyrdom to support for the martyr's cause.

In contrast, for the side that punished the martyr, the story will be about a challenge to the natural order in which those with power stand to lose power and status to those who challenge them. This zero-sum conflict (one side stands to lose, the other stands to gain—there can be no compromise), painted by the martyr in moral tones, presents a difficult choice for those in power. Either they have to admit they have done wrong in persecuting the peaceful martyr, admitting their moral failure and giving up their political standing, or they have to deny the moral failure and hold on to the power with everything they've got. As you may guess, the latter is a far more common choice than the former.

For that reason, peaceful martyrdoms of Gandhi, Martin Luther King, and Nelson Mandela resulted in escalation of violence from those who attacked them, leading to armed conflict between the sides where before the martyrdom there was only political tension.

In other words, martyrdoms radicalize their supporters, their opponents, and passive bystanders in the conflict they represent. The conflict that often follows a martyrdom radicalizes sides even further.

Are suicide bombers martyrs as they claim?

The tactic of suicide bombing has become increasingly common in recent decades. Suicide bombers often record themselves before their missions in "martyrdom videos" or in writing (e.g., Atta's Manual, a document found in the baggage of the apparent ringleader of the 9/11 attackers, Mohammad Atta). Islamist suicide bombers call themselves "shaheeds." The translation from Arabic *shaheed* to English "martyr" trespassed cultural differences in understanding of martyrdom and resulted in an added clout for suicide bombers.

Unlike the martyrs of the West that followed the Christian tradition of martyrdom embodied by Jesus Christ, suicide bombers use violence—indiscriminate violence at that. Where Gandhi could be a symbol of purity of motives, where Nelson Mandela painted his persecutors as cruel and unjust, suicide bombers share only one characteristic with the martyrs of the West: They give up their lives for their cause.

At best, that puts them in the same category as soldiers—they can be seen as heroes by supporters of their cause. But they are not martyrs. Their sacrifice is no testament to the purity of their motives because mass murderers can't claim purity. Their sacrifice is no indictment on the evil of their targets because the attacked did nothing to enact the bombers' claim of their evil.

The use of the word martyr to describe suicide bombers is an unwarranted mantle to them and an undeserved threat to their Western targets.

What is a political frame and how can it radicalize a mass public?

Reality is complex, and conflicts have an added layer of complexity in which each side attempts to represent reality in a way most beneficial to its own interests. Even something as routine as a car accident can be viewed completely differently by the two drivers involved in it. Who was at fault? Who hit whom? Who was speeding or driving recklessly? Police need to get involved to resolve these questions, and they can't always do so definitively. The complexity of political conflicts is infinitely greater. Framing is a way to capture the conflict in simple terms.

Of course, with simplification, some of the facts are left out. What the frame captures and what it leaves out will determine how the audience will perceive the conflict, which side it is likely to support, and which emotions it is likely to experience. Without altering the facts in any way, framings can sway the audience in opposite directions.

Consider the contentious issue of the US prison at Guantanamo Bay, Cuba. One framing of this prison emphasizes the fact that people detained there are terrorism suspects who are dangerous and must be kept far from our homeland where they can do us harm. They may have information about terrorists at large with plans to harm the United States. Therefore, any efforts at getting this information, however brutal, are necessary to keep us safe.

An alternative framing emphasizes the fact that many of the Guantanamo Bay prisoners have not been tied to terrorism; instead, they are victims of mistaken identity or of being in the wrong place at the wrong time. However, because of the special status of the prison, they are kept there without the legal due process that other US prisoners get. The brutal treatment they receive is likely to turn them into radicals with a grudge against the US government at whose hands they suffer, turning them into new threats to US security. Reports and photographs documenting maltreatment at Guantanamo Bay are used by terrorists to radicalize new recruits and mass publics.

As you can see, each frame is comprised of facts, not fiction. And yet they lead to opposite conclusions. One suggests Guantanamo Bay must be kept operational; the other suggests it must be closed. One frame suggests Guantanamo Bay makes the United States safer; the other suggests it creates new threats.

Long-standing conflicts consist of many contentious issues like Guantanamo Bay, and each can be framed in a way to emphasize some facts and de-emphasize other facts. As a result, framing of a conflict is a way of guiding perceptions of it in a particular direction.

Framing can emphasize mechanisms of radicalization—grievance, group polarization, martyrdom, and dehumanization. A demonstration that started peacefully ended with clashes between the protesters and police. One framing will emphasize the peacefulness of the protests, leading to the conclusion that police were unjustified in using violence and creating a political grievance among those who agree with this framing. Another framing will emphasize the protesters' throwing rocks and Molotov cocktails at the police, justifying police action and creating a different kind of grievance among those who subscribe to this frame. Those who support protesters will, in the process of group polarization, drift further in their sentiment from those who support the police. Both protestors and police will see themselves as victims and the other side as perpetrators of injustice and perhaps even inhuman. At this point, what started out as framing will end up as radicalization.

What is a political narrative and how can it radicalize a mass public?

A frame is static; it describes things as they *are*. A narrative is dynamic; it describes *how* and *why* things got this way.

A narrative is a story. "Why do they hate us?" was the question then President George W. Bush asked in response to the 9/11 attacks. His answer was "They hate us for our freedoms." The narrative suggested by this answer depicts the United States as having elicited envy in the 9/11 attackers (and those who supported them), which led to their plotting the acts of terrorism. Why did they attack? "Because of our freedoms" was the answer proposed by the Bush administration.

Of course, the attackers' narrative, evident in their writing and in their leader Osama bin Laden's recorded video speeches, was completely different. It described how the United States supported corrupt puppet regimes throughout the Muslim world that pumped cheap oil for the West at the price of poverty in the Middle East, dividing the Muslim *umma* (community), and bringing bad morals to Muslim lands.

Talking about the cause of the same event, one narrative paints the United States as a shining city on the hill; the other paints the United States as a sinister spider gorging itself on everything good that the Muslim nations have. The emotional alliances and implications that would stem from these narratives are radically different as well. In one case, protecting the freedoms that the United States exemplifies is the right thing to do. In the other case, fighting against US hegemony is the right thing.

So narratives are different from frames in that they describe not the "what" but the "why" and "how." Instead of taking a snapshot of the events, narratives talk about the causes of the present and the likely trajectory into the future.

Another difference between narratives and frames is that while frames talk about facts, albeit simplified and cut to a particular form, narratives don't have to adhere to facts and can instead rely on mythology. Narratives often use sweeping generalizations, such as "All X are Y" or "X always does Y to us."

Those who subscribe to a particular narrative often do so because the emotional connotations of the narrative resonate with their own emotional and political commitments.

A narrative often heard in Western countries is that terrorism is about Islam.

"They [Muslims] are the reason this is happening." This part of the narrative answers the "why" of terrorist attacks. The reason for the attacks, according to this narrative, is that there is something fundamentally wrong with Muslims and with their religion of Islam.

Notice how this falls into the mechanism of mass radicalization that we call dehumanization. When someone has a "bad essence," an immutable integral part of them, then the only way to protect against the bad essence is to get rid of those who carry it.

A common conclusion of this narrative is a demand that all Muslims be banned from travel to Western countries, deported, walled off, or even bombed out of existence. Notice also that, should a government follow this path—deporting Muslims, putting them in internment camps, or engaging in a war with Muslim nations, another mechanism of radicalization, jujitsu politics, is likely to gain momentum. A narrative radicalizes through the same 12 mechanisms of radicalization as were laid out in Chapters 3 and 4.

6

WHAT IS THE RELATION
BETWEEN RADICAL IDEAS
AND RADICAL ACTION?

*I know someone who has radical ideas; Is this
person dangerous?*

Not all radical ideas are connected with violence. A radical
opinion challenges the basic assumptions of a culture; so a
radical is someone who wants deep change in society. Women
seeking the vote were once considered radicals. Antiwar activism is a radical idea for many people, although it justifies
nonviolence rather than violence. Radical ideas are common;
political violence is rare.

Of course, some radical ideas are invoked to justify violence.
In the United States, there are currently three kinds of radical ideas that have been linked with terrorist attacks: jihadist
ideas (e.g., 9/11 attackers), right-wing ideas (e.g., Timothy
McVeigh), and left-wing ideas (e.g., Animal Liberation Front
and Environmental Liberation Front).

As we will show in the next section, only a few of those
who justify violence for a cause ever try to perpetrate violence.
Therefore, the connection between radical ideas and terrorism
is weak in three ways: Many radical ideas are not linked with
violence (i.e., pacifism), few who justify violence ever actually
perpetrate violence (see the following section), and many terrorists don't engage in violence because of radical ideas (e.g.,
status-seeking, unfreezing, and love; see Chapter 3). Taken

together, these three weaknesses mean that the likelihood that an individual holding radical ideas is dangerous is about the same as being struck by lightning.

Is there a conveyor belt from extreme opinion to extreme action?

"Extreme opinion" and "extreme action" are often used interchangeably with "radical opinion" and "radical action." Especially the US government's efforts to fight terrorism have been framed as a program of "countering violent extremism."[1]

A "conveyor belt" from extreme opinion to extreme action implies that everyone with radical ideas will sooner or later move to radical action. In fact, the connection between ideas and action is generally weak, except in special circumstances, such as a voting booth.

Research in social psychology finds that the correlation between attitude and behavior is weak because behavior is determined by many factors besides attitude: social norms, perceived control, means and opportunity, and moral judgment. My attitude toward helping others is positive, but perhaps I worry that others will think me a sucker for trying to help a street person, or I don't know what to do to help this person, or I don't have time today to stop to help, or I don't want to be responsible for helping a drunk stay drunk.

Similarly, terrorism research has found that few individuals with radical ideas ever engage in violence. In the United States, about 10 percent of Muslims believe that suicide bombing of civilian targets is often or sometimes justified in defense of Islam. That 10 percent translates to about 100,000 US Muslims. But the number indicted or convicted for jihadist plots targeting the United States is only in the hundreds. In other words, less than 1 in 100 who justify suicide bombing will actually try to perpetrate violence.

*How do individuals with radical opinions ever move
to radical action?*

The weak connection between ideas and action can be seen in studies of individual terrorists. Many had no radical ideas, or indeed anything like an ideology, before they joined a terrorist group. Some joined for excitement and status, some for love of a friend or relative or lover already in the group who asked for help, some for personal revenge, some to escape trouble with police or family, or to escape loneliness.

On top of individual motivation is the power of group dynamics. Both in-group dynamics and intergroup conflict dynamics can move individuals to terrorist action. In-group dynamics begin to work as soon as an individual joins an existing terrorist group; the individual learns the ideology and norms of the group and competes for status by trying to do more and risk more than other members. This competition leads the whole group, including the new member, toward escalating violence. The power of the group over its members, the power of in-group dynamics, is increased if the group becomes isolated, as when a radical group goes underground to evade government power.

Intergroup dynamics emerge from the conflict between a protest group and security forces. Once either protestors or police resort to violence, the conflict is likely to escalate, with both sides using increasing violence. Escalation occurs because each side sees its own violence as less than the enemy's violence, so what looks like tit for tat to one side looks like tit for two tats to the other side.

Escalation also occurs because the stakes of the conflict change from material goals to status goals—for instance, from pro- and anti-nuclear missiles to who determines national policy, us or them. Material goals can be divided in a compromise (how many missiles? based where?) but "who will blink first" is not subject to compromise. They win or we win.

So, there are two ways group dynamics push for extreme actions: In-group dynamics give more status to individuals on the extreme end of opinion and behavior, and the dynamics of intergroup conflict can move a whole group from radical ideas to escalating levels of extreme action.

The same in-group dynamics and intergroup conflict dynamics that move individuals and groups toward violence also move individuals and groups on the government side of the conflict. Conflict escalation afflicts both sides of the conflict. We return to this point in a later section.

How does radicalization of action affect radicalization of opinion?

Radicalization of opinion only rarely translates into radical action, but it would be a mistake to conclude that the relation between ideas and actions is always weak. One direction of this relation is relatively strong: Radical actions are likely to lead to radical opinions. Humans tend to justify what we do. If an individual joins a terrorist group and joins in perpetrating violence, that individual will find reasons to justify the violence.

This tendency has been much studied in social psychology in relation to "cognitive dissonance theory." According to this theory, doing something that goes against our positive self-image—something stupid or sleazy—gives rise to an uncomfortable feeling of dissonance. To get rid of this feeling, we seek new cognitions that will justify and make sense of what we did.

Normal people—and the great majority of terrorists are not suffering any kind of psychopathology—are likely to feel some dissonance about killing, especially killing women and children. Dissonance pushes terrorists to find new and stronger reasons for their violence. As already noted, many individuals join a terrorist group for reasons that are not ideological—for status and excitement, to help a loved one, to escape troubles

or loneliness. Once involved in terrorist violence, these individuals will learn at least a simple version of whatever ideology justifies the group's violence.

In short, radical action pushes individuals and groups toward more radical ideas and opinions. This tendency is strong,
in contrast with the weak push from radical ideas to radical
action.

One way to think about the strength of the path from action
to opinion, and the weakness of the path from opinion to action, is to agree with Aristotle that virtue lies in doing what we
find reason for, whereas dissonance is rationalizing what we
do. Research, and everyday experience, suggest that virtue is
more difficult and less common than rationalization.

Why is radicalization of opinion a different psychology from radicalization of action?

Radicalization of opinion and radicalization of action are separately represented in our two-pyramids model. The opinion
pyramid has four levels: no support for a political cause; sympathy for the cause; justification of violence in support of the
cause; and, at the apex of the pyramid, personal moral obligation to take up violence for the cause. The first three levels can
be tracked in poll results. For US Muslims, about 60 percent do
not believe that the US War on Terrorism is a war on Islam (no
support), 40 percent believe the War on Terrorism is a war on
Islam (sympathizers), and 10 percent say that suicide bombing
against civilians is often or sometimes justified in defense of
Islam (justifiers). Changes in these percentages register success
and failure in the war of ideas against neo-jihadists such as al-
Qaeda and Islamic State.

The action pyramid also has four levels: inert, legal activism,
illegal activism without killing (sit-ins, property destruction),
and terrorism (killing). These levels can be tracked in case histories of individuals and groups moving to terrorism—and
moving back from terrorism.

It is important to notice that neither pyramid is a staircase or stage model that requires an individual or a group to traverse each lower level to reach a higher level of radicalization. For instance, an apolitical individual may go from inert to terrorist in one step if his brother, a terrorist, calls on him for help.

The two pyramids depend on very different psychologies. Radicalization to action almost always involves participation in a small group, bringing in the power of intragroup dynamics and intergroup conflict dynamics. (Lone wolf terrorists are a relatively rare exception discussed in Chapter 7.) Radicalization of opinion, described in Chapter 5, is a mass-level phenomenon that can be tracked by opinion polls. Radicalization of opinion occurs via mass-level events such as jujitsu politics, martyrdoms, and development of an essentialist perception of the enemy (hate).

Is Hizb ut-Tahrir the best Western ally against al-Qaeda and Islamic State?

An important implication of the two-pyramids model, with its contradiction of the conveyor belt from radical ideas to radical actions, is that anyone who opposes violent action is a potential ally. This is important because only a minority of Salafi (fundamentalist) Muslims justify violence against the West. Most Salafi, like many Orthodox Jews and some fundamentalist Christians, are quietist; they wish only to separate themselves from the impurities of modern Western ways. Rather than pointing to Salafi beliefs as the source of neo-jihadi violence, Western security services might better let quietist Salafi work to draw Muslims to their communities.

Similarly, there is an important potential ally in Hizb ut-Tahrir (Party of Liberation). Hizb is an international Sunni Muslim organization that was founded by Palestinians in Jerusalem in 1953. It aims for restoration of an international caliphate—that is, it has the same aim as al-Qaeda and the same aim as Islamic State. There is a crucial difference, however.

Al-Qaeda and Islamic State are committed to terrorist attacks against the West, but Hizb has condemned attacks on civilians, including condemnation of both the 9/11 attacks in the United States in 2001 and the 7/7 attacks in London in 2005. Hizb does believe, however, that attacks on US troops in Afghanistan and Iraq, including suicide bombing attacks, are justified as defensive jihad.

Thus, Hizb ut-Tahrir is not against violence in principle but is against terrorist attacks in the West. It has the same goals as al-Qaeda and Islamic State, but different tactics. Hizb has been banned in several European countries and in most predominantly Muslim countries; it has not been banned in the United States or the United Kingdom. Those who believe that Hizb is a conveyor belt to terrorism want Hizb declared a terrorist organization because its ideology is dangerous. As we have explained, the conveyor belt is a myth. Ninety-nine percent of those with radical ideas never move to radical action.

Those who believe in the conveyor belt claim that young Muslims become impatient with Hizb's slow-moving and non-violent progress toward a caliphate and form splinter groups that get involved in terrorist attacks in the West. They have one example: In the United Kingdom, a small group broke off from Hizb to form al-Muhajiroun, whose members have been convicted of terrorism offenses. One example since Hizb was founded in 1953 does not suggest a serious threat, and in any case no organization can be responsible for those who leave it.[2]

Precisely because Hizb wants what al-Qaeda and Islamic State want, Hizb competes with these organizations for status and recruits. Better they should go to Hizb. Western governments that ban Hizb are banning the strongest Muslim organization that stands against terrorist attacks in the West.

How does the internet encourage radicalization and terrorism?

The internet is important—for commerce, for politics, for networking. The problem is not that it is difficult to imagine how the internet supports radicalization, the problem is that it is too easy.

Here are some of the possible internet contributions to radicalization that are suggested by the US Department of Justice in an "Awareness Brief."[3] For each possibility, we offer a parenthetical interpretation as an attempt to radicalize ideas or actions:

Using a combination of traditional websites; mainstream social media platforms like Facebook, Twitter, and YouTube; and other online services, extremists broadcast their views [ideas], provoke negative sentiment toward enemies [ideas], incite people to violence [actions], glorify martyrs [ideas], create virtual communities with like-minded individuals [ideas], provide religious or legal justifications for proposed actions [actions], and communicate with and groom new recruits [ideas and actions]. Extremists post incendiary materials such as educational videos about how to construct explosives and operate weapons [actions], videos of successful attacks [actions], lectures espousing radical views [ideas], blog posts and messages supporting and further encouraging attacks and acts of violence [actions]. For example, terrorist groups have used Facebook to exchange private messages and information to coordinate attacks [actions] and Facebook pages that individuals can "like" to show their support [ideas], have disseminated propaganda and press releases on Twitter [ideas], and have uploaded extremists' sermons [ideas] and training videos [actions] on YouTube. They have also used online message boards, chat rooms, and dating sites to meet and interact with one other and spread their messages [ideas].

There are several things to notice about this list. First is that the list is long: 17 possible ways that the internet contributes to radicalization, including 1 (communicate with and groom new recruits) that seems to be about both ideas and actions. Second, 10 of the cited internet contributions to radicalization are focused on transmission of ideas, whereas 8 relate to encouraging action. Third, notice that 3 of the possible contributions to radical action stand out as providing means and opportunity for action (educational videos about how to construct explosives and operate weapons, videos of successful attacks, messages to coordinate attacks).

The length of the list indicates the size of the problem: We do not yet have research that tries to test the effect of each possible internet contribution to radicalization, let alone research to determine which are more and less important contributions.

The fact that internet uses aimed at radicalization of action are almost as many as uses aimed at radicalization of ideas (8 vs. 10) points again to the importance of distinguishing radicalization of ideas from radicalization of action; terrorists are not just selling ideology on the internet, they are pushing action. In particular, 3 of the 8 possible contributions to radical action are of a special kind: They provide means and opportunity for violent action. Terrorism analysts usually focus on motivation—why individuals and groups turn to terrorism—but terrorists seem to recognize as well the importance of means and opportunity for violence.

What kind of internet content radicalized Sidique Khan and the 7/7 bombers?

Case histories of individual radicalization with sufficient detail to see the role of internet content are rare. Beginning with the 7/7 bombers, we look at three cases of radicalization to terrorism that do tell us something about what internet content was most important: victim videos and jihad videos.

Mohammed Sidique Khan is generally thought to be the leader of the group of suicide bombers who killed 52 and injured more than 700 in their July 7, 2005, attack in the London underground. Here is what the BBC had to say about how Khan was radicalized:[4]

While his path into terrorism had been linked to radical mosques, close friends reveal this was not the case.

They say he became part of a tight-knit group of young radicals who watched violent videos about Muslim suffering.

The documentary *Biography of a Bomber* spoke to a former member of his inner circle who tells of violent Jihadi videos being played in an attempt to radicalise young men.

. . .

The men used to spend time paintballing, trips that would take place immediately after watching extremely violent videos depicting Muslim suffering around the world.

What kind of internet content radicalized Jihad Jane?

Colleen LaRose ran away from a home in which her father was raping her and her sister. She did drugs. She prostituted herself. She found a boyfriend who indulged her, and moved in with him. Five years later, she argued with him in a bar in Amsterdam and went home with a Muslim man. After this one-night experience of Islam, she spent time on the internet learning more about the religion. She made her profession of faith to Islam on a whim, in an email, in early 2008. But she never went to a mosque, and her pledge to give up alcohol was soon lost; she spent her time flirting with men on websites and watching warrior films such as *Braveheart* and *Spartacus*.

For more detail, we move to an excerpt from Shiffman's (2012) study of LaRose, which has a special claim on our attention because Shiffman was the only person to obtain an interview with LaRose after her indictment for terrorist offenses:[5]

> Not until six months after the online conversion to Islam would she re-engage. In addition to passing time watching action movies, LaRose became riveted by violent YouTube videos of Israeli attacks on Palestinians and American attacks on Iraqis.
>
> The videos of dead and wounded children moved her most. Sometimes while she watched she could hear the young American children in the duplex below hers, laughing and playing. The disconnect infuriated her. No one seemed to know or care about the plight of the Palestinians. It was so unfair.
>
> By summer 2008, LaRose was posting jihadist videos on YouTube and MySpace. She used various names online, including Sister of Terror, Ms. Machiavelli and Jihad Jane. During the next year she exchanged messages with avowed jihadists.

They asked her to give money for jihad. She gave. They asked her to become a martyr. She agreed to travel to Europe to kill a Swedish artist who had blasphemed Prophet Mohammed. She traveled to Europe, but things didn't work out, and she received a 10-year prison sentence for terrorism-related crimes.

LaRose left a trail of emails and postings that illuminate her trajectory of radicalization. An infatuation with Islam and Muslim men was transformed to action through the power of victim videos—especially Muslim child victims no one cared about, just as LaRose had been a child victim no one cared about. From watching victim videos to posting jihad videos, to giving money for jihad, to promising to kill for Islam and departing for Europe to do so—this is a progression of increasing radical action built from YouTube videos of Muslim victims of Israeli and US military actions in the Middle East.

What kind of internet content radicalized Momin Khawaja?

Momin Khawaja's thoughts and actions leading to his 2004 arrest for terrorism were recorded in his emails and his blog. A Pakistan-Canadian with a good job in information technology, he loved to write about both personal and political issues, especially to his fiancé in Pakistan. His emails became part of the court record when he was arrested for participation in a militant jihadist group seeking to detonate a bomb in London. He is serving a life sentence in a Canadian prison.

Tom Quiggin is a Canadian investigator who testified in court as an expert witness at Khawaja's trial. The following are two excerpts from Quiggin's description of Khawaja's trajectory of radicalization.[6] The first excerpt points to the importance of seeing Muslims as victims. As Khawaja describes his life prior to his arrest, he had a fairly normal upbringing. In an email to his fiancé, he states:

"[I] was once a normal kid too. I played basketball, went swimming, bike-riding, and did all the things that naughty kids do. But once I grew up, I felt that something was wrong, terribly wrong. Right around the age of 21, I realized that all the fun pastime activities that everyone was into were a waste of time and did not benefit Islam and the Muslims in any way. So I left everything. When the Palestinian Intifada happened, I started looking into my own life and questioning myself as to why our situation was so bad. I realized that 'I' must change myself first, I must be willing to make a difference."

To Momin Khawaja, the Intifada highlighted the contradictions between his own life and that of other Muslims in the world. He was living a life of relative

luxury and safety, whilst others were living lives of oppression and fear. He was healthy and well fed, while
others were dying or leading lives of deprivation.
Perhaps most glaring was the fact that he was a Muslim
leading a good and safe life while living in a country that
was—in his mind—collectively responsible for the suffering of Muslims overseas. (pp. 87–88)

By this account, Khawaja's radicalization began with his reaction to the Second Intifada, which unfolded between 2000 and
2005 (Khawaja's 21st birthday was April 14, 2000). We do not
know exactly what Khawaja was watching as the Intifada unfolded, although the 5:1 preponderance of Palestinian to Israeli
Jewish deaths was broadly covered in Western reporting of the
Intifada. We do know, however, the particulars of some of the
internet videos to which Khawaja was exposed. Again we turn
to Quiggin's description:

In addition to the personal political, religious and economic narrative, a series of five "motivational" videos
produced by Ibn Khattab in Chechnya played an important role in the life and the subsequent criminal
conviction of Momin Khawaja. Ibn Khattab was from a
mixed Bedouin–Circassian family and has never been a
member of or a follower of al-Qaeda, despite al-Qaeda's
attempts to co-opt him. Notwithstanding his lack of allegiance to al-Qaeda, his videos, depicting attacks against
the Russian military in Chechnya, were popular among
extremist Muslims and had great influence.

The videos are commonly referred to as the "Russian
Hell" series and together they present a clear narrative.
The videos suggest that with just a few of the "brothers"
and some hand carried weapons, the oppressors can be
defeated. In a typical scene from the videos, the group's
leader, Ibn Khattab, gives a military style pre-mission

brief to his "soldiers." Following the briefing, the soldiers are seen moving to the ambush site from which they will attack a convoy of Russian soldiers. The scenes are almost cheery and ooze with camaraderie and optimism. The videos also have a rich symbolism found in the overlaid graphics as well as inspirational music (*nasheeds*) playing in the background.

For Momin Khawaja, the videos must have formed part of his "education" of the ways in which the *Mujahideen* could defeat the oppressors and their forces. Not only did he have copies of the videos on his hard drives, he is also known to have given copies to a woman that he was recruiting. Her role was to assist him in financial transfers relating to the planned attacks. One video extract was played in court to demonstrate the nature of the material he was using in his recruiting efforts. (p. 89)

The woman Khawaja tried to recruit testified at Khawaja's trial that he gave her several DVDs depicting jihadi activities and suggested that she "play them for others." At least one of the videos Khawaja gave her was entered in evidence at the trial: *Russian Hell I: Chechnya*. We can be confident that Khawaja believed the *Russian Hell* videos were a strong call to action because he recommended them to others.

Why might victim videos and jihad videos be particularly powerful in moving individuals to extremist action?

One possibility is to recognize that these two kinds of video are complementary parts of what social movement theorists refer to as a "mobilization frame."[7] A frame is a view of history and experience that allows us to make sense of and react to new events. An effective political frame accomplishes three functions: It identifies an injustice or grievance and the perpetrator (diagnostic), it identifies what must be done to right the wrong (prognostic), and it calls for individuals to participate in the solution (motivational) while providing knowledge and skills required for participation (means and opportunity). A frame thus has emotional value: Empathy and sympathy for victims bring anger toward the perceived perpetrator, and the call to participate in the solution can bring shame for not joining. Victim and jihad videos together create such a frame.

A victim video shows injustice in human terms: US attacks on Muslims that injure and kill women and children, or scenes purporting to show US soldiers raping a Muslim woman. A victim video also makes clear the perpetrator of injustice: US uniforms, weapons, and made-in-USA shell casings are made salient. Therefore, a victim video has intense diagnostic value, including emotion-arousing blood, pain, and destruction. US efforts to limit collateral damage of strikes against militants do nothing to reduce the power of images of suffering women and children. The emotional effect of these images is anger and outrage for viewers who identify with the victims.

A jihad video picks up where victim videos leave off: a dramatization of violent response to attacks on Muslims, with attractive militants inviting viewers to join them. A salient example of jihad videos is the *Russian Hell* series, which shows jihadists fighting Russians in Chechnya (1 hour 32 minutes, available on YouTube). These videos feature scenes of camaraderie and successful attacks, arousing music, and an explicit invitation: Join us, the brave, who are risking our lives to defend Muslim women and children. These videos show what to do and how to do it—the prognostic function.

Jihad videos are also motivational. They convey hope: The enemy can be attacked and killed despite their greater material strength. The men in the videos are models: If they can do it, so can I. As models, the men provoke a social comparison that can shame inaction: Am I less a man than they? The camaraderie and cohesion of a small group in combat is conveyed in the videos: I can join a band of brothers. The status of warrior is conveyed: I can be someone women look up to and men fear to challenge—a man with combat skills and brothers behind him.

The music of *nasheed* on the sound track is a stirring chant of male voices. The sounds and images of rocket and automatic weapons offer war-movie action; enemy trucks go up in noise, fire, and smoke. Close-ups of Russian bodies appear, booted up for inspection by the victors, then finished off with a few bullets. A helicopter, representative of Russian technological advantage, is shot down and falls dramatically from the sky. A dead mujahedeen is shown, unmarked with serene face, on a draped bier to convey the reality and nobility of sacrifice.

In sum, victim videos are diagnostic frames that elicit outrage against the perpetrators of injustice; jihad videos are prognostic and motivational frames that funnel outrage into joining the heroes who fight injustice. Social movement theory and especially framing theory make sense of our case histories, in which individuals who moved to join in jihadist violence point to victim videos and jihad videos as particularly powerful internet content.

Before moving on, it is worth noting what kind of content does *not* appear as important in our case histories. Study of the Koran and fundamentalist forms of Islam are not turning points in the trajectory to violent extremist action. From these examples, it is difficult to take seriously the popular idea that the center of gravity of jihadist extremism is Salafist, Wahabist, or other fundamentalist or extremist forms of Islam. Beyond some fighting verses from the Koran ("strive hard against the disbelievers and hypocrites"), Islam is represented in the *Russian Hell* videos only in the militants' beards and their shouts of "Allahu akbar" on the attack. Victim videos and jihad videos are about intergroup violence represented in emotion-eliciting images and music—about empathy for victims and outrage against perpetrators. In our opinion, some neo-jihadist terrorists may be religious Muslims and some may not. Religion is not the source of the violence, identification with victim Muslims is the source.

Why does ISIS post videos of beheadings and other barbaric acts?

ISIS has posted some barbaric execution videos, such as the video of burning to death a captured Jordanian pilot. It is important to remember that public beheading was commonplace in Europe for centuries—recall the guillotine of the French revolution—and is still practiced in Saudi Arabia. On one notorious day—January 2, 2016—the Saudis beheaded 43 prisoners for terrorism offenses. Many Muslims oppose Saudi beheadings and especially oppose terrorists' use of beheading. In 2002, al-Qaeda released a video of the beheading of Daniel Pearl, but so many Muslims reacted with revulsion that al-Qaeda no longer uses beheading videos.

If Western audiences find public beheading barbaric, and many Muslims agree, why does ISIS continue to post execution videos? One answer is free publicity, as much of the world gasps in horror at each new video. But al-Qaeda's turning away from beheading videos indicates that even among Muslims, much of the publicity is negative.

Another possibility is that ISIS aims to put fear in the hearts of its enemies. Fear must outweigh outrage and revulsion to make beheading videos a success for ISIS. We suspect that fear will indeed predominate in areas of Iraq and Syria controlled by ISIS but that outrage and revulsion will predominate among Western audiences, including Western Muslims. In this case, ISIS would be well advised to post the videos in their own areas but not post for Western audiences.

So why does ISIS use beheading videos? Who will they appeal to? Our answer is that the videos bring positive reactions and even recruits from a narrow range of Western Muslims who feel that the West is attacking Islam and feel the humiliation that Muslims do not have the power to retaliate. Beheading videos show power: ISIS is powerful enough to retaliate against the West with public executions. For the

Muslims feeling most anger and most humiliation, the power message of a beheading video is its main attraction.

Unfortunately, many Muslims believe that the West is trying to weaken and destroy Islam. Many believe that the War on Terrorism is actually a war on Islam.[8] Polls in 2006 and 2007 by the National Consortium for the Study of Terrorism and Responses to Terrorism (START) found that over half of respondents in Egypt, Morocco, Pakistan, and Indonesia believed that the US-led War on Terrorism was aimed at weakening Islam or controlling Middle East resources. Only 10–22 percent in these countries believed that the primary goal of the War on Terrorism was protection from terrorism. Similarly, the 2007 Pew poll of US Muslims found that only 26 percent believed that the War on Terrorism was a sincere effort to reduce terrorism; 55 percent said it was insincere.

Because many Muslims believe that the West is waging a war on Muslims, those most desperate to retaliate will see ISIS beheading videos as inspiring.

What about the video showing a captured Jordanian pilot being burned to death in a steel cage? ISIS released this video in February 2015. The video is 22 minutes long, and the death by fire appears at the end. Earlier in the video, the pilot is shown in an orange jumpsuit being taken through bombed out buildings supposedly destroyed in air attacks by the United States and its allies. The logic of the video is justice and revenge: Muslims die horrible deaths in buildings crushed and burned by air attacks; now one of the pilots responsible for such attacks dies a similar death. The orange jumpsuit is another piece of payback: Prisoners at Guantanamo Bay wear orange jumpsuits.

Like the beheading videos, the death by fire video will bring revulsion to most viewers but will appeal to the small number of Muslims who are desperate to avenge Muslim victims of Western attacks. This is the audience from which new recruits are drawn to ISIS.

How can we protect young people from online radicalization?

If our analysis is correct, it will be very difficult to prevent on-line radicalization. The West could try to keep victim and jihad videos off the internet, or at least prevent access to these videos in Western countries. This might lead Western countries to the same techniques of information control that China imposes on its citizens.

At the bottom of radicalization is identification: caring about a group enough that what happens to them produces emotional reactions in us. The West might try to prevent young Muslims from identifying with other Muslims, or at least prevent Western Muslims from identifying with Muslims in non-Western countries. This is a tall order but perhaps not impossible. Identification requires feeling similar to that group, and common religion is not usually enough similarity to produce strong identification. In recent centuries, common blood and common culture have been stronger than religion as a source of political mobilization. That is, nationalism has been a stronger force than religion in mobilizing people for conflict.

Perhaps Western Muslims can be turned away from identification with Muslims whose blood and culture are seen as different from their own. The West might try to raise ethnic nationalism as an antidote to a religious nationalism that aims to make Muslim identity the foundation of a multinational caliphate. In predominantly Muslim countries, most Muslims probably feel more attachment to their country than to the umma; most Moroccans, for instance, are probably not willing to sacrifice for an international umma as much as they would sacrifice for the welfare of Morocco and Moroccans.

We know that this will not always work. Momin Khawaja, born in Canada, made fun of Muslims "off the boat" for their baggy clothes and crude manners yet in the end tried to join the Taliban to fight the US invasion of Afghanistan.

Another and perhaps more practical possibility is to make Western Muslims feel more welcome as immigrants. Momin Khawaja, despite being the son of a professor and despite his own educational and occupational successes, did not feel welcome in Canada. He felt that his darker skin, his religion, and his foreign name kept him from being a "real" Canadian. This feeling led him to turn to his religion as his political identity: If he was no longer Pakistani and could not be Canadian, what could he be but Muslim? Identifying more with his religion than with Canada and Canadians led him to see the Canadian armed forces engaged in Afghanistan as part of the Western war on Islam—which pushed him still further from caring about Canadians and toward caring about Muslim victims.

In short, it might help reduce identification with Muslim victims in predominantly Muslim countries if Muslim immigrants felt less suspicion and more acceptance in Western countries. ISIS realizes this and tries to use jujitsu politics to keep walls between Muslims and non-Muslims. Every time a Muslim engages in a terrorist attack in the West—for instance, the San Bernardino attack—the wall between Muslims and non-Muslims is raised.

Finally, there is the possibility that radicalization of Muslims might be reduced by reducing US military involvement in predominantly Muslim countries. In recent years, US drones have brought death from the sky in Afghanistan, Iraq, Libya, Pakistan, Syria, Somalia, and Yemen. It is not possible to avoid civilian casualties when pressing a button in the United States produces explosions half a world away. The collateral damage from US drone attacks brings hatred of the United States and new victim videos.

General Stanley McChrystal, commander of US forces in Afghanistan, 2009-2010, had this to say about overreliance on drones:

"What scares me about drone strikes is how they are perceived around the world," he said. "The resentment created by American use of unmanned strikes . . . is much
greater than the average American appreciates. They are
hated on a visceral level, even by people who've never
seen one or seen the effects of one."[9]

7

WHAT IS DIFFERENT ABOUT LONE WOLF TERRORISTS?

Who is a lone wolf terrorist?

Sometimes called a lone actor terrorist, a lone wolf terrorist acts alone, without support from a terrorist group or organization. Modern use of the term goes back to Tom Metzger, founder of the White Aryan Resistance, who argued in the 1980s for "lone wolf" resistance to the US government.[1] The same idea was earlier advanced by another right-wing theorist, Louis Beam, in an essay titled "Leaderless Resistance" that called for "very small or even one man cells of resistance."[2]

In the 1980s, right-wing extremist organizations in the United States were being crushed by law enforcement agencies using informers and infiltrators. The lone wolf idea was that violent acts by anonymous individuals would be more difficult for law enforcement to penetrate than acts by members of large and hierarchical organizations such as the Ku Klux Klan. The cells were to be anonymous even to one another, with no communication or connection. The only commonality would be willingness to act against oppressive government. Metzger and Beam suggested that lone wolves should avoid membership cards, tattoos, letters to the editor, and participation in demonstrations—anything that would give authorities a link to the cause for which they would act.

From the beginning, then, a small cell—two or three individuals acting together—could be seen as lone wolf terrorists so long as they planned and carried out an attack without help from any larger group or organization. Deadly examples of lone wolf terrorists in the United States include Theodore Kaczynski (Unabomber; killed 3 and injured 23 between 1978 and 1995), Eric Rudolf (bombed 1996 Atlanta Olympics; killed 3 and wounded 117), and Omar Mateen (killed 49 and wounded 58 in 2016 mass shooting in a gay night club in Orlando, Florida).

Are lone wolf terrorist attacks increasing?

This is not an easy question because it is not always clear whether an attack is politically motivated. Sometimes an individual perpetrates violence for personal reasons. A student who shoots up his school, for instance, is not usually seen as having a political cause. A disgruntled employee who attacks co-workers is not usually seen as having a political cause. But some cases are not clear-cut.

In November 2009, Major Nidal Malik Hasan killed 13 and wounded more than 30 in a mass shooting at the Soldier Readiness Center at Fort Hood, Texas. Although Hasan reportedly shouted "Allahu akbar" ("Allah is great") during the attack, the US Department of Defense categorized the attack as "workplace violence." It was not until 6 years later, in December 2015, that President Obama declared that the attack was an act of terrorism. Hasan acted alone, making him a lone wolf terrorist.

In February 2010, Andrew Joseph Stack III, a 53-year-old computer engineer, flew a small plane into Internal Revenue Service (IRS) offices in a building in Austin, Texas. He killed one person and injured 13. He left behind a manifesto in which he blamed the US government, big business, and especially the IRS for taking his savings. The US government did not call this a terrorist incident because there was no sign of terrorist ideology and Stack was not associated with any extremist political group. If, as we have argued, grievance and anger rather than ideology are the key to understanding terrorism, then Stack was indeed a terrorist.

Despite occasional controversy over what counts as lone wolf terrorism, there are best-effort attempts to catalog examples of lone wolf attacks. A report by Frontline started with a database of possible lone wolf attacks in the United States, then excluded attacks that never came to fruition, were hoaxes, or did not seem to include any political intent. Results indicated that lone wolf attacks are rare but show a clear increase by decade, from 2 in the 1940s to 23 in the 2000s and 35 in the 2010s.[3]

The trend is not so clear in Europe, although lone wolf terrorism includes two salient cases. In July 2011, in Norway, Anders Breivik killed 77 in two attacks, the first a bomb and the second a mass shooting. And in July 2016, Mohamed Bouhlel killed 86 and injured 458 by driving a truck into crowds celebrating Bastille Day in Nice, France.

Security officials and citizens are alike in their increasing concerns about the threat of lone wolf attacks. As Metzger and Beam promised, these attacks are difficult to anticipate and prevent. President Obama recognized the threat in 2011:

The biggest concern we have right now is not the launching of a major terrorist operation, although that risk is always there, the risk that we're especially concerned over right now is the lone wolf terrorist, somebody with a single weapon being able to carry out wide-scale massacres of the sort that we saw in Norway recently. You know, when you've got one person who is deranged or driven by a hateful ideology, they can do a lot of damage, and it's a lot harder to trace those lone wolf operators.[4]

Why are lone wolf terrorists a challenge to theories of radicalization?

Lone actor terrorists are risking life and liberty for their cause. Why would any individual take this kind of risk? Why would any individual choose to sacrifice for a cause?

The usual answer to these questions is that group, organizational, and cultural pressures move us to do what we would not choose to do if we considered only our personal welfare. As described in Chapter 4, small group dynamics can provide rewards for those who take risks and make sacrifices for the group, and punishments for those who do not. Organizations similarly provide rewards for those—firefighters, police officers, soldiers—who take risks for organizational goals, and punishments for those who shirk their duty.

The puzzle presented by the lone actor terrorist is that the individual takes risks and makes sacrifices as a free choice, not subject to social pressures. The lone actor does not feel the power of group dynamics and group pressures and does not have organizational support. The puzzle is why an individual would freely choose violence for a cause, knowing that the choice will be costly: Prison, torture, and death are likely outcomes for an individual taking up violence against the power of a state.

A popular answer to the puzzle is that extreme or fanatic beliefs push some individuals to violence. This answer implies a single dimension of radicalization, ranging from individuals who care nothing about a cause to those who believe in the cause so strongly that they are ready to risk their lives for it. It is plausible that radical ideas produce radical behavior, and Silber and Bhatt popularized the single-dimension model in their 2007 New York Police Department report, "Radicalization in the West: The Homegrown Threat." The single-dimension model is similarly embodied in the metaphor that groups advancing extremist ideas are a "conveyor belt" to terrorism.

In this view, terrorist violence is the radical behavior that proceeds from radical ideas.

As we already showed in Chapter 6, however, three kinds of evidence have contradicted the single-dimension model of radicalization. First, there are individuals who move to violence without support of radical ideas. At the individual level, mechanisms of radicalization include personal grievance, group grievance, love, escape, slippery slope, risk and status seeking, and social disconnection (unfreezing). Five of these seven mechanisms—group grievance, personal grievance, risk and status seeking, social disconnection, and escape from personal problems—can potentially move an individual to lone wolf terrorism without any help from radical ideas or political ideology. Love for someone already a member of a militant group is irrelevant for the lone wolf terrorist. Similarly, a slippery slope of increasingly extreme action is irrelevant for lone wolf terrorists, whose first radical act is usually their first and only attack.

Second, radical opinions are common but terrorists are few, lone actor terrorists even fewer. In 2007 and 2011 polls, about 8 percent of US Muslims said that suicide bombing of civilian targets is often or sometimes justified. Eight percent of the approximately 1 million adult US Muslims projects to approximately 80,000 who justify suicide bombing. But only hundreds of US Muslims have been arrested for violence-related offenses, and only about a dozen of these might qualify as lone wolf terrorists.

Third, research on deradicalization has highlighted the difference between extreme action and extreme opinion.[5] Some captured jihadists are willing to give up violent action but not ready to give up extremist opinions. Others are willing to give up both violent action and extremist opinions. The first kind of change is deradicalization of action without deradicalization of opinion. The second kind of change is deradicalization of both action and opinion. The disjunction of action and opinion is not consistent with the idea that it is extreme opinion that produces extreme action.

Thus, three kinds of evidence weigh against the single-dimension view of radicalization that assumes bad behavior begins in bad ideas. Many individuals move to terrorism before they acquire extreme ideas. Ninety-nine percent of those with extreme ideas never act. And individuals can give up extreme action without giving up extreme ideas.

This is the evidence that led us, in Chapter 6, to the two-pyramids model of radicalization in which ideas—even the most extreme ideas—are not a sufficient explanation of extremist violence. If extreme ideas are not a useful explanation of extreme action, then the puzzle remains: How are we to understand lone wolf terrorists?

Can individual-level mechanisms explain lone wolf terrorists?

Five mechanisms of radicalization might move an individual to lone wolf terrorism: group grievance, personal grievance, risk and status seeking, disconnection (unfreezing), and escape from personal problems. These mechanisms can be seen in some case histories of lone wolf terrorists. Major Hasan, for instance, had a group grievance that Western forces were victimizing Muslims. He also had some personal grievances. He felt discriminated against as a Muslim, and his automobile was vandalized. He was ordered to go to Afghanistan to support soldiers fighting there against Muslims; his attack was an escape from this order. He was working on an Army base in Texas far from his family on the East Coast; he seems to have had no friends in Texas, so he was disconnected from the kinds of ties that keep most of us in our tracks. There is nothing in his history, however, to suggest he sought risk taking and status. So, to sum up, Hasan showed evidence of four of five possible mechanisms of radicalization at work in his trajectory to lone wolf terrorism.

What about Andrew Joseph Stack, the software engineer who flew his plane into an IRS office? There is no doubt he felt a personal grievance against the IRS and the US government in general. He was losing his business in a tax case. He felt that his life was ruined, so a suicide attack could seem an escape from an intolerable situation. But there is no sign that he was seeking risk and status, and he was not disconnected. His wife and stepdaughter left home for a hotel only the night before his attack, after he had begun work on his suicide note. Here is a case with evidence of only two of the five possible individual mechanisms of radicalization.

It is interesting to notice that Stack did express more than personal grievance against the IRS in his suicide note. He talked about other engineers who had suffered from IRS rulings and about how government bails out big businesses such as General Motors but lets the small businessman be crushed. Whether Stack is a suicide terrorist or just a suicide depends on how seriously we take the group grievance part of his suicide note. Here is a key passage:

I can only hope that the numbers quickly get too big to be white washed and ignored that the American zombies wake up and revolt; it will take nothing less. I would only hope that by striking a nerve that stimulates the inevitable double standard, knee-jerk government reaction that results in more stupid draconian restrictions people wake up and begin to see the pompous political thugs and their mindless minions for what they are. Sadly, though I spent my entire life trying to believe it wasn't so, but violence not only is the answer, it is the only answer.[6]

We recommend reading the whole suicide note at the website given in note 6, then decide for yourself whether there is enough political intent to see Stack as a suicide terrorist.

Beyond case materials, there is a cumulation of information about lone wolf terrorists in Israel. In about 12-months from October 2015 to 2016, Israel experienced attacks by Palestinians that killed 40 and injured about 500. Most of the attacks were perpetrated by individuals using a knife or a hatchet. The preponderance of knife attacks led this year to be called "the knifing intifada." Most individuals attempting knife attacks (150 of 250 assailants) were shot dead at the scene of the attack; these individuals are thus not just lone wolf terrorists but suicide lone wolf terrorists. Here is a description, from *The American Interest*, of what Israeli security forces learned about the attackers:

Most perpetrators have been quite young, between the ages of 17 and 22. Almost all of them have been unaffiliated with any Palestinian political faction. They embarked upon spontaneous individual initiatives, typically without sharing their plans of attack with friends or relatives. Often, they fit the definition of "from zero to hero" terrorists: They came mostly from the margins of their social groups; few if any were recognized as political activists or leaders among their peers. Social media, primarily Facebook, served as their platform rather than any of the many politically sponsored media outlets.

In most cases they were motivated by personal circumstances, striving to avenge and imitate previous attackers, and in some cases seeking to gain recognition as martyrs. Although many were driven to act by the widespread allegations that Israel was seeking to change the status quo at the al-Aqsa mosque, very few were devout Muslims. Patriotic sentiment trumped religion as the strongest driving force, coupled as always with feelings of indignation and humiliation at the presence of Israeli troops.[7]

Here is a similar description from *The Economist*:

> After reviewing the profiles of scores of attackers, the intelligence officers found that they often acted on the spur of the moment. They were rarely linked to militant factions, and were not especially religious or poor. Many had a grievance: a son who felt unjustly treated, a brother who was disinherited, a bride who was beaten by her husband, and so on.[8]

Spur-of-the-moment action suggests action based on emotion and points away from ideology or religion. Rarely connected to a militant group and not especially religious also point away from ideology or religion. Low-status individuals seeking the glory of martyrdom are status seeking. Indignation and humiliation are emotional reactions to the group grievance that Israeli troops control Palestinians. Some attackers were motivated to revenge a relative or friend killed attempting to attack Israelis—that is, had a personal grievance as well as a group grievance.

What *The Economist* calls a grievance is not a grievance against Israeli Jews. In our terms, unjust treatment from a family member is a humiliation to be escaped and a signal of social disconnection; the relevant mechanisms of radicalization are thus disconnection and escape. It is important to notice that some of the attackers were seeking death in a manner described in the United States as "suicide by cop." For instance, a young woman approached armed Israeli soldiers and waved scissors at them while too far away to reach them. Suicide is an extreme form of escape from personal problems.

Israeli experience with lone wolf suicide terrorists thus points to the importance of five mechanisms of radicalization: group grievance, personal grievance, status seeking, escape, and social disconnection. Unfortunately, we have no way to count how many individuals may show these same mechanisms but do not become lone wolf terrorists. We turn now from case study material to statistical studies of lone wolf terrorists.

What are the personal characteristics of lone wolf terrorists?

The disconnected–disordered profile

The preceding section indicated that at least some of the five individual mechanisms of radicalization can be found in the lives of lone wolf terrorists. In this section, we try to find other and possibly more specific characteristics that may be common among lone wolf terrorists.

In an early example of this kind of research, Hewitt (2003) identified 27 lone actor US terrorists between 1955 and 2001 and suggested that the rate of psychological disturbance was higher (6 of 27) among the loners than among other US terrorists.[9] More recent studies of lone actor terrorists point in the same direction.

Spaaij (2012) examined 88 cases of lone actor terrorists aggregated across 15 Western countries and found that lone actors are likely to suffer from some form of psychological disturbance and tend to be loners with few friends.[10] Gill, Horgan, and Deckert put together an international collection of 119 mostly lone actor terrorists (including also isolated dyads and some individuals with loose group connections). No single profile was identified, but many of the lone actors seemed to be socially isolated.[11] In the most methodologically sophisticated study yet conducted, Gruenewald, Chermak, and Freilich compared lethal attacks by lone actor and group actor US far-right extremists. Results indicated that the lone actors were younger; more likely to have a military background; more likely to suffer mental illness; and more likely to experience disconnection by separation, divorce, or death of a partner.[12]

Expanding the search, McCauley, Moskalenko, and Van Son sought to develop hypotheses about the characteristics of lone wolf terrorists by looking for the common characteristics of two kinds of mostly lone actor violent offenders: assassins and school attackers.[13] The study used existing US government-sponsored reports to examine these two kinds of offenders.

The logic of comparing school attackers with assassins is that these two groups of offenders are like lone actor terrorists in perpetrating planful violence fueled by grievance. To the extent that assassins and school attackers share common characteristics, these characteristics may be risk factors for lone actor terrorism as well. The obvious demographic differences between the two groups (teenagers vs. adults) are actually a strength of the comparison: Any commonalities uncovered are the more striking and unlikely to be a reflection of life status or demographic factors.

The common characteristics of assassins and school attackers included grievance, depression, unfreezing (broken social ties), and weapons use outside the military. These four characteristics suggest the importance of means and opportunity for perpetrating violence. Grievance is a motive for violence, weapons experience provides a means, and depression and unfreezing lower the opportunity cost of violence as the perpetrator has less to lose.

An illustration of these characteristics can be made for the case of Major Nidal Malik Hasan. Hasan turned to the Koran after the death of his parents, seems to have had no close relationships after he was transferred to Fort Hood, and was about to be transferred to Afghanistan (*unfreezing*). He saw himself discriminated against as a Muslim (*personal grievance*) and saw the War on Terrorism as a war on Islam (*political grievance*). He brought two weapons to his attack, one a sophisticated "cop-killer" pistol for which he purchased a laser sight—indicating *experience with weapons* beyond whatever slight weapons training the US Army provides for physician–psychiatrists.

As far as we can ascertain, Hasan showed no signs of depression. So Hasan had three of the four characteristics common to assassins and school attackers: unfreezing, grievance, and weapons experience.

Taken together, these results indicate that grievance-fueled lone attackers are likely to have weapons experience, depression or other mental disorder, and temporary or chronic social isolation. We have called this the *disconnected–disordered* profile: socially disconnected loners with mental health problems. The two elements of the profile are interactive: feeling alone is painful and perhaps depressing; being depressed frays social connections.

Future research may discover characteristics that differentiate lone actor terrorists from assassins and school attackers, or it may turn out that lone actor terrorists are simply one facet of a larger phenomenon of grievance-motivated lone actor violence. Perhaps what a lone attacker says about his or her grievance determines whether we see the individual as a terrorist. Andrew Joseph Stack was a borderline case: Some saw him as a case of workplace violence, and some saw him as an anti-government terrorist.

The caring–compelled profile

There are lone actor terrorists who do not fit the disconnected–disordered profile—individuals who are not loners and not suffering mental disorder but who nonetheless undertake lone actor terrorist violence.

One such case is Vera Zazulich. A young Russian woman who had spent time in Siberia for anti-tsarist political activities, Zazulich heard about a student prisoner beaten for failing to doff his cap to the prison governor. Zazulich was outraged; she tried to learn if the terrorist group People's Will was going to bring vengeance against the governor. The militants brushed her off. She decided someone had to do something, so she procured a pistol, went to see the governor, and shot him.

After a tumultuous trial, she was acquitted and spirited out of Russia before the tsar could countermand the acquittal. In exile, she wrote and debated with the likes of Vladimir Lenin; she showed no sign of mental disorder and was connected with many political activists in exile.

Another such case is Clayton Waagner. Beginning in the 1970s, Waagner was convicted of various acts of theft and burglary, and in 1992 he was sentenced to 4 years in prison for attempted robbery. After serving his prison sentence, he was in Pittsburgh in January 1999 when his daughter Emily went into premature labor, giving birth to a granddaughter, Cierra, born dead at 24 weeks. Waagner's commitment to fight abortion began when he held Cierra, touched her soft skin, and looked at her tiny but perfectly formed face and body. He says that he heard an internal voice—the voice of God: "How can you grieve so hard for this one when millions are killed each year and you do nothing."

In September 1999, he was driving with his wife and children in a Winnebago that broke down. Police found stolen firearms in the stolen vehicle, and Waagner admitted that he was planning to use the weapons to kill abortion providers. Convicted for theft and firearms violations, he escaped from prison in February 2001. He described tracking and finding an easy shot at several abortion clinic doctors, but he could not bring himself to pull the trigger. He kept on the run by committing auto theft and robbery, and changed his plans: He would use fear instead of bullets.

In October 2001, Waagner mailed 285 letters to abortion clinics throughout the United States. Each letter contained a quarter-teaspoon of white flour and an anthrax threat. Coming soon after the still-unsolved anthrax attacks that followed the 9/11 attacks, the letters were taken seriously and seriously disrupted clinic operations. In November 2001, still on the run, he mailed 269 more letters to abortion clinics. Anticipating doubts and accelerated testing after the first hoax, he included in the white powder traces of a substance known to test positive in the most common test for anthrax. Again, he succeeded in shutting down many clinics. Captured in December 2001, he is serving a 30-year jail sentence in the US Penitentiary at Lewisburg, Pennsylvania.

Before holding his dead granddaughter, Waagner was at the second or third level of radicalization in the opinion pyramid: He sympathized with those fighting abortion and may even have seen violence against abortion providers as justified. But he was doing nothing in the fight against abortion—that is, he was inert in the base layer of the action pyramid. His grief holding his dead granddaughter turned to guilt for doing nothing about the millions aborted, and from grief and guilt came radicalization in both the opinion and the action pyramids. As with Zazulich, strong emotion made the personal political; he felt suddenly a personal responsibility for action that radicalized him to the apex of the opinion pyramid. He moved also to the apex of the action pyramid (terrorists) as he stalked abortion providers.

Interesting here is the fact that Waagner had targets in his sights but could not pull the trigger. He was forced down the action pyramid to fight abortion with threats of violence that were in fact harmless. With his anthrax letters, he moved from the terrorist apex of the action pyramid to the radicals level of illegal political action without violence.

The two cases described—the tender-hearted secretary and the man of action—offer several clues for understanding how individuals can leave self-interest and loved ones behind to take risks in lone actor terrorism. Both were sympathizers with a cause and perhaps justifiers of violence in support of that cause. That is, both were in the middle levels of radicalization in the opinion pyramid. Zazulich had already reached the third level of the action pyramid in illegal anti-tsarist activism. Waagner, too, had broken laws but remained in the inert base of the action pyramid doing nothing to fight abortion. For both, something of great emotional significance occurred—unpunished violation of a student, the death of a granddaughter—and the political became personal. In both cases, the emotion came from identifying with—caring about—the welfare of others. Both were radicalized to feeling a personal moral obligation—the apex of the opinion pyramid—and both attacked perceived perpetrators of violence against those they cared about—the apex of the action pyramid.

What moved both, while others who shared their convictions did nothing, seems to have been an unusual capacity to care about the suffering of others. Both had solid social connections and no signs of mental disorder. We have called this the *caring–compelled profile* of lone actor terrorism. The capacity for empathy or sympathy is generally seen as quintessentially human and eminently humane. Here, we have a hint that there can be a dark side to caring greatly about others. Individuals can kill for love, including love of strangers seen as victimized.

What is different about lone wolf terrorists?

We have found a number of ways in which lone wolf terrorists differ from the more common group-based terrorists. Lone wolf terrorists are more difficult to understand, because they are not subject to the pressures of group dynamics and group norms that are the usual way we explain how individuals can put a group or cause above self-preservation.

Group terrorists are predominantly normal individuals with no common characteristics that might provide a profile. In contrast, lone wolf terrorists do have some common characteristics, and we have suggested two possible characteristic profiles—the disconnected–disordered and the caring–compelled. Both profiles point to a kind of abnormality—the first in social disconnection and depression, and the second in an overwhelming sympathy with the sufferings of others.

Both profiles point to the importance of emotion in moving individuals to terrorism. The disconnected–disordered feel the sadness that goes with loneliness and depression. They are in pain and are pushed to action to escape their pain; they have little to lose. The caring–compelled feel sadness over the suffering of those they see as victims, and anger or outrage at those perceived as perpetrating suffering on the victims. These emotions push them to act despite the risk to their careers and families. For lone wolf terrorists as for group-based terrorists, it is extreme emotion rather than extreme ideas that moves these individuals to violent action.

8

ARE SUICIDE BOMBERS SUICIDAL?

Answering this question requires knowing a little about suicide.

What percentage of suicidal individuals kill themselves?

The 2015 National Survey on Drug Use and Health found that 4 percent of US adults (18 or older) reported having "serious thoughts of committing suicide" and 0.6 percent reported attempting suicide.[1] These percentages represent 9.8 million adults who thought about suicide and 1.4 million who attempted suicide. So, only one of seven individuals with thoughts of suicide actually attempts suicide. Here is another example of the difference between extreme ideas and extreme action.

Why do people commit suicide?

In brief, people commit suicide because they are in pain and despair of life getting any better. The National Institutes of Health website on suicide prevention describes the feelings that lead to suicide as feeling empty, hopeless, or having no reason to live; feeling great guilt or shame; feeling trapped or that there are no solutions; feeling unbearable pain (emotional pain or physical pain); and feeling oneself a burden to others.[2]

These feelings amount to seeing death as an escape from endless suffering.

Who is a suicide bomber?

A suicide bomber is one who expects to detonate an explosive that will kill the bomber as well as his or her targets. More generally, a suicide terrorist is one who expects to die in the performance of an attack. Suicide terrorists often use a bomb strapped to their bodies, or drive and detonate an explosives-laden vehicle. Suicide terrorists sometimes use a firearm to attack a superior force with no escape route planned or attempted, as Major Nidal Malik Hasan did at Fort Hood, Texas. In the case of the Palestinian "stabbing intifada," individuals attack armed soldiers with knives. Here, we want to try to understand suicide terrorists in general, most of whom are suicide bombers but some of whom do not use a bomb.

Those who sympathize with the terrorist cause are likely to call the suicide terrorist a martyr—*shahid* in Arabic. Shahid literally means witness, in a close parallel to the Greek word for witness that came to refer to Christian martyrs in the New Testament. Of course, the victims of a suicide terrorist attack are likely to deny that the attacker is a martyr and instead see the attacker as mentally disturbed or otherwise suicidal. In Europe, suicide terrorists are sometimes called "kamikaze terrorists" in recognition that they may be motivated by nationalism and obedience, as were the Japanese who made suicide attacks on US ships during World War II.

About 15 percent of suicide terrorists are female. Attacks carried out by female terrorists tend to be deadlier than those carried out by males, because females are usually seen as less likely to be violent and because of a reluctance to search females, especially those who appear to be pregnant. For a militant organization, using female suicide attackers has three additional advantages. First, as they are less common, female attackers tend to produce more media coverage for the organization that claims them. Second, female attackers signal the desperation and commitment of the organization that uses them, especially in a male-dominated culture. And third, female attackers shame males into doing more, especially in a male-dominated culture. Martyrs rally sympathizers to their cause, and female martyrs tend to have a greater rallying effect than males.

Although the popular image of a suicide bomber is an individual attacking alone, in fact there are many attacks in which two, three, or even eight or more suicide bombers attack one target or nearby targets at about the same time. These multiple suicide attacks are particularly dangerous, not only because of the difficulty of stopping multiple attackers but also because of the group dynamics that make it difficult for any one of the attackers to have second thoughts. If your friends are all sacrificing themselves in an attack, how can you decide at the last minute that they should die without you?

The larger point here is that few suicide terrorists are lone wolf terrorists. The individual Palestinian attacking Israeli soldiers with a knife can be a lone wolf because no organizational help is required. Anyone can find a knife. Similarly, anyone can find a motor vehicle and use it as a weapon to mow down pedestrians. But most suicide attackers and nearly all suicide bombers need help to find means and opportunity for their attack. A militant organization has to supply the bomb, select the target, and transport the bomber to the target. Suicide bombers are not lone wolf terrorists but human weapons prepared and used by a militant organization.

When do terrorists use suicide attacks?

Suicide attacks are increasing. From 1981 to 2016, there were about 5400 suicide attacks in over 40 countries. These attacks killed about 55,000 and wounded about 135,000 people, which means about 10 dead and 25 wounded from each suicide attack.[3] In short, suicide attacks are a deadly weapon. These attacks have been increasing, from about 3 per year in the 1980s to 1 per day in 2016.

Suicide attacks have increased as a response to the numerical and technical superiority of state security forces. Led by the United States, state forces now employ drones equipped with powerful sensing equipment and powerful missiles; these can put high explosives on targets half a world away without risking a single soldier. Unfortunately, pushing a button in the United States to hit a target in Syria, Afghanistan, or Libya is not an exact science; mistakes are referred to as "collateral damage" by the United States but seen as murder from the skies by victims and their families.

In the context of drone attacks and other "smart bombs" deployed by the United States, terrorists have deployed suicide bombers as their own smart bombs. As US technical superiority grows, terrorists increasingly rely on suicide attacks.

Suicide attackers, male or female, can bring fear to those attacked. No place seems safe anymore. But creating fear in the enemy is not the only and perhaps not the major value of using suicide attackers. As described in Chapter 5, those attacked feel anger and hostility toward the group the attackers come from. Suicide attacks raise fear and anger against the whole group the terrorist comes from, especially if that group has ethnic markers that distinguish it from the terrorist's targets. Suicide attacks from Arabs or South Asians against Euro-origin targets quickly produce fear and anger toward those with darker skin.

This is the jujitsu politics described in Chapter 5: Terrorists want to move more of their own people to support and join them, and hope that their attacks will build a wall between their people and others. Suicide terrorism is particularly effective for building walls; when everyone who even looks like "them" is a potential suicide terrorist, walls, checkpoints, and discrimination will soon appear.

In short, militant groups use suicide attackers because they are inexpensive and relatively effective against the superior strength of state forces. Suicide attackers are the poor man's smart bomb, but they are more than that. Their effect in jujitsu politics, in building a wall between groups, is more than any missile or drone can accomplish.

Why do individuals agree to sacrifice their lives in a suicide attack?

It is relatively easy to understand why a small and desperate group would want to use suicide attackers against state forces. The motives of individual attackers are not so straightforward. As with most human behavior, possible motives are many and interactive.

Perhaps the best review of the motivations of suicide bombing was conducted by sociologist Riaz Hassan, who reviewed statistical material and case histories of suicide bombers in Iraq, Israel–Palestine, Afghanistan, Pakistan, and Sri Lanka.[4] He argues that suicide bombing is above all political—a response to repressive occupation and humiliation by foreign forces. These are the situational factors that make a population ready to support suicide bombing and make individuals ready to give their lives to fight for the group. This is altruistic suicide: The bomber believes that death in an attack will help the group.

It is perhaps not obvious how a suicide attack helps the group. Even a successful suicide attack does not usually move the target group to change policy toward the group the terrorists aim to represent. Palestinian suicide attacks have led Israel to ever harsher treatment of Palestinians, with checkpoints, embargoes, and prison making life for ordinary Palestinians ever more difficult and painful.

As Hasan notes, this accounting leaves out the cost of humiliation and domination by a victimizing perpetrator. Humiliation, described in Chapter 5, is a corrosive interaction of anger for maltreatment and shame for not striking back.

Anger is satisfied and shame is reduced when a suicide terrorist strikes the perceived perpetrator of injustice. The payoff is not material gain, but restored self-respect and the beginnings of justice in giving the perpetrator a taste of the violence the perpetrator dishes out. This payoff is not dependent on deterring the perpetrator, which, in the Palestinian case and many others, does not happen.

The situational factors are very broad and affect all or most of a group: Iraqis, Afghans, Pakistanis, Palestinians, or Sri Lankans. Situational factors prepare the foundation for suicide attacks but cannot tell us much about why and how a few individuals commit to these attacks.

Hasan finds a variety of individual motives for suicide attacks. Some individuals seek the glory and status of martyrdom. If a population or a large part of it supports suicide bombing and other forms of suicide attacks, then the bomber can expect the status of a martyr. This is the mechanism of status seeking discussed in Chapter 3. The glory of martyrdom is especially attractive to individuals with a "spoiled identity." For males, this might be charges of fraud or incest or some other honor failure. For females, the spoiled identity might be the stigma of sex outside of marriage, including rape, or simply failure to produce children. Those with low status are particularly susceptible to the status claim of martyrdom.

Personal revenge is another motive common among suicide attackers. If the enemy killed my brother, my children, or my best friend, I am likely in my anguish to seek revenge even at the cost of my life. The loss of loved ones indeed leaves life empty such that the individual feels that there is little left in life to lose. This is the mechanism of personal grievance discussed in Chapter 3.

Status seeking and personal grievance do not replace the situational factors that lead to feelings of domination and humiliation; rather, individual mechanisms of radicalization add to and interact with the situational factors to help us understand the few who commit to suicide attacks.

Do suicide terrorists have personality problems?

Another individual explanation of suicide attackers might be that they are suffering from some kind of mental disorder. There have been two notable versions of this explanation, one from psychologist Ariel Merari and one from criminologist Adam Lankford.

No one has studied suicide terrorists longer than Ariel Merari, who has had the advantage of working in Israel during three decades in which suicide terrorism has been all too common. In Chapter 5 of his 2010 book, *Driven to Death*, he raised the possibility that there is a psychological profile that distinguishes suicide bombers from other terrorists.[5]

Merari's study compared 15 failed or foiled Palestinian suicide bombers with a control group of 12 Palestinian terrorists imprisoned for offenses unrelated to suicide bombing. The control group was matched to would-be suicide bombers on age, time spent in prison, education, marital status, and organizational affiliation. The two groups were compared using a number of psychological tests and an interview with a clinical psychologist fluent in Arabic.

Results indicated systematic differences between the two groups. More would-be suicide bombers were diagnosed with avoidant-dependent personality disorder, more showed suicidal tendencies, and more showed depressive symptoms. Avoidant personality disorder (APD) is characterized by avoidance of new activities that might bring embarrassment; excessive attachment to friends leaves the individual fearful of humiliation or embarrassment. In dependent personality disorder (DPD), individuals tend to be passive and allow others to take initiative and assume responsibility for their lives. When APD and DPD co-occur in the same individual, the clinical picture is of a person completely engulfed by the will of another person or group, unwilling and unable to express and assert his or her own opinion for fear of criticism or embarrassment.

These results are suggestive but not definitive. The groups compared are small, and there is no comparison with nonterrorist Palestinians. The clinical picture of APD–DPD suggests an individual easily recruited into the role of suicide terrorist, but we know from Merari's interviews with terrorist recruiters that about half of suicide terrorists were self-initiated volunteers rather than volunteers solicited by the organization.

Interestingly, the recruiters also said that they would not take criminals, mentally unstable candidates, or suicidal people who wanted to die for personal reasons. The recruiters agreed that the predominant motive for suicide bombers was more nationalist than religious: Striking back against Israeli treatment of Palestinians was the driver; religion was for some an important reinforcer.

Taken together, Merari's results suggest that suicide bombers may be unusually susceptible to influence by those around them, but whatever their personality weaknesses, the would-be bombers have above all a political motive for becoming a suicide bomber.

Are terrorists suicidal?

Adam Lankford's book, *The Myth of Martyrdom*, offers a startlingly simple message: Suicide bombers are suicidal.[6] They want to die to escape personal problems the way a patient with end-stage cancer wants to escape pain. Dying in an attack on the enemy provides a socially acceptable form of suicide, and earlier analyses of suicide bombing have erred in seeing the bomber's cause as the cause of the bomber's act.

Lankford takes several tacks in advancing his thesis. First, he argues that suicide bombers are suicidal because they orchestrate their own deaths: "As a starting point for a more sophisticated theory, this book takes the view that, by definition, all suicide terrorists are suicidal" (p. 10).

This shortcut is quickly left behind, however, in order to examine more specific issues relating to the motivations of suicide bombers. Lankford argues that suicide bombers are not heroes because heroes—the soldier who falls on a grenade, the Secret Service officer who takes a bullet for the president—act to save others rather than to harm others, and they act on trained reflexes with no intention of dying. This is an odd argument in two ways. There are heroes, like Audie Murphy, who are awarded the United States Medal of Honor for extraordinary risk-taking in attacking and killing the enemy. And it is not obvious why the individual who acts without thinking is more heroic than one who chooses death.

Lankford further argues that US suicide terrorists ($n = 12$) are similar to US rampage shooters ($n = 18$) and to US school shooters ($n = 16$). In Lankford's coding of these cases, the vast majority of all three groups have mental health problems, most die in the course of their attacks, and many are socially marginalized or suffering from school or work or family problems. In this portrait, suicide terrorists are not heroes but troubled loners with mental health problems.

This portrait is similar to our disconnected–disordered profile of lone wolf terrorists, but as already mentioned, the vast majority of suicide terrorists are not lone wolves. It is unlikely that suicide bombers, embedded in an organization, have the same motives as lone actor rampage and school shooters.

There are other issues here. The small numbers make generalization difficult. Although the suicide terrorists are identified by name, the rampage shooters and school shooters are not identified. Readers must trust that the author has included all relevant cases and that definitions of social marginalization, family problems, work/school problems, and mental health problems were consistently and reliably coded across the three groups.

Finally, Lankford's thesis must stand or fall with evidence about the motivations of suicide bombers. Willing to die for a cause is martyrdom. Wanting to die to escape human travail is suicide—condemned by major religions and, to varying extents, by the social norms of most cultures.

When Lankford's book was published in 2011, the world total of suicide terrorism cases was about 3,000.[7] Lankford raises the question, How many of the 3,000 were suicidal? His Appendix A ("Partial List of Suicide Terrorists with Risk Factors for Suicide") contains 142 cases, but only 40 have enough detail to be cited in a chapter. These 40 cases are not representative of the 3,000 in terms of country origins (e.g., no cases from Iraq). And the causal value of the risk factors identified for these 40 cases can be questionable because many individuals with risk factors for suicide never attempt suicide.

But let us suppose that all 40 cases were persuasively shown to be suicidal. What should we conclude about the 3,000 suicide terrorists? One possibility is to estimate that approximately 1 or 2 percent of suicide bombers are suicidal. Lankford believes that close to 100 percent are suicidal. Readers will decide for themselves which is the more reasonable estimate.

Given the uncertain evidence that suicide bombers are suicidal, it is worth asking why Lankford's book has attracted attention. We believe that the appeal of Lankford's thesis is psychological and political. Psychologically, it is reassuring to think that our enemies are not so committed to their cause as they seem. They do not generate martyrs for their cause; they only channel suicides to masquerade as martyrs. Their commitment to their cause is no stronger than our commitment to our cause; they are not going to outlast us. Politically, it is reassuring to think that "As a form of psychological warfare, [this book] could be used to smear the reputations of suicide terrorists by portraying them as weak, cowardly, and suicidal" (p. 172). The enemy won't be listening to this, but it can play well with US voters. It has always been easy to see terrorists as crazy.

9

IS IT POSSIBLE TO PREVENT RADICALIZATION TO TERRORISM?

What if we just jailed every ISIS sympathizer?

How many ISIS sympathizers are there? A 2017 internet poll of about 200 US Muslims asked two questions about ISIS:[1]

> "Overall, do you have a favorable or unfavorable opinion of the Islamic State of Iraq and Syria (ISIS)?" Thirteen percent were very or somewhat favorable.
>
> "How do you feel about U.S. Muslims going to Syria to join ISIS?" Nine percent felt that "I would not do it myself, but I would not condemn anyone who did." One percent felt that "It is morally justified to join ISIS." And three percent felt that "Joining ISIS is required for any Muslim who can do it."

The same 2017 internet poll also found that 13 percent of US Muslims believe that suicide bombing and other forms of violence against civilians are often or sometimes justified in defense of Islam.

The two ISIS questions and the suicide bombing question agree in showing about 13 percent of US Muslims with some level of sympathy for jihadist terrorism. Thirteen percent of about 1 million adult US Muslims projects to about 130,000 US Muslims. We think it is not practical to arrest and jail 130,000

US Muslims with radical opinions in order to prevent terrorism. We are back to the same problem represented in the two-pyramids model of radicalization: Radical opinions are common, but radical action, especially violent action, is rare.

How rare? John Mueller counts 92 cases of jihadist terrorist attacks or plots in the United States between 9/11 and December 2016, or about 6 plots per year over 16 years.[2] About 113 individuals were involved in these plots. This size of threat cannot justify action against the approximately 130,000 US Muslims with radical opinions.

Can we identify violent political actors before they act?

Preventing radicalization to political violence might be possible if we knew how violent radicals differ from nonviolent radicals. Perhaps the largest comparison of violent and nonviolent political actors examined nearly 1,500 individuals convicted in the United States of crimes judged to be politically motivated.[3] The crimes were 68 percent violent and 32 percent nonviolent, and they included left-wing, right-wing, jihadist, and single-issue offenders. Examples of violent offenses included assault, armed robbery, kidnapping, and murder. Examples of nonviolent offenses included money laundering, tax fraud, and providing weapons.

Results have to be taken cautiously, as most of the measures used to compare violent and nonviolent offenders had missing data for 50 percent or more of the individuals in the study. The strongest difference uncovered was that violent offenders were more likely to have a lover or friend engaged in political violence. Violent offenders also tended to be younger and unemployed.

Can these results help us prevent radicalization to violence? We think not. It isn't surprising that individuals involved in political violence have lovers and friends similarly engaged, but prevention is too late by the time a violent network has emerged. Nor does it seem useful to target individuals for anti-radicalization interventions on the basis of characteristics as general as youth and unemployment.

This study basically confirms the familiar conclusion that there is no profile that distinguishes terrorists from others.

Does the British Prevent program work?

Radicalization prevention programs vary in three ways.[4] Some are run by government, others by civil society organizations or nongovernmental organizations (NGOs). Some are active in targeting particular individuals (referrals), others are passive in the sense that they advertise their work but wait to be contacted by individuals seeking help in leaving an extremist group or organization (e.g., exit hotlines). And some directly target ideology, while others focus on action by helping an individual to reintegrate with family, work, and nonviolent politics.

We begin with a look at the UK Prevent program, perhaps the best known attempt to prevent radicalization in an English-speaking country. Prevent has been a model for similar programs in the United States and Canada.

Here is how a UK newspaper, *The Telegraph*, described the program in 2017:[5]

The [UK] government introduced Prevent in 2003, but it wasn't made public for some years. . . . It is intended to stop vulnerable people from becoming radicalised, joining extremist groups and carrying out terrorist activities.

The programme was expanded greatly in the wake of the 2005 London bombings, with almost £80 million spent on 1,000 schemes in the six years after the attacks. . . . The cash has gone into a broad range of areas. In 2010, it emerged that CCTV cameras in Muslim areas of Birmingham—72 of them hidden—were partly funded by Home Office counter-terrorism funding.

Last year [2016] the Guardian [newspaper] reported that one component of Prevent has been a covert propaganda campaign [dozens of websites, leaflets, videos, films, Facebook pages, Twitter feeds, and online radio content, with titles such as *The Truth About Isis*] that aims to bring about "attitudinal and behavioural change" among young British Muslims.

The Prevent program also includes advertising for both an email and a telephone hotline for reporting cases of suspected radicalization.

Related to the Prevent program is the Channel program that was rolled out in the United Kingdom in 2012 and 2013.[6] Individuals identified by Prevent as at risk for extremist ideas or actions are referred to Channel for further risk assessment and, if needed, intervention against incipient extremism. About 20 percent of individuals referred to Channel are required to participate in deradicalization sessions, and about 30 percent of those referred in 2015 were children 14 years old or younger. Most are referred for jihadist sympathies, but about 25 percent are right wing.

Since 2015, the UK government has required by statute that public institutions and officials have a Prevent Duty to assess the risk of individuals being drawn into terrorism, including support for extremist ideas that are part of terrorist ideology, and to refer at-risk individuals to the Channel program. Public officials include teachers in privately and publicly funded schools, including universities, as well as doctors and nurses of the National Health Service, youth and social workers, probation officers, and childcare providers. More than 500,000 of these employees have received training in how to spot and report potential radicalization.

Prevent has been controversial. Some claim that Prevent is a "toxic brand" in UK Muslim communities, and see Prevent as government surveillance aimed at them. Some say that the Prevent Duty was mandated by law because of low levels of voluntary cooperation with the program. The National Union of Teachers, the United Kingdom's largest union of school staff, voted for a motion criticizing Prevent for trying to make teachers the "secret service of the public sector."

Do Prevent and Channel prevent radicalization to political violence? The short answer is that the case for effectiveness is not clear. In principle, Prevent and Channel can be useful for both jihadist and right-wing radicalization, but in practice the emphasis since the 2005 London subway bombings has been on jihadist radicalization. UK officials believe that Prevent and Channel have stopped hundreds of individuals, including many children, from traveling to Syria to join ISIS. This would be partial success given that by 2015, the UK government had reported that 600 British citizens had gone to fight in Syria.

Another possible indicator of success is that the number of referrals to Channel went from about 1,700 in 2014 to about 4,000 in 2015, after the Prevent Duty was mandated to public officials. As already noted, these referrals were mostly judged not at risk, which means that a large number of individuals were left feeling that the government has targeted them unfairly, perhaps because of their religion or ethnicity.

The UK government has advanced a controversial definition of extremism: "the vocal or active opposition to our fundamental values, including democracy, the rule of law, individual liberty and the mutual respect and tolerance of different faiths and beliefs." (HM Government Prevent Strategy, 2011, https://www.icslearn.co.uk/policies/prevent/). This broad definition may contribute to the increase in referrals for extremist beliefs, both jihadist and right wing, as criticism of UK values may be seen as extremist thinking.

But do Prevent and Channel prevent terrorist attacks? In 2017, the United Kingdom experienced four jihadist terrorist attacks:

On March 22, 2017, Khalid Masood jumped the curb in a hired car and drove into pedestrians on Westminster Bridge, and then he stabbed a policeman. He killed 5 and injured 50 before being shot dead.

On May 22, 2017, a suicide bomber, Salman Abedi, killed 22 and injured 59 at a concert in Manchester.

On June 3, 2017, three men in a white van hit pedestrians on London Bridge and then began stabbing people nearby. Khuram Butt, Rachid Redouane, and Youssef Zaghba killed 7 and injured 48 before being shot dead.

On September 22, 2017, an improvised explosive device produced injuries to approximately 25 people in a London Underground commuter train. In October 2017, police announced that Ahmed Hassan Mohammed Ali would stand trial for this attack.

These attacks indicate that whatever its success in preventing travel to Syria, Prevent has not prevented terrorist violence in the United Kingdom. Perhaps most discouraging, suicide bomber Salman Abedi was reported to the authorities as an extremist by two of his friends, who each called the Prevent hotline twice—once 5 years before the bombing and again about 1 year before the bombing. Abedi was also reported to the authorities after being banned from a mosque for confronting an imam who was criticizing ISIS.

Prevent and Channel may even make jihadist terrorism more likely by causing UK Muslims to feel profiled and discriminated against. Two NGOs, Rights Watch UK and US-based Open Society Justice Initiative, have issued reports criticizing Prevent for violations of citizen rights.[7]

As of 2019, it appears that Prevent stops a minority of those who would travel to fight in Syria and is far from stopping terrorist attacks in the United Kingdom. In addition, controversy about the program suggests that it may produce a backlash that makes the United Kingdom less safe.

In the next three sections, we will look at programs in Denmark, the United Kingdom, and the United States that, like Prevent, try to mobilize civil society resources to prevent radicalization but, unlike Prevent, operate without requiring government employees to report suspected extremism.

Does the Aarhus model work?

The Aarhus program (Aarhus is Denmark's second largest city) is unusual in that it aims at both prevention of radicalization and deradicalization of those already caught up in extremist ideas and actions. The program does not target ideology but aims to move individuals—right wing or jihadist—to legal means of satisfying their human needs. The program is built on 40 years of experience with SSP programs in which Schools, Social authorities, and Police collaborate in crime prevention. The Aarhus SSP was enlarged to include political radicalization and operates in consultation with social scientists at Aarhus university.[8]

Perhaps most controversial is the Danish treatment of individuals who return from fighting in Syria or Somalia, often fighting for ISIS. Many governments are concerned that such individuals, with new skills for perpetrating violence, represent a new terrorist threat on return to a Western country; many Western countries put returnees in prison for violating laws against joining a terrorist organization. In Denmark, beginning in 2013, returning foreign fighters are placed in the Aarhus program, provided with a mentor, and offered help with education, employment, housing, counseling, and medical care.

The Aarhus program has not ended terrorist attacks in Denmark. But it survived public reactions to the February 2015 attacks in Copenhagen, in which Omar el-Hussein killed two and wounded five before being shot to death.

The program has one important advantage. Most returning fighters return disillusioned with the cause or the violence they experienced in Syria. They can provide strong testimony against joining Islamic State that may discourage others from going. This kind of testimony is not available from individuals who return to a jail cell, as happens to foreign fighters who return to countries, including the United States, that have made it illegal for citizens to fight for ISIS in Syria or al-Shabab in Somalia.

Does the Quilliam program work?

The Quilliam Foundation was founded by UK-born Maajid Hawaz and Mohamed "Ed" Hussein. Quilliam had UK government support until 2011, but in 2019 it was supported by funds from the John Templeton Foundation and other private donors. Quilliam focuses on countering extremist Muslim ideology with reports, public debates, and workshops that forward a modern moderate Islam as the antidote to extremism.

Hawaz and Hussein describe themselves as former radical Islamists, able to see both the attractions and defects of extremism. Both were members of Hizb ut-Tahrir, which does in fact seek the international caliphate that al-Qaeda seeks and that ISIS tried to raise in Syria and Iraq beginning in 2014. But Hizb does not support terrorist violence and has not been banned in the United Kingdom as a terrorist organization. Hawaz and Hussein have experience of extreme ideas but no experience of extremist violence. Their work rests on the assumption that jihadist terrorism depends on an extremist version of Islam such as that forwarded by Hizb, and Quilliam has fought the idea that Hizb may be useful as a nonviolent competitor drawing recruits from al-Qaeda and ISIS.

Whether Quilliam succeeds in preventing jihadist terrorism is unclear; to our knowledge, there is no empirical research to show its effectiveness in turning individuals from either radical ideas or violent action. Contrary to Quilliam's logic, we believe that radicalization of ideas is a different problem than radicalization of action.

Does the WORDE program work?

An NGO fighting radicalization in the United States is the Muslim-led World Organization for Resource Development and Education (WORDE). Based in the Washington, DC, suburb of Montgomery County, Maryland, WORDE receives funding from both federal and county governments to develop a network of trusted adults, including faith community leaders, public officials, law enforcement officers, educators, social service providers, and civic activists. WORDE workshops generate awareness of various public safety threats, including radicalization and recruitment to violent extremism. The network of trusted adults receives referrals of individuals thought to be at risk for political extremism, and connects these individuals with resources and interventions that can move them away from extremism.

Like Quilliam, WORDE focuses on extremist ideas and ideology. WORDE programs try to encourage moderate Islam as an antidote to extremist Islam and to raise perceptions of moderate Islam in other faith communities. The larger goal is community cohesion and resilience to stereotyping and racism when a jihadist terrorist attack hits the news.

Beginning in 2014, the US Department of Justice funded an evaluation of WORDE programs. The resulting report concluded that "WORDE's volunteer-service and multicultural programming had intended effects on 12 of 14 outcomes believed to be CVE-relevant. . . . To wit, these results make WORDE's volunteer-service and multicultural programming the first evidence-based CVE-relevant programming in the United States."[9]

Unfortunately, the results cited are not relevant to countering violent extremism (CVE). The WORDE programs included in the study are designed to build community cohesion by bringing Muslims together with individuals of other faiths in community volunteer work and multicultural workshops. These activities did not focus on political beliefs, and the survey questions used to assess these activities did not assess political beliefs. Survey items were about liking for the activity—for example, "I feel welcome" and "I make friends with people from other races." A comparison group of individuals who participated in activities not sponsored by WORDE did not differ from the WORDE volunteers: Both showed high liking for the activity they engaged in.

In short, the evaluation of WORDE programs is not an evidence-based demonstration of countering violent extremism. The evaluation did not assess political beliefs, and results show only that WORDE participants had high levels of liking for the program they experienced.

In addition to WORDE, the US Department of Justice supports community-based programs to prevent political radicalization in Boston, Los Angeles, and Minneapolis. These programs are loosely modeled on the UK Prevent program, except that Prevent's explicit attitude change interventions and government-required participation of public officials cannot be applied in the United States. First Amendment protections of free speech in the United States mean that government intervention against extremist ideas cannot be as explicit in the United States as in the United Kingdom, which does not have US-style free speech protections. This limitation means that the programs in Boston, Los Angeles and Minneapolis—and WORDE programs—depend more on community initiatives than on government direction. As with the WORDE programs, there is no systematic evidence that programs in Boston, Los

Angeles, and Minneapolis prevent radicalization of either ideas or actions.

How many US terrorists are arrested with the help of tips from private citizens?

Between 1999 and 2009, there were 86 terrorist plots targeting Americans living in the United States. Of these, 18 reached execution and tried or succeeded in harming people or infrastructure; 68 plots were foiled. The initial clue leading to a foiled plot came mostly from federal law enforcement (20 cases), local law enforcement (15 cases), and a tip by a member of the public who was not an informant (20 cases). In other words, tips volunteered by members of the public were as important as intel developed by federal or local law enforcement.[10]

Focusing only on jihadist terrorist plots shows a similar result. Between 2001 and 2010, 120 Muslim Americans were arrested for suspicion of terrorism in cases in which the government has disclosed the initial source of suspicion. For 48 of those arrested, the initial tip came from the Muslim American community: "In some communities, Muslim-Americans have been so concerned about extremists in their midst that they have turned in people who turned out to be undercover informants."[11]

If terrorism tips from the general public are an important component of success in the War on Terrorism, overreactions to the terrorist threat can undermine trust in the authorities in the subcultures and communities from which tips come.

How many US terrorists are arrested with the help of undercover agents and informants?

Sensitivities about government intervention against free speech in the United States have not blocked government efforts to prevent actual terrorist attacks. The FBI and state and local police intervene directly to prevent radicalization to political violence by arresting individuals involved in terrorist plots.

John Mueller's list of 92 jihadist plots and attacks targeting the US homeland from 9/11 through 2016 can help us understand how security officials try to prevent terrorist attacks. Of the 92 cases, 43 (47 percent) involved use of an undercover agent or informant. Of these 43 cases in which a plot was infiltrated by the FBI or police, in 28 cases (65 percent) perpetrators were convicted for using some kind of explosives, usually a bomb but sometimes a grenade. From these results, we learn that almost half the jihadist plots targeting the United States are prevented by use of an undercover agent or informant, and that two-thirds of the infiltrated plots involve an explosive.

In comparison, Mueller's list includes 21 cases in which perpetrators got as far as committing or attempting to commit an attack that was *not* infiltrated. Of these 21 cases, only 5 involved some kind of explosive. Two of these 5 cases involved explosives brought from abroad (the "shoe bomber" and "underwear bomber"), and 1 of the 5 cases involved training in Pakistan for building a bomb (the "Times Square bomber"). Only 2 of 21 cases (10 percent) involved a home-made bomb (the Boston Marathon bombers and the Chelsea bomber).

Comparison between infiltrated and non-infiltrated plots reveals a striking disparity: Two-thirds of informant cases involve explosives, but only 1 in 10 of no-informant cases involves explosives. Why are there so many bomb plots involving informants and so few bombs in plots without informants?

There are several advantages for FBI and police in having an undercover agent or informer help a would-be jihadist toward a bomb plot. First, few civilians know anything about bombs or how to make one, so the undercover agent can promise or provide a fake bomb that will not be dangerous. The would-be perpetrator does not know how to determine whether the bomb is real. Second, there is more publicity value in uncovering a bomb plot; a bomb seems more threatening than a firearm. And third, a bomb or even a hand grenade—any kind of explosive weapon—qualifies in law as a weapon of mass destruction, which qualifies the perpetrator for a longer prison sentence.

It is useful to remember that undercover agents and informers are the chief law enforcement tool of the war on drugs. Using the same tools for preventing terrorist attacks helps law enforcement officials profit by their experience in the war on drugs to prosecute the War on Terrorism. Less positive is the implication that the War on Terrorism is unlikely to be more successful than the war on drugs.

How does CVE compare with military counterinsurgency programs?

There is a strong parallel between countering violent extremism and countering insurgency. The *US Army/Marine Corps Counterinsurgency Field Manual*[12] gives close attention to the insurgent strategy that aims to mobilize new support by eliciting government overreaction to insurgent attacks. The need to recognize and counter this strategy comes through in the first five paradoxes of counterinsurgency operations:

Sometimes, the more you protect your force, the less secure you may be.

Sometimes, the more force is used, the less effective it is.

The more successful the counterinsurgency is, the less force can be used and the more risk must be accepted.

Sometimes doing nothing is the best reaction.

Some of the best weapons for counterinsurgents do not shoot.

Surprisingly, military forces facing insurgency may be more alert to the danger of overreaction than security forces facing domestic terrorism. The five paradoxes amount to recognition of the limits of military force and a caution against unintended casualties—the "collateral damage" from military operations that kill civilians. Collateral damage can produce increased support for insurgents, and it can produce increased support for terrorists. Collateral damage is the key to jujitsu politics because collateral damage turns nonmilitants into militants and supporters of militants.

To sum up, counterinsurgency and counterterrorism are both forms of political conflict. Mao Zedong's slogan is perhaps the shortest summary of the road to success for both counterinsurgency and counterterrorism: "Politics takes command." Politics requires taking account of the costs of overreaction, avoiding the trap of jujitsu politics by avoiding collateral damage.

Is it possible to prevent radicalization to terrorism?

In this final section, we return to the basic question of this chapter. The radicalization prevention programs reviewed in this chapter are of unknown value; there is no persuasive empirical evidence of success for any of these programs. We might simply conclude with a Scots verdict of "not proven." But it is possible to use what we know about radicalization to point to some further possibilities for preventing radicalization to political violence. A similar case might be made for right-wing or left-wing terrorism; here, we continue our focus on radicalization to jihadist terrorism.

We begin with the distinction between radicalization of ideas and radicalization of action. How to reduce radicalization of ideas is one question; how to reduce radicalization to terrorist action is a different question.

As described in Chapter 6, radicalization of ideas distinguishes two levels: sympathizing with a terrorist cause and justifying terrorist violence for the cause. In the case of jihadist terrorism, sympathizing with the cause means perceiving the War on Terrorism as a war on Islam. More extreme radicalization of opinion is seeing suicide bombing of civilians as justified in defense of Islam. We have emphasized that many Muslims have these radical opinions: About 30 percent of US Muslims see a war on Islam, and about 10 percent of US Muslims justify suicide bombing in defense of Islam.

Polling data indicate that seeing a war on Islam is related to feeling discriminated against as a Muslim and opposition to US foreign policies. In other words, seeing a war on Islam seems to have two separate sources: personal experience of hostility to Muslims in the US, and US foreign policies seen as hostile to Muslims.

In principle, then, decreasing discrimination against Muslims in the United States could reduce perceptions of a war on Islam. But decades of stereotype research indicate that changing public stereotypes of US Muslims would not be easy. Also not easy would be changing the level of surveillance of US Muslims that occurs in mosques and airports.

Changing US foreign policies could also reduce perceptions of a war on Islam. US troops are stationed in many Muslim countries. In the Middle East, these countries include Syria, Iraq, Jordan, Yemen, Oman, Kuwait, United Arab Emirates, and Qatar.[13] US troops are also stationed in Afghanistan, Niger, and Libya. US forces in these countries sometimes carry out missions that produce casualties, including civilian casualties, and often raise local feelings against what many Muslims view as a kind of US military occupation. Drone attacks are particularly salient sources of collateral damage.[14] A wedding party is mistaken for a party of militants. Women and children traveling in a vehicle with a militant are killed in a drone attack targeting the militant.

As with reducing discrimination against US Muslims, reducing US military operations in Muslim countries would not be easy. Without change in stereotyping of US Muslims and change in US military operations, change in Muslim perceptions of a war on Islam does not seem likely.

What about the 10 percent of US Muslims who justify suicide bombing in defense of Islam? Where do they get this opinion?

Polling data show that justifying suicide bombing is related to feeling socially disconnected and to feelings of depression.[15] These are the same characteristics we found associated with the disconnected–disordered profile of lone wolf terrorists. It seems that loners with personal problems are more likely to get involved in both extremist ideas and lone wolf violence.

Can feelings of disconnection and depression be prevented or changed? Possibly, but not easily. Change would require a better safety net and more community support for individuals suffering from these feelings. Something more like public health intervention than political intervention would be called for. Again, not an easy change to accomplish.

Finally, what can we do to prevent radicalization to violent action, to terrorism?

We have emphasized that 99 percent of those with radical opinions will never turn to violence. Only a few of the 10 percent of US Muslims who justify suicide bombing will ever try to mount a terrorist attack.

Nevertheless, those with radical opinions do contribute to violent action in that these opinions allow especially young male Muslims to see themselves as heroes for defending Islam while others only talk. Loners/losers can see themselves going "from zero to hero" by taking up violence in defense of Islam. John Mueller, in his Introduction to the 92 cases of jihadist attacks targeting the US, describes the motivation of the perpetrators:[16]

The overwhelming driving force was simmering, and more commonly boiling, outrage at American foreign policy—the wars in Iraq and Afghanistan in particular and also the country's support for Israel in the Palestinian conflict. Religion was a key part of the consideration for most, but it was not that they had a burning urge to spread Islam and Sharia law or to establish caliphates. Rather it was the desire to protect the religion against what was commonly seen to be a concentrated war upon it in the Middle East by the United States government and military.

In stark contrast, there is remarkably little hostility to American culture or society or to its values or, certainly, to democracy. This is particularly impressive because many of the people under examination (though certainly not all) were misfits, suffered from personal identity crises, were friendless, came from broken homes, were often desperate for money, had difficulty holding jobs, were on drugs, were petty criminals, experienced various forms of discrimination, and were, to use a word that pops up in quite a few of the case studies and fits even more of them, "losers."

What we know about radicalization brings us to a pessimistic view of prevention. Reducing stereotyping of US Muslims and reducing US military operations in Muslim countries might reduce perception of a war on Islam and, in time, reduce the number of loser/loners trying to be terrorist heroes. Reducing the number of disconnected–disordered Muslims in the United States might reduce support for jihadist violence and, in time, reduce the number trying to be terrorist heroes.

Unfortunately, none of these possibilities is easy in practice. We are forced to say that for US Muslims, there is no easy way to prevent either radicalization of ideas or radicalization of action.

10

IS IT POSSIBLE TO DERADICALIZE TERRORISTS?

What is the difference between deradicalization and desistence?

Many assume that deradicalization requires giving up both radical political ideas and radical action. In particular, it is often assumed that giving up radical ideas is the only or best pathway to giving up terrorist violence. This is the same mistake that psychologists used to make, before research showed the weakness of the link between attitudes and action.

In terrorism research, this mistake has been exposed by talking with former terrorists, including members of the Irish Republican Army, 1970s student radicals, and ex-jihadists. Many have given up violence but still believe that their cause was just. They gave up violence for non-ideological reasons: Violence isn't t producing political change, terrorist leaders are venal or stupid, police have identified and jailed them, they are tired of the strain of underground life and want a more normal life and perhaps a family. These are good reasons for quitting violence without doubting the justice of the terrorist cause or even doubting that violence for the cause is justified.

Non-ideological reasons for quitting violence should remind us of the non-ideological reasons for joining a violent group in the first place, including revenge, love, escape, and comradeship.

Talking with former terrorists led to a distinction between *deradicalization* and *desistence*. Deradicalization today is usually understood to mean change of ideology: giving up radical ideas. Desistence or disengagement is understood to mean change in behavior: giving up violent action. In the past 10 years, understanding of how some individuals leave terrorism has converged with understanding of how some individuals turn to terrorism: Both on the way into terrorism and on the way out, bad ideas are only weakly associated with bad actions.

How many countries have some form of deradicalization/ disengagement program for convicted terrorists?

Almost as many countries as have experienced terrorist attacks! Perhaps the best known for research and media attention are programs in Saudi Arabia, Singapore, and Sri Lanka. Other countries that have or have had programs include the United Kingdom, Denmark, Northern Ireland, the Netherlands, Germany, France, Sweden, Austria, Spain, Belgium, Columbia, Yemen, Iraq, Sudan, Uganda, Kenya, Nigeria, Somalia, Morocco, Algeria, Pakistan, Malaysia, Thailand, Bangladesh, India, and Australia.

Many countries have established an "exit hotline" that individuals can call for help in leaving an extremist group. But individuals calling for help in leaving an extremist group are already effectively deradicalized, and so are not relevant to understanding programs to deradicalize detained or convicted militants. Exit programs are not considered in this chapter.

As with programs to prevent radicalization (see Chapter 9, this volume), programs aiming to reverse radicalization can have one or both of two goals. Some program activities aim to oppose radical ideas, other activities aim to oppose extremist violence. Most programs use some combination of these activities. And most programs aim for more than the end of dangerous ideas and violent action; the goal is not just deradicalization or disengagement but *reintegration*.

Reintegration means a former militant rejoins family, neighborhood, and employment as a loyal citizen of the state. Reintegration is an ambitious goal because success depends on the reactions of others to the deradicalized or disengaged individual. If family, friends, neighbors, and employers see interaction with an ex-militant as a threat—subjecting them to government scrutiny—then reintegration will fail. If family, friends, neighbors, and employers see an ex-militant as irretrievably flawed, bad, or evil, then reintegration will fail.

What do we know about the effectiveness of the best studied deradicalization programs?

Perhaps the largest and best studied deradicalization program is in Germany. The German government greatly increased funding for right-wing deradicalization after an arson attack on a synagogue in Dusseldorf in October 2000. In 2017, Germany had 18 different neo-Nazi deradicalization programs, some run by national or state government agencies and some run by nongovernmental organizations. Germany also has some of the best statistical data relating to political extremists and politically motivated violence. Daniel Kohler, Director of the German Institute on Radicalization and Deradicalization, provides an overview of these programs and their success.[1]

Kohler estimates that during the period 2000–2016, the various programs have helped approximately 2,000 individuals leave right-wing extremist groups. Some programs, both government and nongovernment, have reported high rates (near 40 percent) of individuals dropping out of counseling. But other programs, both government and nongovernment, have reported low dropout rates. The good news is that the number of right-wing extremists in Germany (by government estimates) has dropped steadily from about 50,000 in 2000 to about 20,000 in 2014. This decline is not necessarily a result of the deradicalization programs in Germany but is at least consistent with the idea that the programs are working.

The rest of the news is not so good. The number of violent right-wing extremists (again by government estimates) has remained constant at about 10,000 each year from 2000 to 2014. The number of German-language right-wing websites was little changed during the same period. The number of right-wing posts in social media increased from 0 in 2006 to about 5,000 in 2014. Right-wing music concerts showed an erratic but not declining pattern from 2000 to 2015. Right-wing periodicals showed only slight decline from 2000 to 2012, when the government banned these publications. The number of right-wing extremist demonstrations varied around 100 per year from 2005 to 2014, with no sign of a trend for decline. Perhaps most important, the number of politically motivated violent crimes varied around 1,000 per year from 2001 to 2014, with no trend for decline.

In short, 15 years of strong efforts against neo-Nazi extremists in Germany have reduced the overall number of right-wing extremists, but right-wing demonstrations, the number of violent right-wing extremists, and the number of politically motivated violent crimes have not declined. It appears that German programs targeting neo-Nazis have succeeded in reducing radicalization of ideas (fewer right-wing extremists) but have had no effect on radicalization of action (violent extremists and politically motivated violent crime).

Can deradicalization success be measured in terms of how many militants return to terrorism?

If reintegration is the maximal goal of deradicalization programs, disengagement is the minimal goal. Officials and citizens alike will find it difficult to support a program in which a high proportion of "graduates" return to extremist violence. Thus, a common measure of success for deradicalization programs is the recidivism rate—the percentage of program graduates who return to extremist ideas or actions. Most countries with deradicalization programs report success—low recidivism rates.

There are several reasons to take these reports with a grain of salt. No country has fully opened its deradicalization programs to researchers. Much depends on who enters the program: the proportion who are perpetrators of violence and terrorism versus the proportion who are in trouble for extremist ideas or nonviolent offenses such as financial support of a government-banned organization. Of course, more violent offenders are more likely to return to violence.

What counts as recidivism is often left unclear. Is it any criminal offense after leaving the program? Or do only violent offenses count as recidivism? Or do only politically motivated violent offenses count, so as to exclude bar brawls and partner abuse?

A big problem with interpreting recidivism measures is that we don't know the recidivism rate for imprisoned extremists who do *not* participate in a deradicalization program. In the United States, about 30 percent of released violent offenders will be re-arrested within 5 years for another violent crime. So the recidivism rate for violent crime in the United States is about 30 percent.[2] But there have been suggestions that recidivism for political extremism offenses is less than that for nonpolitical violence.

How does the Saudi program work?

Perhaps the best known deradicalization program is operated by the government of Saudi Arabia. The program began in 2004 and, thanks to Saudi oil income, has exceptional resources and support. The program has three phases: prevention, rehabilitation, and after-care.

The prevention phase is open to anyone suspected of extremism and has enrolled perhaps 10,000 detainees. Individual counseling for 2 weeks is conducted by a team that includes a Muslim cleric, a psychologist, and a security official. Group education lectures with 6–10 detainees may continue for up to 6 weeks. These interventions are based on the assumption that extremist actions are the result of a misunderstanding of Islam under the influence of extremist propaganda, with personal problems as a contributing cause. The goal of the prevention phase is to contest and debate extremist ideas, and to replace these with a more moderate form of Islam

It is important to recognize that the more moderate form of Islam sought is the Wahabist state religion of Saudi Arabia. Wahabist Islam is a form of Sunni Islam that is only one step less fundamentalist than Salafi Islam. A major difference is that Wahabists acknowledge the authority of the Saudi king, whereas Salafis do not see the king as a legitimate caliph. With regard to deradicalization, the Saudi goal is that extremists should give up violent jihad that is not sanctioned by the Saudi king, and in particular should give up violence within the Kingdom. But they do not have to give up violent jihad entirely, and may even argue that violent jihad is justified in Muslim lands occupied by unbelievers (including Shi'a Islam as unbelievers).

Those who have made progress in accepting this nuanced version of moderate Islam, and who have not committed serious crimes such as murder, are admitted into the rehabilitation phase—a halfway house where participants are referred to as "beneficiaries." Several thousand detainees have been admitted to this phase, in which they continue individual and group counseling that has both psychological and religious components. The rehabilitation phase also includes secular education, vocational training, and even art therapy. Detainees are encouraged to reconnect with their families, and families are encouraged to reconnect with them.

The third phase, aftercare, aims for reintegration of freed detainees into family and work. Perhaps 700 detainees have been released into aftercare, which provides substantial financial support that may include living expenses and help with housing, health care, and purchase of a car. Individuals are encouraged to marry and start a family, and help is available for marriage expenses, possibly including a dowry.

The success rate for this elaborate program is not clear. The Saudis claimed 100 percent success until 2009, when several detainees released from Guantanamo into the program returned to al-Qaeda after graduating from the program. The program has not been opened to researchers, but informed observers estimate that success rates are perhaps 80–90 percent, with perhaps 10–20 percent recidivism rates. In this case, it seems that recidivism means returning to jihadist violence.

Given its early start, its size, and its resources, the Saudi program has been a model for deradicalization programs in other predominantly Muslim countries, including Yemen, Singapore, Algeria, and Egypt. Success of these programs is even less clear than Saudi success.

How did the US program in Iraq work?

Little known but worth noting is the US program for deradicalizing security detainees in Iraq, which began in 2008 and ended with the departure of US troops from Iraq in 2011. This program has the double distinction of having been designed by a psychologist—Anne Speckhard—and having operated with strong human rights standards, including voluntary participation and informed consent. Although voluntary, the program promised a fast track to release.

The 20,000 security detainees were a varied lot that included juveniles as well as adults, perpetrators of sectarian violence (mostly Sunni/Shi'a violence), perpetrators of violence for hire, and 5–15 percent "hard core" jihadists. The program included education in moderate Islam to counter jihadist ideology, as well as psychological counseling for traumatic experiences before and after entering detainment. For the religious component, imams with former jihadist experience were

sought in order to provide an insider challenge to jihadist ideology. A literacy and job skills component was also included.

The program lasted 4–6 weeks; owing to the large numbers
involved, interventions were mostly with small groups rather
than with individuals. The following is Speckhard's description of the results:

> Initial results were very promising, with 6,000 detainees
> released nine months after program commencement, al-
> though most of these were low security risks rather than
> "hard core." Of the original group released, only 12 of
> these inmates were rearrested—much lower than the
> usual recidivism rate from previous years of close to 200.[3]

It is unfortunate that this promising program ended before
research could test its effectiveness with "hard core" militants,
although Speckhard believes that some of these were indeed
deradicalized.

What does the United Kingdom do?

From 9/11 to 2017, there were about 3,500 arrests for terrorism-
related offenses in the United Kingdom. About 80 percent of
these arrests were for "international terrorism" (jihadist) offenses. Only 646 of these arrests resulted in conviction for a
terrorism-related offense. Of those convicted, 186 terrorism
or extremism prisoners were still being held in prison in
March 2017.[4]

Based on these data, 460 individuals imprisoned for
terrorism-related offenses after 9/11 have already been released (646 – 186). A further implication is that most of the
offenses were relatively minor because terrorists convicted of
murder or attempted murder receive long sentences. So those
released were mostly guilty of supporting terrorism in ways
that did not include violence (e.g., money or other material

support and hate speech). After relatively brief periods in prison, then, 460 individuals convicted of terrorism-related offenses—the great majority jihadist offenders—became prospects for deradicalization.

Deradicalization of individuals convicted of terrorist offenses in the United Kingdom is in the hands of probation officers, often working with community groups that try to provide support and mentoring for probationers. Sarah Marsden has interviewed more than 30 of these frontline deradicalization workers to learn what they do and what they think works. The results are interview examples rather than statistics about success and failure.[5]

As earlier suggested, the radicalizing issue for many probationers is foreign policy. Here is a senior probation officer talking:

> Social exclusion, racism, things like that, you know, diversity's a big part of it, foreign policy, perceived injustice, and grievance . . . grievance is an important part, foreign policy, it's about the impact factors, that people are seeing Muslim children dying on the TV, these can have big impacts on people.

A notable result of the interviews is that probation officers and community mentors report some success with interventions that do not directly challenge jihadist ideology. Instead, interventions aim for disengagement and desistence by debating not the grievance but the violent response to grievance. Here is a community mentor talking:

> If they want to talk about foreign policy, we'll just join their argument, you know, I think you're right about Afghanistan or Iraq, why should other people go into Afghanistan or Iraq and kill innocent people, they've no right to go there—yes you're right. So then these people

start thinking, well hang on we've got the same views, at the end then, when the conversation finishes on that particular subject, what we have both agreed is that, yes, we don't like it what's happening, but what is the action we can take, to stop that from happening?

This kind of intervention may be particularly helpful with individuals who feel strongly the suffering of others. Rather than insist the probationer deny Western victimization of Muslims, or deny that this suffering justifies violence in return, the debate turns on whether violence or support for violence is the most effective response for the probationer.

A probation officer reflects on the limits of the possible in deradicalization: "He's always gonna have strong political beliefs, that's the way he is, and he's got a really strong sense of injustice, but I think what he's learned now, is that he can't channel those in the way he was."

To summarize, we still don't know anything about recidivism rates for UK probationers with convictions for terrorist offenses, but the practitioners working with these individuals seem to have developed some useful ideas about deradicalization and its limits.

How does terrorism end?

Previous sections of this chapter focused on deradicalization of individual militants. Of course, there is another kind of desistence, at the group level. A number of possible outcomes can mark the end of a terrorist group or at least the end of a group's use of terrorism as a tactic of political conflict. These outcomes may be conveniently divided into those that leave the group and its organization largely intact or even expanded, and those that leave the terrorist group and its organization reduced to the point that terrorist action is much reduced or impossible (Table 10.1).

Table 10.1 Terrorist Group Outcomes[a]

Terrorist decision to desist from terrorism

Achieve final goals (Irgun, FLN)

Achieve intermediate goals of attention and status for the cause (PLO, ISIS)

Transition to nonviolent politics (Provisional IRA, Egyptian Islamic Group)

Expansion to mass protest, guerrilla war, insurgency, or revolution (Viet Cong)

Transition to criminality (FARC, Abu Sayyaf)

Terrorist organizational breakdown—disabling

Decapitation (Sendero Luminoso after capture of Ibimael Guzman)

Loss of members in action (Asad bombs Hama to crush militants)

Loss of members by defection and burnout (1980s Red Brigades penitenti)

Loss of safe havens (ASALA loses bases when IDF enters Lebanon)

Dwindling mass support (Red Brigades after killing Aldo Moro)

[a]Examples in parentheses.

ASALA, Armenian Secret Army for the Liberation of Armenia; FARC, Revolutionary Armed Forces of Colombia; FLN, National Liberation Front; IDF, Israel Defense Forces; IRA, Irish Republican Army; ISIS, Islamic State of Iraq and Syria; PLO, Palestine Liberation Organization.

Intact group outcomes

Decline of terrorism can be associated with a number of outcomes that preserve the group, its organization, and its leaders. These outcomes include achievement of the explicit goals of the terrorist group, achievement of intermediate goals such as attention and status won for the terrorist group and its cause, and transition to nonviolent politics. These three outcomes have in common a group decision to give up violence, but it is also possible that a group can give up terrorism as a tactic in a transition to other forms of violent political action—mass protest, guerrilla war, insurgency, civil war, revolution, or even interstate war. Also possible is transition to apolitical criminality, although this transition can be difficult to assess because many terrorist groups engage in criminal activity such as drug running or kidnapping as a way to get money for the cause.

Disabled group outcomes

Decline of terrorism can also be associated with outcomes in which a group is broken, eliminated, or disbanded. Organizational breakdown is an outcome forced by events the terrorists cannot control, including loss of leaders (decapitation, failure to replace leadership), loss of group members (death, injury, imprisonment, fatigue, disillusionment), defection of group members taking up government amnesty, and dwindling support (loss of sympathizers and supporters, including loss of foreign support or secure bases). The decades-long persistence of infrequent attacks by Greece's 17 November leftist terrorist group is a warning that dwindling support need not mean the end of terrorist attacks.

In general, disabled terrorist groups are likely to suffer more than one disabling event. After the massacre of tourists at Luxor, for instance, Egyptian Islamic Group suffered death and imprisonment of many members, factionalization and leader competition over peacemaking, and loss of public sympathy.

It is perhaps surprising that governments give so much attention to individual-level deradicalization and relatively little attention to group-level deradicalization. Because terrorism is a form of political conflict, governments might usefully consider which outcomes of group deradicalization might be possible or desirable. In other words, it might be useful to imagine how to get to a world beyond terrorism rather than how to decrease the number of terrorists.

11

WHAT ARE MASS IDENTITY MANIPULATIONS (MIMS)— PICTURES, SONGS/CHANTS, RUMORS, RITUALS, AND SYMBOLS?

What is a mass identity?

Imagine having to complete 10 statements that start "I am . . .". Your responses would likely span your individual identity (student, welder), your group identity (mother, union member), and your mass identity (American, Catholic). These identities define many of your opinions, values, and behaviors.

Personal and group identities are tied with personal outcomes. To get a college degree, you must think and act like a student. To maintain friendships, you must shape your attitude and behavior to accommodate your friends. A good life requires nurturing personal and group identities. Not so with mass identity.

In fact, there's no obvious reason to have a mass identity. Mass collectives are impersonal: You will never meet most members of your nation, your ethnic or religious group. Mass collectives are also diverse: Americans in California are different from Americans in Alabama. Finally, these large collectives offer very little in the way of tangible benefits, while they demand a lot for the privilege of belonging. Being an American means paying taxes, serving on jury duty, voting, maybe even risking your life if there is a draft into a military campaign.

You could have a happy and fulfilling life without a mass identity. But most people pledge allegiance to some large and impersonal group, giving their time, money, and even lives for the intangible benefit of that membership—for their mass identity.

Why do we even have a mass identity?

Evolutionary psychologists would say it's a glitch in our brain's programming. For millennia, humans have existed in tight-knit groups where everyone knew everyone else, where survival of an individual depended on belonging. Being cast out meant a quick death by predators, rival groups, cold, or starvation. It wasn't until medieval times that the concept of a nation emerged to define "imagined communities."[1] Evolutionary psychologists would say we repurposed the brain structures that evolved to process small face-to-face group membership for use with large, impersonal groups, where costs are steeper and benefits more elusive.

Another view of mass identity says that it is not a glitch but a feature. Jon Haidt calls this idea hive psychology. He argues that humans are ultrasocial species (like bees) whose brains have a kind of "hive-switch" to turn off individual perspective in favor of the collective and abandon self-interest for the interest of the group.[2] In this view, the cost–benefit analysis extends beyond any one individual to the whole group whose survival depends on its members. We could say that mass identity is activated when the hive switch is turned on.

In a way, radicalization is a process of loosening the hive switch, making mass identity more easily triggered by symbols, slogans, or images referencing the large collective.

Is there scientific evidence of mass identity?

Look around you, and you will likely see an American flag on someone's property, an Irish clover bumper sticker, a sports team logo on a T–shirt, or a star of David on a gold chain around someone's neck. All of these are markers of mass identity. People display them to assert their membership in a large and impersonal collective, such as a sports team fandom, an ethnic group, a religious group, or a nation. You may say these are irrelevant: Who cares what people display on their bumpers, their property, or their clothes? But psychological research shows that mass identities serve an important function: People flock to them when threatened.

In the days following the terrorist attacks of 9/11, American students rated their nation and their university as more important than either before or months after the attacks.[3] The threat of the terrorist attacks made students embrace their mass identities. When their "hive" was endangered, the hive switch was flipped, and the mass identity came forefront.

One study illuminated why that might happen. When people are made to feel bad about themselves because of false-negative feedback, they are especially prone to "bask in reflected glory" (BIRG)—that is, associate themselves with a successful group by using personal pronouns ("we" as opposed to "them") when describing the group's achievements.[4] The threat of bad self-image makes one lean on mass identity.

Similarly, national leaders are more likely to use "we" in speeches leading up to a war than in speeches made during peaceful times.[5] The threat of war produces a more inclusive language that could trigger mass identity to rally the nation against that threat.

A different kind of threat—physical pain—also makes people flock to groups. Thus, when waiting for an electric shock, people prefer to sit in (anonymous and silent) the company of others who are going to be shocked as well, as opposed to sitting alone or sitting with others who are not expecting to be electrocuted.[6] This anonymous collective helps to diffuse anxiety just by being there. Those who were very anxious about the procedure felt less anxious after waiting with others; those who were calm felt more anxious after waiting in company. The mere presence of others who share our fate allows us to share emotions and reduce stress.

Emotional contagion is a tendency of people to pick up on feelings of others around them, even when these feelings are not explicitly expressed.[7] Epidemiology research has demonstrated that not only emotional states (depression,[8] anxiety, loneliness)[9] but also physical conditions (obesity, insomnia)[10] and behaviors (suicide, divorce, illegal drug use)[11] can spread through a population like a virus, with emotional contagion likely playing a large role in transmission.[12]

Recent research on Twitter showcases emotional contagion on a mass level. When aggregated across geographic areas, tweets can be analyzed to see if, for example, curse words appear more frequently in some counties than in others. These results can then be compared with countywide health statistics. The more tweets from a particular county used words expressing negative emotions ("Ass*ole," "bored," or "jealous"), the greater was that county's heart disease mortality rates. Remarkably, these Twitter emotion markers predict cardiovascular mortality better than all other factors combined: demographics, smoking, diabetes, hypertension, race, and marital status. And the surprise is that people who were tweeting were likely different (younger) than people who were dying from heart disease.

In other words, Twitter users, although not themselves afflicted with heart disease, expressed the emotional climate of their larger community. This emotional climate likely contributed to the rates of mortality among those suffering from heart disease in the community. Mass identity has real health consequences.

Another study examined not Twitter but Google Trends, which tracks the popularity of Google searches. Google Trends showed that counties with more frequent searches for "erectile dysfunction," "how to get girls," "penis size," "impotence," and "Viagra" were more likely to have voted for Donald Trump in the 2016 presidential election.[13] This correlation held even when controlling for education and racial composition, as well as for other Google search phrases, such as "breast augmentation" and "menopause." The study authors concluded that Trump appealed to men with "fragile masculinity," anxious about fitting in with the social standard of manliness. The authors suggest that the correlation between fragile masculinity and voting behavior is driven by these men's desire to associate with a strong authoritarian figure (a kind of surrogate for their own masculinity), such as Trump. The correlation between the umbrella of search terms related to fragile masculinity and voting for Republican candidates repeated in 2018 midterm elections, boosting the reliability of the results.[14] As in the Twitter study, we can't assume that the individuals who did the googling are the ones whose votes determined election outcomes in their districts. Yet this meta-data on the county level predicts individual voting behavior, suggesting mass identity at play.

Another study[15] went one step further by demonstrating a relationship between mass radicalization of opinion and radicalization of action—terrorism. The study compared public opinion toward leadership of nine world powers (including the United States, the United Kingdom, Russia, Japan, India, China, and France) among residents of Middle Eastern and North African (MENA) countries. The more disapproval residents of a MENA country expressed (in a Gallup survey) against a world power, the more terrorist attacks against that world power originated from the MENA country. In other words, public opinion in country A about country B predicted rates of terrorism from country A toward country B.

It's fascinating that, as with angry tweets predicting heart attacks, and googling "penis enlargement" predicting voting, people answering Gallup questions are likely not the ones orchestrating and carrying out terrorist attacks. But their opinion—mass opinion—is predictive of radical action among their compatriots who share their mass identity. Mass radicalization is connected with individual radicalization.

If mass identity can affect our emotions, actions, and even mortality, perhaps it is useful to pay attention to it. Perhaps our hive mind is not a glitch, even if we don't quite understand it yet. Perhaps we should try to understand it better.

What are MIMs—mass identity manipulations?

Twelve days before the presidential election of 2016, the Trump campaign analytics team told reporters that Trump had only a 15 percent chance of winning.[16] National polls showed Hillary Clinton 6 points ahead of Trump. The spectacular upset that followed has been the subject of speculations and investigations ever since.

Several factors seem to have contributed to Clinton's defeat, including the vagaries of the electoral college and FBI Director James Comey's reopening of the investigation into Clinton's improper use of email servers.[17] Less objective, but not less important, were (fabricated) internet rumors about Clinton's involvement with an underground pedophile and child trafficking ring operating out of a Washington, DC, pizza restaurant—"Pizzagate."[18] These rumors, advanced by partisan Washington insiders like Eric Prince and Roger Stone and featured on the (now-banned from YouTube) conspiracy site Infowars, were amplified on social media by Russian trolls and bots (automated accounts posing as internet users).[19]

Ten days before the election, combined search terms "Clinton" and "pedophile" registered 0 interest on Google

Trends (a measure of interest ranked from 0 to 100). Only 4 days later, the combination of search terms hit 100 on Google Trends, a maximum among 1.7 billion unique users of the search engine worldwide.[20] Research now estimates that fake news stories such as Pizzagate were successful in swinging undecided voters from Clinton to Trump by a wide enough margin to explain the election going to Trump.[21]

These fake news stories were propped up by Trump, who began calling Clinton "Crooked Hillary," reinforcing the idea that Clinton was a criminal. At Trump rallies, crowds routinely chanted "Lock her up!"—again referencing the idea that Clinton was a criminal who must be put in jail. "That became Trump's closing argument —Watergate, endless investigations, criminal activities and an inability to govern."[22]

The Trump campaign's efforts to stay on this message paid off. For example, in Florida, early voters favored Clinton by about 4 percent, but those who decided on the candidate on the last day before the election (voters likely exposed to internet rumors and Trump campaign's messaging) favored Trump by 13 percent—a 300 percent increase.[23]

Arguably the greatest political upset in American history, Trump's victory was pulled off within 12 days, fueled largely by a rumor, a slogan, and a chant. To many political observers and scholars, this defies rationality and strains credulity.

Yet there are many examples of irrational, counterfactual ideas stirring mass identities and aiding mass radicalization. Attacks on Jews in Europe (*pogroms*) often resulted from rumors about Jews abducting Christian children.[24] The 1917 Russian revolution, born of public frustration with the bloodbath of World War I and czarist oppression of peasants and factory workers, gained momentum with the rallying cry "Peace! Land! Bread!"[25] In recent American history, Barack Obama's presidential run against John McCain was nearly derailed by an advertisement that compared the young and relatively inexperienced candidate to Paris Hilton, a blonde Hollywood socialite.[26]

Mass identity manipulations (MIMs) are messages that, in their simplicity, shortcut through the nuance of political issues straight to the heart of mass identity. "Give me freedom or give me death!"—to hell with the complexity of taxation and representation: Americans want to be free of British rule.

MIMs come in different forms. "Oh say, can you see, by the dawn's early light . . ." summons the memory of the tune and the urge to stand up as we experience the swelling of national pride. The song awakens the American mass identity.

Some of the most powerful MIMs have no words at all. Seeing an American flag when traveling abroad, do you feel pride and joy at being an American? A national flag is a powerful symbol able to rouse the national mass identity.

Other MIMs are all about the experience. Being part of a procession, a protest or a rally, or witnessing a religious or cultural ceremony, a torchlit procession or a military parade, can make participants feel as one, willing to protect one another and sacrifice for strangers.

MIMs are a kind of meme that can spread fast, far and wide. MIMs' success is rooted not in a kitten's cuteness or in a joke's cleverness but in humans' ability to share an identity with perfect strangers. MIMs reach past our individual interests and daily grind and straight into the identification with a large and impersonal collective to which we feel connection: religious group, ethnic group, and national group. Deep inside, most of us carry an allegiance strong enough to sacrifice for it. MIMs are psychological access codes that bypass our normal cynicism and self-preservation, bringing the cherished group to the forefront of our mind and preparing us for sacrifice.

In the following sections, we discuss a variety of MIMs: pictures, symbols, rumors, music/songs/chants, synchronized movements, and slogans. This is not an exhaustive list. In fact, we wrote a whole book about one powerful MIM—martyrdom.[27] Here, we present only the most basic, most frequently used MIMs, whose power to mass radicalize has been documented.

In the wake of revelations about efforts by governments (Russia) and the private sector (Cambridge Analytica) to manipulate mass identity by targeted social media posts that included pictures, rumors, and slogans, time is ripe for researchers and policymakers to become more invested in studying MIMs.

How does visual art (posters, murals, graffiti, cartoons, photographs, films) contribute to mass radicalization?

Through paradox and vulnerability.

They say a picture is worth a thousand words. An entire book about the Holocaust may not have the same gut-wrenching effect as a photograph of starving prisoners behind the barbed wire fences of Auschwitz. In the universe of images, some pictures are worth a million words.

A single image can have the power to undermine a military campaign. In 1972, the photo of a Vietnam girl running naked from a South Vietnamese Air Force napalm bomb on her village became iconic for its power to turn Americans against the Vietnam War.[28] Attempting to put a dent in the public outcry about the photo, President Nixon mused that the image might have been altered by the photographer. The photographer, Nick Ut, responded, in print, "The horror of the Vietnam War recorded by me did not have to be fixed." The war ended the same year.

Similarly, images of American soldiers, dragged through the streets of Mogadishu after they were captured and killed in the Black Hawk Down operation, shattered Americans' positive view about US involvement in Somalia. This public sentiment contributed to the withdrawal of US troops from Somalia the next day and continued to inform US foreign policy for years afterward.[29]

Other images have the opposite effect: to incite people into battle. Notoriously, the Nazi Ministry of Propaganda created an entire campaign of posters to radicalize the German nation for war. Many of these posters depicted blonde and beautiful Germans suffering at the hands of sickly, ugly, or inhuman-looking Jews or communists.

More recently, we have witnessed iconic images move mass opinion and action toward empathy. The photo of a drowned little boy, whose body washed up on a beach in Greece, changed the rhetoric about Syrian refugees in Europe.[30] The average daily amount of donations to the Red Cross for the Syrian refugees was 55 times greater in the week following the release of the photograph than in the weeks prior. Even 6 weeks later, donations continued at a rate twice as high. Additionally, there was a 10-fold increase in donors signing up for monthly contributions to the Red Cross campaign asking support for refugees. Six months later, 99.9 percent of these donors remained committed to monthly contributions. The study's authors attribute the increased giving for refuges to the emotional impact of the photograph, especially for people in Europe. Supporting this argument is the fact that at the same time as donations for refugees increased, so did the number of Google searches for "Syria," Refugee," and "Aylan" (the boy's name).[31]

Google "iconic images," and you may discover that you have already seen many: a Viet Cong officer, bloodied and tied up, being shot in the head by a South Vietnamese general;[32] police dogs attacking an unarmed Black protestor in Birmingham, Alabama;[33] a young woman screaming over the body of a student shot dead during the Kent State protests;[34] a Chinese man with a plastic grocery bag in each hand confronting a tank in Tiananmen Square.[35]

One measure of an image's impact is how many people recognize it from even a brief verbal description. This familiarity suggests that many people have been emotionally moved by these images and then moved to share their experience with others.

Not only are these images emotionally powerful, they are politically powerful as well. Each image we have mentioned supports one side in a political conflict. The fact that many people have shared them is evidence that these images have shaped opinions about the conflicts they represented.

Each of these pictures forces the indifferent to pick a side in the conflict, and moves those already committed higher in the pyramid of opinion radicalization.[36] How could an image do that, and what about these particular images made them so powerful? We believe that the radicalizing power of iconic images lies in their combining two elements: paradox and vulnerability.

The *paradox* in the picture engages the mind. A dead toddler on an idyllic beach, a naked girl running from a blazing fire, or a man confronting a tank with nothing but grocery bags— the paradox brings our thoughts back to the picture again and again.[37] Research on visual advertisements found that incongruous images made people change their perspectives by challenging habitual thinking. Not only does a paradoxical picture challenge one's opinions but also it leaves a lasting impression: Images with incongruencies in them are more memorable than images that do not violate expectations.[38] Like an unsolved puzzle, the incongruency nags at our order-seeking mind,[39] making us think about the image and what it represents, making us remember it.

The second element of iconic images, *vulnerability*, engages our heart. A small child distressed or dead; a tied-up, bruised and bloodied prisoner being shot; an unarmed man attacked by vicious-looking dogs—these portray powerlessness juxtaposed with power. We sympathize with the powerless in these images, feeling pity and sadness, and we empathize, sharing their helplessness, hopelessness, and humiliation.

These emotions amplify the cognitive processes stirred by the paradox in the image. The cognitive pull and the emotional push motivate us do something to resolve both. As a result, we are likely to form a more radical opinion about the political conflict portrayed in the image and sometimes even to engage in radical action.

How does music (songs, chants) contribute to mass radicalization?

Through familiarity, message, and synchronicity.

Marching songs seem to be as old as war. Revolutions often have distinct songs associated with them, sometimes specifically commissioned for radicalizing the masses.

The most famous and time-tested is "La Marseillaise," commissioned by the mayor of Strasbourg, France, in the face of an imminent invasion by Austrian forces intent on rolling back the French Revolution and restoring Louis XIV to the throne. The author, Rouget de Lisle, a soldier and violinist, reportedly stole the music from a popular song and stole half the lyrics from graffiti plastered around the city.[40] The result was a MIM so successful that a French general once said "La Marseillaise" was worth 1,000 extra men in battle.[41] To this day, the French sing it at protests and parades to inspire unity, and all over the world, people sang it to express solidarity with the French in the wake of the 2015 terrorist attacks in Paris.

How can a song be worth 1,000 soldiers? We suggest that there are three forces behind the radicalizing power of songs and chants. The first is *familiarity*.

In the chaos and uncertainty of the battle, a street protest, or a violent riot, anxiety is high. To act together, people must overcome their fear.

Research finds that familiarity reduces anxiety.[42] Patients awaiting medical procedures, for example, feel less anxious when they are told exactly what will happen to them and in what order—expectations create perceived familiarity. So, too, a familiar song can reduce fear.

Familiarity with a musical piece activates pleasure circuits in the brain.[43] Across varied pieces of music, familiarity correlates with both self-reported pleasure and physiological activity in the brain's pleasure centers.[44] The more familiar the music, the more pleasure it brings.[45] A song as familiar as "La

Marseillaise" would produce a wave of pleasure, reducing anxiety as it makes people feel good.

This effect might be stronger for simple songs than for songs with complicated melody.[46] Marching songs or chants such as the soccer fans' favorite "Olé Olé Olé" are especially useful as MIMs because of their simplicity.

But music is capable of eliciting all kinds of emotions.[47] A sad song can make you cry, a theme to a horror movie can make your skin crawl, and happy music can bring joy. People manning the barricades or trenches choose music and lyrics that build up unity and courage. "La Marseillaise," for example, begins with energetic chords and the words, "Arise, children of fatherland." The refrain goes, "To arms, citizens, form your battalions! Let's march! Let's march!"

Radicalizing songs and chants offer a measure of comfort and pleasure to people in the uncertainty of a conflict. At the same time, they reinforce a radicalizing message through the lyrics. *Message* is the second radicalizing force behind songs and chants.

The Russian Bolshevik revolution of 1917 relied on the MIM power of "The International." It begins with rhythmic and rousing beats, "Rise, you branded and cursed world of the hungry and the slaves." The radicalizing rhetoric is powerful, wrapped into familiar, pleasure-producing music.

The Nazis popularized the catchy tune of "Horst Wessel Leid," the official song of Hitler Youth whose refrain says, "Today, Germany is ours, and tomorrow, the whole world." "Kampflied der Nationalsozialisten" ("Battle Hymn of the National Socialists"), another popular Nazi song, begins with a blare of brass and the words, "We are the army of the swastika." Both of these songs are banned in Germany and Austria today because their radicalizing power has been, unfortunately, well documented. A chilling re-creation of the power of such songs is available in a YouTube clip from the 1972 film *Cabaret*.[48]

In the 1960s, the US civil rights movement produced several songs that became anthems, sung by crowds at protests, sit-ins, and rallies. Among these are "We Shall Overcome" and "A Change Is Gonna Come."

In the United States today, presidential candidates often use simple, familiar songs with a political message at rallies to rouse their followers' mass identity—like Bruce Springsteen's "Born in the USA"[49] or John Mellencamp's "Our Country."[50] At Obama's campaign rallies, people chanted "Yes we can!"—a simple message with a simple beat, familiar to all. At Trump's rallies, people often chanted "Lock her up"—another simple message (about Hillary Clinton), albeit of a very different nature.

The familiarity of a song's tune or a chant's beat brings comfort in an unfamiliar setting. The message of the song or chant informs the mass identity of the crowd. But there's an added benefit in singing or chanting together.

In a crowd of hundreds or thousands, the act of chanting or singing together creates an instant community. These strangers know the same song you know; they feel the same passion for its message as you feel; you can see on their faces the emotions you feel inside. The familiarity of the song or chant, shared with others, creates an instant community.

The third force behind songs' and chants' mass-radicalizing power, *synchronicity*, completes this transition from individual to mass identity. Synchronicity is a human tendency to involuntarily sync posture, speaking patterns, and physiology, including skin conductivity, breathing, and heart rates.[51] Research has found a variety of stimuli that produce synchronicity: holding hands,[52] staring at each other while sitting silently face-to-face,[53] and moving in rhythm with another, such as tapping on the table in the same pattern.[54] One powerful path to synchronicity is singing or chanting together. Choir singers develop synchronicity so complete that their hearts literally "beat as one," rising or falling simultaneously as they sing or chant.[55]

What does synchronicity have to do with mass radicalization and the power of songs and chants to manipulate mass identity?

To answer this question, consider the effects of synchronicity. In small groups, synchronicity predicts cooperation, conflict regulation, and motivation for group goals.[56] Synchronicity also moderates risk-taking behaviors and boosts performance of group members.[57] One study even demonstrated that synchronicity can reduce pain.[58]

Extrapolating these effects to large impersonal collectives, you can imagine how synchronicity can contribute to mass radicalization. Singing or chanting together, people in a street protest or on a battlefield sync their heart rates, brain waves, and levels of hormones that regulate stress, aggression, and joy. They begin to feel more unity, acting more cooperatively, striving to achieve group goals and moderating risky behaviors. If they get injured, synchronicity helps reduce their pain. Through synchronicity, a large crowd begins to act like a single organism—sharing emotions, motivations, and action.

Songs and chants are thus powerful MIMs. Through familiarity, message, and synchronicity, they activate the hive switch that unleashes mass identity, enabling large collectives of people to act as one, to submerge individual interests for the interest of the larger group. A marching song or a protest chant radicalizes en masse, preparing the community for battle.

How does rumor contribute to mass radicalization?

Through stirring mass emotions, putting mass identities in conflict, and suggesting radical action.

The British East India Company represented the British colonial rule in India in 1757. In the battle of Plassey, the East India Company overthrew the Nawab of Bengal and established a military presence through the formation of the East India Company's Bengal Native Army. The soldiers in the army were mostly Hindu or Muslims, while the senior officers were British. A hundred years later, in 1857, native soldiers had accumulated a number of grievances against the company, including low pay and frequent deployments far from their families. New rules added to the dissatisfaction: a law permitting remarriage by Hindu widows, seen by Hindu soldiers as an affront to their religion, and a regulation that a soldier unfit for foreign service would be ineligible for pensions. These grievances, both economic and religious, were widely shared—and yet it was a rumor that sparked a rebellion.[59]

The rumor had nothing to do with any of the grievances of the past. Instead, it was about something the British were allegedly about to do. And it was atrocious. The rumor was that the British were about to start using cartridges greased with pig fat and beef tallow. The soldiers had to tear the cartridges open with their teeth before they could pour the gunpowder into their rifles. The idea that the British were about to make them touch pig fat (forbidden for Muslims) or beef tallow (forbidden for Hindus) with their lips led to a series of violent riots against the East India Company, with two-thirds of the native regiments mutinying.

What was so powerful about a rumor that legitimate economic and religious grievances lacked? How could a rumor radicalize the majority of the Hindu and Muslim soldiers against the British?

A rumor is a particular kind of story. It is different from news: Unlike news, a rumor is false or at least unsubstantiated. It's different from gossip: Gossip is only relevant to a few individuals, whereas rumor is important to a larger group.[60] A rumor is a story that stirs collective emotions: fear, outrage, disgust, and anger.[61] It is especially effective in uncertain or anxiety-producing situations[62] because it reduces uncertainty and anxiety through a process of communal sense-making.[63] A few elements mark successful (widely shared) rumors: plausibility, simplicity, suitability (how applicable to the anxiety-producing situation), vividness, and suggestiveness (how straightforward are the implications for opinion/action).[64]

The rumor that triggered mutiny among East India soldiers in 1857 fit the profile of a successful rumor: It was unsubstantiated but important to all soldiers. It stirred communal emotions, including outrage and anger. It was plausible, simple, vivid, and suitable for a community already aggrieved against the British. And it was highly suggestive: No Hindu or Muslim soldier could in good conscience obey orders to put forbidden animal fat in his mouth—the only course of action was rebellion.

Before, soldiers' grievances were personal—*my* pension, *my* deployment, *my* widow now allowed to remarry. The rumor brought into the mix a collective grievance—*our* religious identity. The moral dimension of the rumored violation by the British opened the floodgates to the moral outrage that could be expressed and shared with other soldiers.

Modern historians have shown that regiments rebelled shortly after soldiers engaged in a religious gathering or procession; the British had permitted such rituals for both Hindu and Muslim soldiers.[65] The timing of rebellions across regiments indicates that the time and space dedicated for mass gathering and celebrating of the mass identity allowed also for the sharing and amplification of the emotions stirred by the rumor. In other words, a rumor elicited a shared emotion, and with it, highlighted a mass identity. The simplicity of the rumor drew a line between *us* and *them*: the Indians versus the Brits. The suggestiveness of the rumor laid out the choice of action: Violate your religious belief and betray your mass identity, or rise up against those who threaten it.

Rumors are often thought of as stories circulating from person to person. But the rise of the internet as a medium of news that competes with traditional news outlets has undermined the distinction between person-to-person communication and mass media communication. We began with consideration of a rumor that surely spread person to person; the British controlled the telegraph system in India and did their best to block the story about cartridges greased with pig and cow fat. We move now to discussion of misinformation and disinformation campaigns—stories—that are launched and disseminated using mass media, including the internet. These stories depend on both mass media and person-to-person communication, and we believe that the same factors that make a rumor successful are important to the success of a misinformation campaign.

The power of a good story was not lost on the Nazi Minister of Propaganda, Joseph Goebbels, who crafted a story of martyrdom out of a street thug murdered for unpaid rent.[66] Goebbels wrote newspaper stories and delivered a eulogy that painted Horst Wessel as an embodiment of all that was good and pure in Germany, and his communist killers as intent on stifling Germany's innocence and grace. The story, although fabricated, was effective: Horst Wessel became a national hero. After his death, stories that he was still fighting on one front or another gave birth to a euphemism for dying in battle: "He joined the Horst Wessel battalion."

Goebbels' story had all the necessary elements to go viral: It was simple (a good boy, killed by an anonymous enemy threatening us all), it stirred collective emotions (outrage and fear), it was plausible (Horst Wessel was indeed killed), it was suitable (many Germans felt threatened by communism), it was vivid (portraits of smiling, Aryan-looking Horst Wessel were widely publicized), and it was suggestive. Celebrating Horst Wessel's martyrdom in annual pilgrimages to his grave and naming streets, military units, and ships after him, Germans fortified and radicalized their mass identity in conflict with their enemies' identity.

In more recent examples, propagandistic misinformation has been weaponized by the Russian government for an internet era. After the Ukrainian revolution of 2014 threw off Russian influence, Russian media disseminated a story purportedly from Eastern Ukraine. According to the Russian "news," Ukrainian armed forces crucified a 4-year-old boy on his town's news stand,[67] later driving around a tank with the boy's lifeless body hanging off the turret. This story, told by "an eyewitness" in convincing detail (she claimed the boy was crucified wearing only his underwear), became a rallying cry for Russian volunteers to join a military campaign against Ukraine.

Similarly, after Russian forces occupied Eastern Ukraine and accidentally downed a passenger plane, the Russian propaganda mill put out a host of rumors to deflect the blame. These ranged from suggestions that the plane was downed by Ukrainians to stories that the plane was not carrying any people and that dead bodies had been brought to the field where the plane crashed—for publicity.[68]

Most recently, the US public has been on the receiving end of the Russian rumor mill—through social media including Twitter, Facebook, and Instagram. Simple stories designed to stir mass identity and rouse emotions divided the US public into conflicting camps, radicalizing Whites against Blacks, liberals against conservatives, straight against LGBT.[69] Some researchers believe that Russian "discourse saboteurs" were instrumental in changing the outcome of the 2016 election.[70] According to communications professor Kathleen Hall Jamieson, extensive studies of past campaigns have demonstrated that "you can affect people, who then change their decision, and that alters the outcome." She continued, "I'm not arguing that Russians pulled the voting levers. I'm arguing that they persuaded enough people to either vote a certain way or not vote at all."[71]

Perhaps a story of a crucified 4-year-old boy or a rumor of the British using pig fat for cartridge lubricant sound ridiculous to you. But these were effective MIMs among people who shared a mass identity that the rumor threatened. In an era in which our mass identities are easily identified and targeted through the internet, dismissing the radicalizing power of ridiculous stories is unwise. Especially in times of uncertainty and anxiety, rumors and misinformation campaigns are powerful MIMs that can rouse people to riots, lead to war, and change election outcomes.

How does mass ritual (demonstrations, rallies, parades, marches, dances) contribute to mass radicalization?

Through synchronicity and basking in reflected glory.

The Maori, native New Zealanders, perform the *haka*, a ceremonial group dance and chant, for a variety of occasions. Perhaps the most famous haka is the one the New Zealand rugby team has traditionally performed before games. A war haka's elements include scary facial contortions (pocking of the tongue and bulging of the eyes), stomping of the feet, grunting, and slapping of hands on thighs. Originally, warriors performed this haka before a battle to build up their spirits and to intimidate their opponents. It is a choreographed display of unity, ferocity, and athletic prowess.

Other traditional cultures have war rituals that also include choreographed group movements, designed to display skill, strength, and unity[72] and to be performed in front of a large audience. Modern Western militaries stage parades where soldiers march in formations as citizens watch. Even during pretend war—sports—teams and fans alike often ritualize their pregame chants accompanied by synchronized movements.[73] Football and soccer fans create stadium "waves," rising and sitting down in a pattern.

Mass ritualized movement, be it haka, a *hopak*,[74] or a parade, is used by a variety of cultures throughout the world to prepare for battle. What about mass ritual affects mass identity, and how can mass ritual radicalize? We propose two ways.

The first is *synchronicity*, the synchronization of movement, speech patterns, and biorhythms. (See the section on songs and chants.) Just as singing together or chanting together can synchronize people's heartbeats and brain waves, so can moving together in time.

Synchronicity has profound and far-reaching effects on unifying and motivating a group. Research shows that spontaneously synchronized movements correspond with greater rapport among strangers meeting for the first time.[75] The effects go beyond rapport and are especially strong when synchronicity is induced rather than spontaneous. Dancing together in synchrony produces cooperation, especially when people are intentionally trying to synchronize their movements (compared to when they spontaneously fall into synchronicity because of a rhythm they hear).[76]

When cleverly orchestrated, synchronized movements can make strangers act altruistically toward each other. In one experiment, people wore headphones while they tapped on the table the rhythm of audio tones. Some heard the same pattern and tapped in unison; others heard a different pattern, making their tapping distinct. Afterward, given a choice to stay and help their partner with some math problems, those who synchronized through tapping volunteered to help at almost three times the rate of unsynchronized participants.[77] Synchronized movement makes group members give time and effort for group members' benefit.

Driving this point further, another experiment re-created traditional military-style movements, asking some participants to march together around campus in unison, while other participants walked the same route for the same amount of time but without synchronization. Afterward, participants played economic games where they could maximize their own earnings or give up personal profit for the benefit of the group. Those who synchronized were 50 percent more likely to give up personal benefit for the group than were those who didn't synchronize.[78] A follow-up study established the reason for the difference: Synchronization created a feeling of unity—cohesion—which resulted in greater altruism.[79]

Mass rituals bring strangers together and engage them in synchronizing actions: singing, dancing, marching. The synchronization of movement in these mass collectives leads to greater unity, cooperation, and altruism, reinforcing mass identity and preparing self-sacrifice for the group. Active participation in the ritualized movement is not even necessary. Observing it from the sidelines is enough to achieve a boost in mass identity through mass ritual.

One study of Spanish fire-walking, a ceremonial feat in which courageous (or crazy) individuals walk on burning coals barefoot, demonstrated that the biomarkers of stress (elevated heart rate, cortisol, adrenaline) synchronized between the walkers and their fellow villagers who watched their performance.[80] Visiting spectators with no ties with the village or the fire-walker did not synchronize. Lacking a shared identity, these spectators didn't benefit from a ritual that was a powerful MIM for villagers.

A study of soccer fans in Europe found that fans of a winning team experienced a surge in testosterone—the hormone marker of dominance—even though they only observed their team dominate an opposing team.[81] At the same time, testosterone dropped in fans of a losing team, marking the submissive status of their team. The mass identity shared between the team and the fans shines through in biochemical reactions to the team's successes and failures. If mass identity sometimes seems mysterious and abstract, these results show it to be concrete and powerful.

Synchronicity is not the only mechanism that drives mass ritual's MIM effects. It is not by accident that ritualized war dances display strength and vigor; it is not by accident that military parades dazzle observers with the sheer number of marching soldiers and the latest and greatest weapons. Mass ritual is especially powerful as a MIM when it allows observers to feel the warm glow of basking in reflected glory (BIRGing), to identify with the successful group.[82] BIRGing allows observers to achieve a boost to their own self-esteem—even though they made no contribution to the group's success. This tendency is evident when individuals whose self-esteem is threatened use second-person pronouns ("we") to describe their favorite team's winning game.[83] For mass identities of ethnicity, religion, or nationality, ritualized displays of a group's size and power invite spectators to partake of the power by identifying with the group, boosting their mass identity.

The flip side of BIRGing is CORFing—cutting off reflected failure. Individuals use more third-person pronouns ("they") to describe their team's losing game; they protect their self-esteem by reducing group identification. The problem is that no team always wins, and no ethnic, religious, or national group always wins. If self-esteem were the only thing people cared about, no amount of mass ritual could keep up mass identification against a trend of losses.

But many people do maintain mass identification despite losses and even humiliations experienced by their ethnic, religious, or national group. How is this possible? The obvious answer is that self-esteem is not the only reward of mass identification.

One possibility is that a mass identity is an answer to mortality.[84] Most religions offer an explicit answer to mortality with promise of an afterlife. Ethnic and national groups offer a kind of civil religion in which an individual continues after death as part of the progress of a group with a long history and an indefinitely long future. Mass identity offers symbolic immortality. No wonder we are ready to kill and die for it.

How do group symbols (flags, pictograms, salutes, gestures) contribute to mass radicalization?

By highlighting mass identity's boundary, leading to out-group discrimination, and fostering pluralistic ignorance.

Symbols are a diverse category. They include letters of the alphabet, numbers, and words; pictograms like the smiley face; abbreviations like USA; animals such as rats (traitors) or bulls (fearless); and historical figures—heroes (Paul Revere), martyrs (Gandhi), or villains (Hitler). Symbols are simple representations of complex ideas. They help us communicate and navigate the world.

Mass identities often rely on symbols to communicate the complexity of social identities. And mass identity can sometimes be manipulated through these symbols. Indeed, symbols are a particularly powerful kind of MIM.

Every nation has a unique symbol associated with it: the flag. Often, there is another graphic representation of national identity, such as the bald eagle for Americans, the two-headed crowned eagle for Russians, the Ukrainian trident, or the French fleur-de-lis. Among religions, Christians revere the cross, Jews the star of David, and Muslims a star inside a crescent moon. Political parties and movements use symbolic representations as well: donkey stands for US Democrats, elephant for Republicans, a peace sign for hippies, a MAGA hat for Trump supporters. LGBT's symbol is a rainbow, neo-Nazis favor swastikas, and anarchists identify with the pentagram.

But mass identity symbols are not limited to pictographs. Some are hand gestures. The Nazis invented the Nazi salute; the Black Power fist denotes Black nationalism. At the Brett Kavanaugh Senate confirmation hearings, Zena Bash, seated behind him, repeatedly flashed an upside-down OK gesture that many recognized as a White Power salute.[85]

How do mass identity symbols move us?

Symbols are the simplest, most basic representations of a mass identity. Being Ukrainian means many things. Are you ethnic Ukrainian, Russian, or mixed? Catholic or Orthodox? From the mountains in the West or the plains in the East? Big city or small village? These sub-identities of the mass identity are so different as to be in direct conflict at times. So what does a national flag convey to all whose nation it represents? What is the lowest common denominator among all of our loyalties and affiliations? The Ukrainian flag's blue and gold fields highlight the one thing all Ukrainians have in common: their Ukrainian citizenship.

Mass identities—national, religious, ethnic—are so diverse that the only thing *all* members share is their membership. A mass identity is therefore defined less by the in-group than by the out-group. Being Black means *not* being White or Hispanic; being Jewish means *not* being Muslim or Christian; being a Democrat means *not* being a Republican. Us versus them is the simplest way to define a mass identity; symbols, in their abstract simplicity, are uniquely suited for this task.

Highlighting the divide between the in-group and the out-group(s), MIM symbols set the stage for mass identity radicalization. Experiments on minimal groups showed that highlighting the group boundary makes people likely to favor the in-group and discriminate against the out-group. This is true even if the groups are formed arbitrarily for the duration of the experiment, and the divide is irrelevant to any real-life conflicts (a preference for paintings of Klee vs. Kandinsky, or even assignment by coin flip).[86]

When we see a national flag, it reminds us of our national identity, defined by its difference from other national identities. As a result, we favor the in-group (our nation) and denigrate the out-group (foreigners). Seeing an American flag makes American students more nationalistic (negative toward the out-group) and makes them feel superior to non-Americans.[87] Likewise, exposure to the German flag increased out-group prejudice among Germans.[88] Across different nations, then, national flags, symbol MIMs, increase negativity toward those who don't share that mass identity.

The effect of exposure to the flag doesn't end with out-group discrimination: It can lead to greater unity within the in-group and even to changes in political behavior. A study in Israel assessed participants' political positions before subliminally exposing some participants to the Israeli flag. Glimpsing the flag reduced political differences among participants, making them more unified than before. This change in attitudes translated into a change in their voting behavior: Those exposed to the flag voted more alike than those who hadn't glimpsed the flag.[89] A study in New Zealand found that subliminally exposing New Zealanders to the national flag made them more mindful of the national values and norms, although this exposure had no similar effect on foreigners.[90]

Seeing the national flag reminds people of their national identity's norms and values, unites them, and prejudices them toward outsiders. These are all markers of mass radicalization. Flags, therefore, are MIM symbols whose mere presence can radicalize a national identity.

Beyond flags, other mass identity symbols have attracted less research. A few studies have examined the effect of religious symbols. A study in France found that more individuals were willing to sign up to be organ donors (consistent with the norms of Christianity) when the individual soliciting the donation wore a Christian cross.[91] Similarly, a study in Chile using an economic game that measures cooperation showed that playing the game in a chapel produced more cooperation than playing it in a lecture hall.[92] Exposure to religious symbols, like exposure to national symbols, leads to greater adherence to group norms.

Like national symbols, religious symbols can lead to greater out-group discrimination. Muslim students in Israel, primed with either symbols of Judaism or symbols of Islam, showed greater stereotyping and rejection of Israeli Jews.[93]

One mechanism of mass radicalization through symbol MIMs is their ability to highlight the mass identity, increasing stereotyping and rejection of the out-group. Another radicalizing effect of MIM symbols is fostering *pluralistic ignorance*. Pluralistic ignorance is a mistaken belief about a social group that is widely shared among group members—for example, college students' mistaken belief that most students don't mind heavy drinking on campus.[94] Princeton University freshman males who shared this mistaken belief became more favorable toward heavy drinking over time, changing their initial attitudes toward the (mis)perceived norm.[95] In other words, pluralistic ignorance is a common misconception about the opinions of other group members (meta-opinions).

Display of group symbols asserts a group's legitimacy and cohesion, making the group seem more unified and fearsome to outsiders.[96] In times of threat, symbol display may help restore the violated mass identity. Thus, Americans displayed the national flag much more frequently on their cars, front lawns, and clothes following the 9/11 terrorist attacks than they did before.[97] The symbol MIM helped us cope with the outside threat.

Display of MIM symbols helps create a false meta-opinion that favors the group represented by the symbol (All these Ukrainian flags in northeast Philadelphia must mean the Ukrainian community is big and powerful here). In turn, meta-opinion can change people's own attitudes toward the group (I guess Ukrainians are cool/important/interesting).

How do mass identity manipulation symbols exaggerate the power of minority groups?

Pluralistic ignorance driven by MIM symbols can help legitimize a marginalized mass identity. The change in meta-opinion is especially likely when the MIM symbol is displayed on a high-power platform.

When we see a White power hand gesture on the US Senate floor, this display raises and legitimizes the alt-right movement. When the gesture is repeated during a Senate confirmation hearing, observers begin to wonder if the inaction of people watching the hearings in real life means they condone the display and condone the group and its norms. Before, the alt-right seemed distant and insignificant. After, it gained immediacy and clout. In 2019, the gesture was repeated at his courtroom hearing by the New Zealand mosque shooter.

Spray-painted swastikas communicate the hostile intentions of those who did the painting, but they also imply support of those who didn't stop them. Perhaps there is no support;

perhaps the swastikas were painted in the darkness, and every passerby since has silently cursed the vandals. But looking at the symbols, all the observers see is an unfettered assertion of one group's claim to power. Supporters of the group will therefore feel reassured, and the opponents threatened, by the symbol's presence. The more swastikas, the bigger and more assertive the group behind them seems.

The Nazi salute "Heil Hitler" began as a marginal group's "secret handshake" and transitioned into a compulsory greeting, serving as a litmus test for loyalty to the Nazi party.[98] The symbolic gesture was more than an alternative to "hello." It asserted a mass identity's ideology and the group's social dominance every time it was used. Eventually, so many people were using it that it became a better test of defection than of loyalty.

Mass identities are fluid constructs. Nations, ethnicities, and religions persist only so long as enough people believe in them. Symbols express not only belief in a mass identity but also a public display of such belief. They prop up mass identities, assuring supporters, threatening opponents, and laying the foundation for mass radicalization.

How do political slogans contribute to mass radicalization?

By creating a collective action frame.

Remember George W. Bush' presidential campaign slogan? Nobody does. Some slogans never catch on.

Others go viral.

Donald Trump's victorious presidential campaign popularized "Make America Great Again!" The abbreviation of the slogan, MAGA, turned into a symbol of Trump support displayed on hats, pins, and bumper stickers. Another slogan, "Lock her up!" became a favorite chant at Trump rallies, affirming his supporters' belief in Hillary Clinton's criminal misconduct. Recently, Trump rallies have been using a different slogan, "build that wall," to support his agenda to fund a wall on the border with Mexico. In a tweet, Trump amended this shorter version by adding a rhyming second line: "Build the wall, and crime will fall."

These slogans may sound ridiculous to Trump's opponents, but they excite and mobilize his supporters. What is it about slogans that can excite crowds, and sometimes even foment a revolution?

The Bolshevik revolution of 1917 was not the first attempt to overthrow the czar. *Friction* describes a decade-long effort by Russian activists to persuade the peasants to rebel. Idealistic young people traveled the countryside convincing peasants that the cause of their miserable existence was the czar, and the cure was revolution. But the peasants refused to listen, often reporting the agitators to the police. This disappointment led some activists to turn to terrorism; People's Will aimed to kill the czar and free the peasants to act on their grievances. They did kill the czar. They failed to move the peasants.

The man who succeeded in moving the peasants shared the goals of People's Will but not their idealism. Vladimir Lenin was a cynic. Instead of schlepping down dirt roads to schmooze with barbarians, Lenin lived in Europe off the rent he charged peasants to use his family land. This while popularizing the slogan "All land to the peasants!"

World War I took able men away from their farmlands. In 1915 and 1916, the czarist military routinely "requisitioned" grain and other food from the peasants—already weakened by the loss of breadwinners. Lenin's slogan fell on fertile ground. He told the peasants what they yearned to hear.

He told them a lie. In his political writing of 1915 and 1916 (writing that illiterate peasants would never read), Lenin advocated state ownership of the land.

Lenin's gift was his understanding of the Russian peasants' mass identity. His slogans spoke to them in the simplest terms, appealing to deep-seated emotions instead of intellectual truths or moral convictions. "All land to the peasants" promised bread. Circuses were promised in another of Lenin's greatest hits: "Communism is Soviet government plus elec-trification of the whole country." At a time when electricity seemed akin to magic, Lenin's branding linked a future utopia with the Soviet government.

Understanding the peasants' mass identity didn't mean Lenin cared about them. When the peasants rebelled against the Bolsheviks' confiscation of bread, Lenin rolled out another slogan. "He who doesn't work, doesn't eat!" placed the re-sponsibility for hunger on the peasants and justified the Red Army's atrocities against them.

To fuel messaging, Lenin started a cultural revolution in the 1920s, sponsoring artists, especially writers and poets. Amid the civil war and mass starvation, artists faced a choice: Create propaganda or perish. Some immigrated, like Ivan Bunin. Others were arrested and executed, like Nikolai Gumilev. But many writers and poets threw their creative power behind the revolution.

Lenin's intuition to invest in talented poets to spread the Party's message was on target. Research shows that rhymed messages are easier to remember and more persuasive than unrhymed messages carrying the same idea.

Slogans are the most basic expression of one side of a po-litical issue. They appeal to widely shared emotions, creating a perception of unity in a crowd of strangers. They prescribe a (simple) course of action that stems from these shared emo-tions, mobilizing the crowd.

"Make America Great Again" condenses complicated ec-onomic and political issues into two basic premises. First, things used to be great, but not anymore. With its wistful "great again," the first premise elicits nostalgia. Second, they better give back our greatness. The second premise, conveyed through the imperative and indiscriminate "Make America" builds anger. Notice how the slogan eludes details: Who is re-sponsible for the not-greatness? What was the greatness that is no more? How to bring it back? There is plenty of room for political maneuvering while the crowd, moved by nostalgia and fired up by anger, throws support behind the politician promising to satisfy these emotions.

"Build that wall, and crime will fall" adds the persuasive power of rhyming to the emotional appeal of crime (fear) and wall-building (safety and ownership).

Gifted messengers create slogans that speak to mass identity in the language it understands: simplified divisions and mobilizing emotions. "Us versus them," where we are threatened and must fight for the glorious future we deserve, is a timeless hit. The Great Wall of China and the remnants of the Berlin Wall testify to the historic appeal of walls—if not to their practicality.

Other countries also have famous slogans. The banner of the French Revolution and the motto of France today is "Liberte, Egalite, Fraternite." For Hitler, the foundational slogan was "Ein volk, ein Reich, ein Fuhrer."

The examples cited show what slogans have in common: They are brief, memorable, and highlight one side of a political conflict. Slogans can be understood as condensations of a political cause and, specifically, of the *collective action frame* of that cause.

Sociology has studied why some social movements persevere and succeed, while others quickly fade and accomplish nothing. To be successful, a social movement needs a collective action frame that can move individuals to sacrifice for the cause. The frame must identify a problem or grievance and who or what is to blame (diagnostic frame), must identify what is to be done (prognostic frame), and must identify who should do what is to be done (motivational frame).[99]

Slogans remind us of the attacks our group has suffered, highlight our glorious goals, and call for action. That is, slogans are diagnostic, prognostic, and motivational framings of a political cause. They are condensed versions of the collective action frames that power social movements.

At the bottom of every successful political slogan is a threat or injustice, and a promise of safety and justice. A good slogan evokes emotion in members of the group threatened or suffering: fear, anger, shame, and humiliation. The promise of common action toward justice and safety evokes positive emotions: pride, hope, and joy.

These emotions are all focused on a particular mass identity. Emotional reactions make the mass identity more salient and better able to radicalize opinion and motivate sacrifice for the group. Most individuals have more than one mass identity—that is, they care what happens to their nation, their ethnicity, their religious, regional, and neighborhood groups. A good slogan raises one identity above all others.

In short, slogans are a form of MIM that can radicalize sentiment and action for a political movement. Chanted in a mass public setting, a slogan joins in the MIM power of song and synchronicity.

What do all mass identity manipulations have in common?

Cognitive simplicity and emotional power.

One thing all MIMs have in common is *simplicity*. No need to think deep thoughts or engage an ideology, no need to spend time studying or interpreting. MIMs require a minimum of effort from the audience. A photo or a few chords of a song, a glimpse of the flag, and we are transported into the political theater, ready to transcend individual interests for a large and impersonal collective. MIMs deliver the biggest bang for the radicalizing buck.

For many observers, this simplicity can be misleading. Sitting in an armchair, surrounded by books and articles about a political conflict, we are likely to downplay the importance of a photograph, newly painted graffiti, or a video of a crowd chanting. Who would fall for that, we may think, dismissing the MIM.

Research has long mapped two routes to persuasion: central and peripheral.[100] Attitudes change via the central route to persuasion when we rely on well-informed arguments, acknowledge both sides of the issue, and trust experts. A debate, the kind we would expect between debate teams, would rely on the central route to persuasion. The central route to persuasion is politics at its *refinest*.

In contrast, the peripheral route to persuasion builds on heuristics instead of algorithms, quick and dirty estimations instead of lengthy calculations, celebrities instead of experts. Attitudes and behavior can change via the peripheral route when we are less attentive to the substance of the argument than to the source and style of its delivery. MIMs rely on the peripheral route to persuasion to radicalize political attitudes and behaviors.

Several factors make the peripheral route to persuasion appealing. These include the audience's inability or unwillingness to devote the resources to central route processing. If a political issue is too complex, if the audience is overwhelmed with other tasks or thoughts, or if the audience doesn't have time or the intellectual capacity to discern the issue's nuances, it's more likely to rely on peripheral route processing. The audience is more likely to be influenced by MIMs.

So, sitting in an armchair studying political issues, we are likely to miss the true power of MIMs: We have the time and inclination to contemplate mass politics; we dedicate our undivided attention and our intellectual capacity to the issue. These are ideal conditions for central-route persuasion. But in the midst of a street protest or a noisy rally, when feeling threatened by a foreign adversary or an authoritarian government, the peripheral route moves us easier and faster. These are the conditions that drive the power of MIMs.

Even in less dramatic circumstances, we may lean on MIMs when we feel overwhelmed. The expanding reach of social media puts pressure on our cognitive resources and absorbs increasing portions of our day. As we struggle to keep up with the influx of complex and conflicting stories, we are more likely subject to peripheral-route persuasion, relying more on MIMs' simplicity than on experts' complex analyses.

The second common factor among MIMs is their appeal to *emotions*. Sober discussions about political issues will cite studies and statistics, speaking to cold rationality rather than to heated emotions. In contrast, MIMs produce gut reactions and irrational behaviors.[101] Policy wonks speak to the issues; MIMs speak to the heart.

Emotions are another political force too often ignored by experts. Politics in the Western world are dominated by White men who've spent lifetimes mastering the ability to control impulses, delay gratification, and prioritize logic and reason above emotion. A political candidate can lose support for appearing too emotional (Gov. Howard Dean lost the presidential nomination for an excited scream).[102] Female politicians are often criticized for appearing too emotional (Rep. Alexandria Ocasio-Cortez was criticized for a video of her dancing in joy).[103] With emotions so costly to political careers, it is not surprising that political players and experts underestimate the impact of emotion-stirring MIMs. Having been trained to control and deprecate emotions, experts and politicians often expect logic and reason to have the final word on political issues.[104]

But psychological research has rejected this idea again and again. It showed instead that attitudes and actions are often irrational, framed in logical terms only after they were born of sensations (warm sensation in the hand makes a stranger seem more likable),[105] social pressures (an authority's order will lead most people to deliver deadly electric shocks to an innocent stranger),[106] and emotions (feeling bad about having done something shameful leads to attitude change that justifies the behavior).[107]

Jon Haidt's apt metaphor describes a rider atop an elephant, where the rider is our logical mind, and the elephant is everything else that drives us outside of conscious awareness: emotions, sensations, and social pressures.[108] Haidt observes that too often in political discourse, we pay attention to the rider and ignore the elephant. Yet the difference between the rider's and the elephant's size and power suggests that trying to persuade the rider to go in a particular direction is much more effective if the elephant can be persuaded first. Once the elephant is willing, persuading the rider is easy; but if the elephant is digging in or dragging its feet, persuading the rider is unlikely to be enough. So, too, we often try to persuade people by informed logical arguments, when the difference that needs settling is within the emotional domain.

MIMs are politically powerful because they persuade the elephant, speaking to our fears and hopes, our loves and hates, our pride, anger, and shame. Shared within the mass identity, individual emotions add up to more than the sum of their parts when they achieve synchronicity. Synchronicity unites strangers into something like a single organism, with individual interests submerged in group interest, and actions coordinated for common goals. That's some mighty horsepower behind silly rumors, crowd chants, and street graffiti.

Failing to account for MIMs, high-brow pundits failed to predict the Arab Spring, the Ukrainian revolution, or Donald Trump's election. Chapter 12 considers mass radicalization in the United States today. Some of the driving forces behind it were MIMs, including MIMs deployed through internet social media by an adversarial foreign power in an effort to destabilize and control American politics.

12

IS MASS RADICALIZATION A PROBLEM IN THE UNITED STATES?

Is there mass radicalization in the United States today?

Yes.

When we published *Friction* in 2011, the book's subtitle, "How Conflict Radicalizes Them and Us" was itself radical.[1] Our idea was that not only the bad guys, the terrorists, but also good Americans can become radicalized. That "our people" could be anything like "them" threatened many Americans' worldview. Seven years later, it is hard to deny radicalization is growing in America.

Consider the facts.

Hate crimes rose 17 percent in 2017, according to the FBI. These data don't include the jurisdictions that do not report hate crime statistics to the FBI. And this increase is unrelated to general crime: in the same period, general crime declined slightly, by 0.02 percent.[2]

Mass shootings in the United States claimed more lives in 2017 than in any other year in the past four decades.[3] Violent riots averaged 2 per year between 2000 and 2015, but their number increased dramatically to 10 in 2016 and 8 in 2017.[4] A company specialized in attire and decals with radical messages was started in 2012; by 2016, it had expanded to a self-reported million customers.[5]

These statistics lay out radicalization in action. A similar picture emerges when considering radicalization of opinion in the United States. Survey data show that hate for the other party has increased from about 17 percent among both Democrats and Republicans in 2000 to about 50 percent in 2016.[6]

Radicalization is also evident in social interactions online: 2016 marked a sharp increase in hate speech, including anti-Semitic and anti-Muslim rhetoric on Twitter and Facebook.[7] Although these social platforms have put in place policies and mechanisms to contain radical speech, there are alternative platforms (e.g., Gab) that attract users precisely because they do not try to sanction hateful rhetoric.

Both in opinion and in action, the United States has transformed in the past few years. We are more radical now than we were before. In America, radicalization emerges out of conflict, not between Americans and terrorists but between groups of Americans. Conflicts arise on the basis of ethnicity, religion, sexual preference, and political party. How is this happening, and why is it happening now?

When we wrote *Friction*, we searched for mechanisms of radicalization that would reach beyond any particular group of terrorists. We studied case histories of terrorists from different religious, cultural, and historical backgrounds, ranging from anti-tsarist terrorists of the 1890s to Islamist terrorists of today. The 12 mechanisms of radicalization that we identified could be seen at work in the history of every terrorist group studied. This generality led us to expect that the same mechanisms would be found on both sides of escalating political conflicts, both old and new. Thus, *Friction* described how radicalization could be seen not only in the terrorists but also in Americans responding to the terrorists. Indeed, we see many of the same mechanisms of radicalization that lead to terrorism at work in US politics today.

Status and thrill seeking motivate mass shooters like the Las Vegas shooter Stephen Paddock,[8] just as they motivate Islamist terrorists like Abu Musab al-Zarquawi. *Personal grievance* motivated incel (involuntarily celibate) Scott Paul Beierle, who shot several women at a yoga studio in Tallahassee, Florida,[9] just as it motivated some Palestinian suicide bombers. *Group polarization* and *group isolation and threat* are at play on radical social media websites in the United States, leading one individual to attack a synagogue in Pittsburgh,[10] just as these mechanisms led 19 al-Qaeda terrorists to the 9/11 attacks.

But it is mass radicalization observed in the United States that is the most striking. In *Friction*, we laid out three mechanisms of mass radicalization: martyrdom, jujitsu, and hate. In the recent selection of a US Supreme Court Justice, Brett Kavanaugh was a martyr for some and a monster for others. President Donald Trump attacks immigrants to instigate Democratic counterreaction and distract from his connections with Russia (jujitsu). Hate implies a bad essence. A belief in the other party's bad essence causes many to want their children to marry within their party: "In 1958, 33 percent of Democrats wanted their daughters to marry a Democrat, and 25 percent of Republicans wanted their daughters to marry a Republican. But by 2016, 60 percent of Democrats and 63 percent of Republicans felt that way."[11]

Recent proliferation of social media offers an unprecedented window into mass psychology. It's possible to see a story spreading in real time—through the rate at which it is shared, commented on, or "liked." It's possible to see which social media profiles are more influential than others—by the number of their "followers" or "friends." We can even track the effects a story, a tweet, or an image has on people—by reading their comments. People interacting on Facebook or Twitter don't know each other personally. They are an imagined community, a part of another imagined community—a country, an ethnic group, or a religion.

It has never been easier to observe mass radicalization in an imagined community. And it has never been easier to produce mass radicalization. The Nazis, the Soviets, and the Chinese used propaganda to mass radicalize their citizens. A traveling theater, a staged street argument, a charismatic speaker, a film, a newspaper article—these could reach crowds, but the size of these crowds fades in comparison to the crowd that can access a viral story on Twitter. The difference between an effective radicalizing story then and now is hundreds versus millions exposed to it, days versus minutes for the exposure, and a handful versus hundreds sharing reactions to it.

This capacity can be exploited by foreign governments and domestic political players who benefit from fractionating the United States into conflicting groups. Private sector research firms such as Cambridge Analytica can harness the power of social media by collecting personal data of users and target-messaging content most likely to radicalize. Paid internet trolls can instigate group divisions in fake social media posts.

Mass radicalization is a counterintuitive notion in a society where we are taught from a young age to take responsibility for our actions and have our own opinions. The past few years demonstrate that even in our individualistic society, mass identity is at play, and mass radicalization is a real danger.

How does mass radicalization differ from individual and group radicalization?

Mass radicalization is more elusive than either individual or group radicalization.

With individual radicalization, all we need to know whether someone is radicalized are the person's opinions (from an interview, a questionnaire, or writing) and actions. Like measuring temperature, we can grade these on a scale and derive a relative value of the individual's radicalization. If a person is stockpiling an arsenal to shoot up a school or posting threats on social media, we know for sure he or she is strongly radicalized.

Similarly, with a face-to-face group, we can collect group members' opinions, including group discussions, and track actions by group members to decide how radical the group is. If a group is discussing a way to blow up a bus stop, we are looking at a radical group.

With mass radicalization, however, the number of individuals sharing a mass identity is too large to query, their actions too diverse. Suppose 5 percent of a nation are ready to go on barricades to overthrow the government; what does it say about the nation's radicalization? Is 5 percent high radicalization or low? What about 10 percent? 20 percent?

Mass radicalization is also hard to understand. Mass radicalization often stems from irrational actions and experiential processes. If we ask ourselves why we feel a certain way about some political issue, we are unlikely to recognize the elation we experienced at a mass rally or the feeling of belonging we derived from some online group discussion. Trained to find rational explanations for our behaviors, we ignore things that defy rationality. Believing we are adults with our own opinions, responsible for our own actions, we discount the influence of others on our attitudes and behaviors. Yet it doesn't make them any less significant.

A man lights himself on fire in protest of government corruption, and within days the entire country erupts in protests, leading to the ousting of the regime and starting a chain reaction of revolutions in neighboring countries. Few people witnessed the self-immolation, few knew the self-immolator, but there was enough mass radicalization in opinion among Arabs at that moment to lead to mass radicalization in action that became the Arab Spring.

Closer to home, the US intelligence community now believes Russia meddled in the 2016 presidential elections, strategically running social media campaigns that targeted voters' attitudes to increase support for Donald Trump.[12] In other words, Russia manipulated mass identity of various groups, playing on racism of some, even as it played on ethnic pride of others, sowing divisions and stoking fears, ultimately increasing mass radicalization. At the same time, these fears were assuaged with promises from the pro-Trump camp. The pundits and political scientists believed Hillary Clinton had the presidency in her pocket,[13] yet mass radicalization changed the expected election outcome. Like gravity, mass radicalization is elusive but powerful, a force to be reckoned with.

What are some of the factors driving mass radicalization in the United States?

In the weeks leading up to the 2018 midterm elections, Trump told an average of seven lies per day.[14] In August 2018, he tweeted, "Over 90% approval rating for your all time favorite (I hope) President within the Republican Party and 52% overall." These numbers seemed to come from thin air because no poll on or near this date had put Trump's overall approval rating above 46 percent.[15] In October 2018, Trump tweeted, "New Fox Poll shows a 40% Approval Rating by African Americans for President Trump, a record for Republicans. Thank you, a great honor!" In reality, according to Gallup, Ipsos/Reuters, and YouGov/Economist, Trump's approval rating among African Americans was closer to 10–15 percent.[16] After the government shutdown of 35 days ended in January 2019, Trump remarked to the press that most civil servants supported the shutdown and that most Democrats and Republicans supported the wall.[17] But according to polling data, the shutdown was extremely unpopular among federal employees, and most Americans did not support the wall.

Why would the president lie about things that can easily be fact-checked against poll results? Because by misrepresenting poll numbers, he can form meta-opinions.

What is a meta-opinion?

A meta-opinion is an opinion about the opinions of others.

Public opinion is usually measured by professional polling, which can be complex in practice but depends on a simple idea—that a random and representative sample of a population can describe the whole population. In the United States, national polls use the opinions of hundreds of respondents to describe the opinions of the approximately 200 million citizens over 18 years old.

For instance, a spring 2018 poll of 750 adult US residents found that 34 percent believed that global warming is real and caused by human activity.[18] Political action to reduce or stop global warming depends on this 34 percent who recognize the problem. But political action also depends on public perceptions of US opinions about global warming. These opinions about opinion are *meta-opinions*.

A 2013 poll of 5,000 Australians shows how meta-opinions can go awry. [19] The topic was global warming; respondents were asked to put themselves into one of four groups: "Climate change is not happening" (6 percent), "It's happening but natural" (40 percent), "It's happening and human induced" (50 percent), and "Don't know" (4 percent). Respondents were then asked to estimate the percentage of Australians in each group. Respondents in the "not happening" group estimated that 40 percent of Australians agreed with them. Those in the "don't know" group believed that 30 percent agreed with them. So respondents in the smaller groups greatly overestimated agreement with their positions (40 percent estimated vs. 6 percent actual and 30 percent estimated vs. 4 percent actual). In contrast, respondents in the larger groups underestimated agreement with their positions (30 percent estimated vs. 40 percent actual for "natural" respondents, and 40 percent estimated by "human induced" respondents vs. 50 percent actual).

In sum, small minorities greatly overestimated agreement with their positions, whereas those with more popular opinions substantially underestimated agreement with their positions. Perhaps support for measures to fight global warming would be greater in Australia if more Australians knew that half the population believes that global warming is real and human induced.

How can meta-opinions affect mass radicalization?

Political opinions are important, as are meta-opinions. But it's the difference between the two that can make all the difference for political action.

Many were surprised by the sudden dissolution of the Soviet Union in 1991. Almost overnight, a global superpower was reduced to its constituent states as squabbling nations. One account of this surprise is that mistaken meta-opinions were suddenly corrected. The Soviet Union was a police state that sanctioned dissent. Even though many Soviet citizens came to detest their government, they did not voice their opinions, fearing persecution. Most citizens thought that most citizens supported the government. When President Mikhail Gorbachev started "Glasnost"—a program of democratization that encouraged citizens to express their opinions— mistaken meta-opinions began correcting. An attempted coup by hard-line communists failed when Russians, newly unafraid to express their opinions, poured into the streets to protest the coup.

There is an iconic photograph of Boris Yeltsin speaking to the crowd from atop a tank parked before the Russian parliament.[20] Behind Yeltsin is the new three-color Russian flag instead of the red Soviet flag with its hammer and sickle. In the hatch of the tank, a uniformed soldier sits, his head bowed and hidden in his hands. This picture is a MIM, a mass identity manipulation. The Soviet identity is cast down; a new Russian identity is raised up. Seeing thousands of citizens protesting finished off what was remaining of the mistaken meta-opinions about the Soviet Union. No longer afraid to voice their dissatisfaction with the status quo, former Soviet republics declared independence.

How do meta-opinions influence individual political opinion and political action?

They convey social norms that induce bandwagon effects.

Once upon a time, an emperor engaged two weavers to make him new clothes. These charlatans promised the most glorious garment ever made, but warned that stupid or incompetent people would not be able to see it. In fact, the weavers made nothing. They delivered an imaginary suit. Neither the emperor nor his people would admit they could not see the suit, for fear of being seen as stupid. Finally, a child cried out, "But he's not wearing anything at all!"

The Emperor's New Clothes, penned by Hans Christian Andersen, is so popular that the phrase "the emperor's new clothes" has become an idiom referring to a situation in which a (falsely) perceived social norm suppresses belief and action contrary to the norm.

Roger Brown described social norms as having a triple regularity: regularity of action, expectation, and prescription.[21] In a particular situation, most people will behave the same way. In that situation, most will expect others to behave in this way. And most will see something wrong with anyone who does not behave in this way, in this situation. For instance, most Americans will stand up as the flag passes by in a Fourth of July parade. Most Americans expect that others will stand. And most will see something wrong with an individual who does not stand.

Research on social norms has emphasized the behavioral and prescriptive regularities that mark a norm, but expectation is an important part of a norm's power. If we didn't expect others to stand for the flag, would we stand ourselves? A meta-opinion is a kind of expectation—an expectation about what others believe, want, feel, or will do. The expectations set up by meta-opinions push individuals toward a bandwagon effect. An experiment using internet polling showed how bandwagon effects work.[22]

Respondents were asked how likely they were to vote for public financing of elections; for reducing US troops in Afghanistan; and for free trade agreements with North, Central, and South American countries. After some distracting questions, respondents received a (bogus) "aggregation of polling results" reporting support for each policy between 20 and 80 percent. Then, they were asked again (in different format) how likely they were to vote for each policy. Averaged across the three policies, a 20-point increase in poll support produced about a 3-point increase in voting for the policy. The bandwagon effect here is small but perhaps enough to sway a close election.

There is another way in which bandwagon effects occur. Meta-opinions can affect not only voter opinions but also donations to political candidates. The candidate perceived as more popular is likely to draw more and bigger donations and more volunteer workers. These in turn feed into bigger and better campaigns, increasing poll numbers, and multiplied bandwagon effects.[23]

The internet has become a battleground of efforts to control meta-opinions to advance e-commerce. Reviews and star ratings can make or break sales of internet products and services. Some reviews are fakes posted by those with financial interest in the product; there are now apps designed to identify fake reviews.[24] The number of Twitter followers or Facebook friends signals popularity and approval. During the 2012 presidential campaign, tens of thousands of @mittromney followers were found to be fake accounts, and—here is the kicker—no one could determine who had paid for them. Social media sharing buttons—with counters—give the impression that everyone who has shared approves of or uses the product or service shown on the page. Facebook users are twice as likely to "like" an update when three unknown users like the update than when one unknown user likes the update.[25] Online as in life, we jump on the bandwagon.

How can the internet help form meta-opinion?

If meta-opinions' norm power is a key to e-commerce success, governments have recognized the power of meta-opinions in attempts to control them. These attempts have been going on for years; the examples that follow are from a 2015 review.[26]

The most famous example of meta-opinion manipulation is China's army of internet commentators, known also as the 50 Cent Party, a reference to how members are paid a small fee per post. These posts are designed to uphold the party line by attacking critics and defending government policies. The hundreds of thousands of individuals who contribute to the work of the 50 Cent Party can create a sense that the party's narrative is everywhere, and everywhere dominant. Undesirable ideas are not just deleted (although this also may happen); they are responded to and argued against wherever they may be—chat rooms, forums, or comment pages.

Showing the broad appeal of the 50 Cent Party's methods, the Chinese government has been forced to investigate internet commentators for abuse of position. With appropriate bribes, a corporation in China can get its own concerns and public relations goals added to a commentator's duties. For those corporations that do not need the powerful (and government-restricted) tools of the 50 Cent Party, the private "Water Armies" offer similar capabilities. The Water Armies train and pay their own commentators in much the same way as does the 50 Cent Party, putting the same rapid and distributed response methods at the disposal of anyone willing to buy their services.

Other countries have shown interest in the methods of the 50 Cent Party. In the fall of 2013, Israel announced a program that Prime Minister Netanyahu described as an element of the public diplomacy front. Students from Israeli universities are given partial scholarships in return for countering critics of Israeli policy. This program is in addition to the previously organized Interactive Media division of the Israeli military, in which dozens of soldiers are similarly tasked.

Also in 2013, Prime Minister Erdogan of Turkey unveiled a program of "social media representatives." Unlike the Chinese and Israeli programs, Erdogan's is meant to work on behalf of his party rather than for the government as a whole. Everything else about the program is familiar; 6,000 young members of Erdogan's party are to be trained to respond to criticism and share the party line across multiple social media platforms.

In South Korea, a team in the National Intelligence Service attempted to influence public opinion before an election with over 1 million blog posts and Twitter messages. South Korean courts did not look kindly on the spy agency involving itself in domestic affairs and convicted the intelligence chief involved.

All of these programs demonstrate a need to counter unwanted opinions informally and at their point of origin—individual internet users. None of them involves massive media campaigns and slick presentations, just patient individuals with a keyboard and an internet connection. The goal is to control perceptions of the distribution of opinions—meta-opinions.

The US Constitution's First Amendment, freedom of speech, prevents the government from suppressing true poll numbers or silencing fact-checkers. But bogus poll numbers can still form meta-opinions. Many won't bother to check the numbers' authenticity, and many will take the high office's word over the media, whom President Trump calls "fake news" and "enemy of the people." With meta-opinions formed in his favor, President Trump can boost his supporters' confidence in him, fueling mass radicalization of opinion.

How can social media contribute to mass radicalization in the United States?

It can do so through group polarization and false consensus.

The news offers a variety of topics to be angry about. Here is one: "The Red Hen restaurant refused to serve Sarah Huckabee Sanders." Chances are, you have used social media to inform your opinion about that story. As it turns out, whether you sided with Sanders or the Red Hen, the social media likely radicalized your opinion, fueling your anger.

For radicalization researchers, social media offer an interesting observational study. Research on face-to-face groups discovered that discussion among like-minded people radicalizes their average opinion. A group that starts out slightly pro-life ends up more pro-life; a group that starts out anti-guns ends up more so.

Two forces radicalize opinions in group discussion. One is informational: People learn new arguments to support the opinions they already hold. The second radicalizing force in group discussion is social: People admire and want to emulate those expressing the most extreme opinions.

Social media discussions carry both informational and social aspects of group polarization. In news-related Twitter threads, tweets that offer new arguments supporting a particular attitude (useful facts, catchy metaphors, moral judgments) get more "likes" and retweets. Twitter users learn relevant arguments to reinforce their own opinions. Users with more radical opinions get larger followings precisely because their tweets use expletives and polarizing rhetoric. More radical individuals have more social influence.

Social media are more radicalizing than face-to-face groups because they are larger collectives (more sources of information) and because in these large collectives there is more likelihood of encountering radical individuals. There is a third reason social media groups are more radicalizing. In a face-to-face group, dissenters can be ignored or expelled—but only with some unpleasantness. On a social media platform, selection has no downside; just press the mute button or the block button.

Some cases of social media radicalization have already come to light. The Arab Spring, the Ukrainian revolution of 2014, and the Armenian revolution of 2018 evolved on social media, where opinions radicalized first and then action was planned and coordinated. ISIS' use of social media to recruit fighters, wives, and supporters around the globe resulted in thousands of Western youths traveling to Syria and Iraq. Russia used Facebook and Twitter to try to twist the US electorate with radicalizing posts. Perhaps the most amazing example is the incel movement, which unites men unable to seduce women and upgrades their personal grievances of sexual failure to the level of a political movement worthy of editorials in *The New York Times*.

More people every day rely on social media for their news, entertainment, and social interactions. What we need is independent research to investigate their potential political effects. Like a Trojan horse, we let these vehicles into our daily lives. We should not close our collective eyes to the danger that they carry.

Were Americans especially vulnerable to radicalization through internet social media?

Yes.

If you are an American, in all likelihood you have been targeted online by Russian propaganda. Facebook estimates that in the months before the 2016 presidential election, 126 million US users saw posts, stories, or other content created by Russian government-backed accounts,[27] and an additional 20 million were exposed to this Russian content on Facebook-owned Instagram.[28] A similar picture emerges from Twitter and YouTube.[29] Russia has weaponized the social media to spread rumors, conspiracy theories, and emotion-stirring images in a coordinated effort to radicalize the United States from within.[30]

Americans were not their only target: former Soviet republics (Ukraine, Georgia, Estonia, Lithuania), as well as countries of the European Union (Poland, France, Germany) have been subjected to the same treatment. In different languages, Russian trolls used the same tactics, planting and amplifying divisive messages, posting fake or doctored photos and made-up stories to stoke fear (vaccinations are killing your kids[31]) and anger (immigrants are coming for your jobs[32]).

But Americans fell for the Russian lies at a much higher rate. Researchers found an average of 1.73 likes, retweets or replies for Russian trolls' posts in Russian or any language other than English, but for English-language posts, the rate was nine times higher (15.25).[33] Americans, it turned out, were easy targets for the Russian propaganda.

American social media giants scramble to defend against the onslaught of Russian troll attacks. One result of their efforts makes it possible now to check if you personally were exposed to the Russian propaganda.[34]

Why were Americans more vulnerable to social media propaganda?

An answer proposed by the authors of the above study was that the former Soviets were "immunized" against the Russian propaganda. Because of their history with Russia, they expect to be lied to and so are generally more cynical than Americans. This is an explanation that cultural psychologists would agree with. There may be some truth to it.

But cynicism can't be the whole answer.

If cultural exposure to propaganda were enough to immunize against it, then we should expect Russians to be laughing at the Kremlin's recent portrayals of supposed Ukrainian aggression against Russia or of supposed NATO plans to attack

Moscow. Instead, cynical as they are, most Russians seem to believe the Kremlin-directed propaganda that targets them.[35] The cynicism, therefore, is not enough to understand what makes Europeans less susceptible than Americans to Russian propaganda.

What if we try another explanation, not from cultural psychology but from mass psychology?

Jon Haidt calls the human ability to forsake individual interests in the name of group interests *the hive mind*.[36] We have a kind of hive switch built-in, Haidt suggests, that can be flipped, turning us from rational individualists into selfless group players. This ability, he argues, has evolved through natural selection because humans live in groups, and groups can persist only when some members are willing to give up their interests, and even their lives, for the benefit of others.

When the hive switch is turned on, we turn away from our individual identity toward a mass identity—ethnic, religious, or national. When the hive switch is turned on, we can become radicalized—more accepting of violence in the name of the large impersonal collective that is our mass identity.

That's what the Russian trolls attempted: to set our mass identities at odds, radicalizing Blacks against Whites, Caucasians against Latinos, WASPs against Jews, and Democrats against Republicans. Then the question becomes, Why was American mass identity more easily radicalized through social media than, say, Ukrainian or Estonian mass identity?

Mass identities are social constructs. We need to know what our fellow X (e.g., Americans, Jews, and Ukrainians) are up to and up against. We need information to maintain and nurture our mass identities. One big difference between the United States and European countries is availability of this kind of information. For Americans, mass identity inputs are less likely to come from personal interactions.

Physically, Americans are more isolated than Europeans. The average population density in the United States is 92 residents per square mile,[37] versus about 143 residents per square mile in Europe.[38] Most US residents (70 percent) live in detached houses[39] in small towns and suburbs where they have to drive to get to work, school, or the grocery store.[40] Compare this with only one-third of Europeans living in detached homes.[41] Also, more Europeans ride public transport or bike or walk to work, school, or the grocery store.[42]

Americans work more hours and take fewer vacation days than do Europeans.[43] Europeans are more willing to give up money for leisure than are Americans.[44] American preferences for personal cars, detached homes, and more income result in long and lonely commutes from home to work, with less time to socialize and fewer venues for socialization. Taken together, these factors contribute to the stark difference in reported loneliness between Americans (46 percent)[45] and Europeans (6 percent).[46]

When real-life social interactions are fewer, virtual interactions have more scope to define and radicalize mass identity. Seventy-one percent of American internet users report using social media, compared with 58 percent in France, Italy, and Spain and 46 percent in Germany and Poland.[47] Three-fourths of American Facebook users say they visit the platform at least once a day.[48]

Russian propaganda masters pounced on the opportunity to use social media to define and mobilize American mass identities. Because Americans are more dependent on social media, they succeeded beyond anyone's expectations. Social isolation made Americans vulnerable to social media manipulation.

Physical isolation is a simple demographic explanation for a complex psychological phenomenon, but the link is not hard to see. The number of people we run into predicts how many social connections we form. Researchers studying undergraduate friendships discovered that the physical location of one's dormitory room determined how many friends one had at the end of the year.[49] Propinquity, or the degree of exposure to people, predicted popularity.

Because we interact with fewer people, we have fewer friends. Americans' number of close confidants decreased from three to two[50] during the past 25 years, nearly tripling the degree of social isolation. With fewer friends and fewer social interactions, we become lonelier, seeking virtual substitutes through the internet.[51] And that is where Russian trolls dwell.

American vulnerability to social media propaganda points to a need for countermeasures. One is increasing public awareness about social media's radicalizing potential. Building up healthy cynicism about online political content can help immunize Americans against Russian ruses and against others trying the same techniques. Cynicism should be easier in a time when new investigations of political malfeasance are announced weekly.

Another countermeasure might be government oversight of the social media. The reach and speed of the internet allowed hostile foreign actors to spread radical ideas far and wide among us. Russian propaganda attacks may help bring an end to the Wild West era online. Algorithms and safeguards to detect and avert similar attacks in the future may be required, although preserving freedom of speech will not be easy.

Finally, we should all get out more. Loneliness is a dangerous condition, with health consequences as dire as 15 cigarettes per day.[52] Until recently, we could dismiss loneliness as a personal problem. But the success of the Russian mass identity manipulations shows that loneliness can be a political problem as well.

It would serve our national interests to spend more tax dollars on events that bring people together. During sports events such as soccer World Cup, football playoffs, or Rugby World Cup, suicide rates decline by as much as 10 percent, with the greatest decline among men aged 30–44 years.[53,54] Especially for sports fans, these spectator events create social exposure and opportunities for socialization even after the games are over.

Sports are not for everyone, but the variety of mass social gatherings is broader than sports. In addition to their already more connected home and work lives, Europeans encounter a wealth of socializing events: regular street fairs, free music performances, open-air art exhibits, and even impromptu yoga and dance sessions. Nations that play together stay together against mass identity manipulations.

What can the government do to lower radicalization in the United States?

Research, oversight, and infrastructure.

How can research help lower radicalization in the United States?

After the terrorist attacks of 9/11, the US government sponsored research initiatives linking academics with security practitioners. Government grants produced research centers and interdisciplinary groups focused on understanding, predicting, and reducing terrorism. Their work resulted in scientific articles, books, and training programs. We now know much more about terrorists than we knew on 9/11. This knowledge helps the FBI and the police to track potential perpetrators and thwart most terrorist attacks before they endanger people's lives.

Mass radicalization inside the United States is a new threat to the country's stability, security, and prosperity. Foreign governments and private research firms are capitalizing on American vulnerability to social media propaganda, directing coordinated attacks designed to divide and radicalize Americans against their fellow Americans. As we write this in January 2019, Facebook has refused to turn over the data it obtains from users or even the user data it has already shared with those using the data against Americans.

It makes no sense that Cambridge Analytica and the Russian internet search engine Yandex have Facebook user data but the US government and researchers in the United States do not.[55] To understand how Americans were targeted, we need access to Facebook data and the data acquired by other social media such as Twitter, YouTube, and Instagram. We need to know how social media messages, including emotion-stirring images, rumors, slogans, and symbols, affect users' attention, opinions, and action. For that, we need research. Initiatives similar to those dedicated to terrorism research need to be dedicated to research on radicalization through social media.

As data accumulate and we understand better what content is particularly dangerous, a system of warnings, similar to the Federal Communications Commission's ratings of movies and computer games, could be applied to social media messages. The warning system can support parental and personal controls to filter particularly dangerous propaganda and block fraudulent accounts and bots. Without this, we are sitting ducks, wide open to manipulation and radicalization on the internet platforms we have come to depend on.

How can oversight help lower radicalization in the United States?

Internet social media have proven to be powerful vehicles for mass radicalization. Paid trolls or internet bots (computer programs designed to impersonate an individual, amplifying a particular political message by retweeting, "liking," or re-posting corresponding content) can aid a political campaign, help incite a rally, or popularize a political position. This power to interfere in our political system requires oversight.

Political candidates in the United States are not allowed to accept campaign donations from foreign sources, and Americans lobbying for foreign governments must register with the US government. But through social media, foreign governments can interfere in US politics, including US elections. Even among US political players, social media open doors to voters' minds in a new form of influence that is not subject to campaign limitations or reporting requirements. Existing laws are not enough to control foreign or domestic political manipulation in the age of the internet. We must write new laws that would reduce the public's vulnerability to manipulation through the social media, especially foreign-origin politicking disguised as American voices.

How can infrastructure help lower radicalization in the United States?

As noted previously, Americans are especially vulnerable to Russian propaganda delivered via social media because they are lonelier and more isolated than, for example, Europeans. Social media offer many Americans what they lack: social connection and a sense of larger community. Infrastructure to increase opportunity for socializing, including social spaces like parks, pedestrian boulevards, and mass attractions like festivals and performances, can increase quality of life at the same time as they will reduce Americans' dependence on social media. Similarly, mass transit offers more opportunity for connection than commuting by private vehicle, and better mass transit might increase quality of life by reducing toxic emissions. Many cities have begun to ban motor vehicles and encourage walking and biking.[56]

As demonstrated by Russian efforts on social media, Americans are vulnerable to radicalization along existing fault lines. The gist of the Russian propaganda emphasized our internal conflicts, inflaming passions of Whites against Blacks, immigrants against native-born, gays against straights, Christians against Muslims, and Democrats against Republicans. Russian internet interventions aimed to exploit these divisions.

This is a new form of warfare. Other countries will try to do what the Russians tried to do. We should work toward reducing the divisions that give enemies an opening. One way to achieve this goal is for the government to sponsor large-scale projects that bring different factions together for the common good. The challenges looming on our collective horizon are serious—climate change, increasing inequality, mass migrations driven by poverty and crime, an aging population, and health care crises. These issues require collective action. Government-led initiatives to address these major challenges could bring us together as a nation and fortify us against hybrid warfare whose battlefield is the internet and whose trophies are our hearts and minds.

13

CONCLUSION

WHAT EVERYONE NEEDS TO KNOW ABOUT RADICALIZATION AND EXTREMISM

What is wrong with radicalization and extremism?

Radicalization is change in beliefs, feelings, or actions toward increased support for one side of an intergroup conflict. *Extremism* refers to beliefs, feelings, or actions that go against the political status quo. What is wrong with radicalization and extremism is the *few* radicals or extremists who move to violent action, especially the violence against civilians that is called terrorism.

What kinds of radicals and extremists are governments concerned about?

Most salient are Islamist jihadists, whose grievance is Western policies toward predominantly Muslim countries. Also important are right-wing radicals who tend to see government as out of control, doing too much for minorities, and ignoring the plight of working-class White males. Since the 9/11 attacks, right-wing terrorist attacks in the United States have been on the rise.

Then there are left-wing radicals. The Animal Liberation Front and the Environmental Liberation Front (with considerable overlap in supporters) believe that animals are being tortured and the environment wasted, often for the profit of large corporations. These organizations attack corporate assets but do not appear in the news because they do not kill anyone.

Finally, there is the radicalization of Americans, not against government or corporations but against other Americans: Black Lives Matter versus Blue [police] Lives Matter, "Stronger Together" (Hillary Clinton's 2016 campaign slogan) versus "Lock Her Up" (Donald Trump slogan), and MAGA ("Make America Great Again") versus ANTIFA (anti-fascist). These are the divisions of Americans that, as we have described, Russian trolls and bots aimed to radicalize—divisions that the politics of the future will continue to play upon.

How has radicalization evolved?

We are on record asserting that the psychology of radicalization has been the same for hundreds of years. The same 12 mechanisms that moved Russian terrorists in the late 1800s can be identified in present-day Islamist terrorists in Syria and Iraq and right-wing terrorists in the United States. But while psychological mechanisms have remained the same, the means for radicalizing have changed.

The internet has opened unprecedented opportunities. Sitting in front of their computers at home, individuals can receive radicalizing messages. They can download instructional videos or manuals for building homemade bombs. They can identify with a radical group and carry out attacks in its name without ever interacting with any other group members.

Internet social media emerged as a channel of mass radicalization when Russia appealed to internal divisions between racial and social groups in the United States to meddle in the 2016 elections. As of January 2019, US intelligence officials state that Russia continues to be an active player in US social media, evolving tools for mass radicalization and plotting another election interference for the 2020 elections. It is likely other countries will use the social media for mass radicalization in the future. So will US politicians.

Feelings, thoughts, and behaviors that lead to radicalization have remained consistent. But with the advent of the internet and social media, there are new ways to appeal to them. Similarly, the audience for radicalizing rhetoric has grown larger than ever before. And the means for carrying out radical actions (e.g., building a bomb) have become more readily available. In the United States, where firearms are plentiful, radicalized lone wolves have an easy option for carrying out attacks.

What is new about radicalizing media today?

Like so many other things these days, radicalizing media are faster paced than ever before. It took Abu Musab al-Zarqawi several years and thousands of miles tracked across Afghanistan to achieve his goal of meeting Osama bin Laden. If it were happening today, that journey may have taken only weeks. Those seeking radical groups and individuals can get to them by clicking on the right websites; following certain Gab, Instagram, or Twitter handles; or watching certain YouTube channels. Speed is one thing that's different about radicalizing media today.

Breadth is another. Billions of people around the world use the internet and participate in social media platforms. Even if the proportion susceptible to radicalization is small, the number affected is much greater now.

Before, radicalization efforts were like cannon fire: heavy and cumbersome to maneuver, their damage localized. Now, radicalization is lighter, faster, and better targeted—like laser weapons.

What is different about mass identity manipulations today?

The speed and spread of radicalization multiplies the power of mass identity manipulations (MIMs). Whether it is an iconic photo, a catchy slogan, a radical song, or a video of a violent riot, MIMs are easier to come by—by accident or choice—on the internet than ever before. With one flick of a finger, by liking, sharing, or retweeting, each of us can spread a radical MIM.

MIMs may have become especially powerful today not only because their supply has grown but because demand for them has grown as well. The pace of living seems to increase all the time. Feeling strapped for time, we are constantly multi-tasking. Twitter has taught us to think in 280-character bursts. Athleisure, Uggs, and sock sneakers appeal to our desire for fuss-free footwear and clothing. Even in the ultimate long form—literature—backstories and long set descriptions have been replaced by quicker-paced action scenes. An average reader is not prepared to muddle through more than a couple of pages before getting to the point. We are gluttons for quick clothes, quick books, and quick ideas.

Tired: Manifestos. Wired: MIMs.

With MIMs gaining traction and power, what's lagging is our understanding of them. We are also behind on curbing or countering MIMs' radicalizing power.

Can we understand radicalization if we focus only on the radicals?

No.

Radicalization is a dynamic process in which both sides are changed. The mechanisms of radicalization described in Chapters 3–5 do not take place in a vacuum. As individuals, groups, and mass publics move to radical beliefs, and a few are radicalized to terrorist action, someone or something is pushing them along. Political grievance cannot happen without perceived injustice. Group isolation and escalation cannot take place without the state's security apparatus pursuing those who challenge the state. Jujitsu cannot radicalize without the government overreacting to the threat posed by protestors or terrorists. Ignoring actions and reactions of the state while trying to understand and control radicalization limits both our understanding and our options by half.

As the history of the Irish Republican Army shows, the state can sometimes engage in successful negotiations with terrorists. As the deradicalization program in Denmark shows, when a state offers terrorists support in the form of housing, counseling, and job training, they are more likely to deradicalize. On the other hand, research demonstrates that majority hostility toward a minority group results in multiplying of grievances and increased radicalization. What the state and its citizens do can incite or dampen radicalization by political grievances.

Can we understand radicalization if we focus on ideology?

No.

As detailed in Chapter 6, radical actions often have nothing to do with radical ideas. People join a radical or even a militant group for many reasons: for personal revenge, for status and thrill, to escape personal problems, and to be a part of a group that offers support and friendship. Individuals undertake lone wolf attacks for group grievance, personal grievance, status and thrill, and to escape personal problems. None of these paths to radical actions require dedication to or, indeed, even knowledge of radical ideology.

Some say that every group grievance is an ideology. We disagree. Attacking those who have harmed us does not require anything as deep as ideology. Justice or revenge are human motives throughout the world, and they do not depend on anything like religious belief or political 'ism.

The exception we have pointed out is that ideological differ-ences within a movement can produce violence, as when ISIS attacks Shi'a, Sufi, and other competing forms of Islam. There are rebel groups, in Syria for instance, that are more likely to fight with groups more ideologically distant.[1]

Once part of a militant group, individuals learn an ideology—a narrative—that supports use of violence. Once in-ternalized, the ideology can affect action, including targeting. But we have argued that ideology is more justification for vi-olence than reason for violence—else everyone with radical ideas would engage in radical action. Unlike what some pop-ular media accounts claim, there is no conveyor belt from rad-ical ideas to radical action.

In fact, the vast majority of people with radical ideas (e.g., justification of suicide bombing in defense of Islam) will never do anything radical. Polls of Muslims in both Western coun-tries and Muslim countries indicate that there are hundreds with radical ideas for every individual engaged in radical action.

Understanding radical ideas may be important for under-standing mass sympathy for terrorism, but not for under-standing terrorists. For that, it is better to focus on past actions, as well as on means and opportunity.

Can we understand terrorism if we define it as an attempt to terrorize us?

Not really.

As discussed in Chapter 2, definitions of terrorism often imply that instilling fear is terrorists' main goal. However, ter-rorists are primarily interested in eliciting other emotions—emotions that can help them radicalize new recruits and supporters. Reactions of anger and humiliation serve their purposes better because angered and humiliated states and publics are more likely to engage in disproportionate response, directing violence against civilians who will then have real grievances that might radicalize them.

Terrorists use violence as a tactic. In the absence of an army or sophisticated weapons, their attacks bring them the attention of enemies far bigger and stronger than they. In this way, terrorists' targets grant them the status they seek and the platform from which to declare their demands. Fear may be helpful to terrorists, but anger is what they are really after.

Can we win against terrorism with the same weapons used in the war on drugs?

Probably not.

Have you watched a police drama on television or cable in recent years? The US war on drugs is featured in shows such as *Hill Street Blues*, *The Wire*, and *Narcos*. For police, FBI, and the Drug Enforcement Administration, the war on drugs is a constant battle against the big-money corruption and violence that drug dealers use to protect their products, salespeople, and turf.

Efforts against illegal drugs cost the United States approximately $50 billion a year. These operations depend on intelligence about the dealers and their operations, and this intel comes from wiretaps (see *The Wire*) and especially from morally ambiguous relations between police officers and their informants. Police officers go undercover to develop friendships with potential informants. Some informants volunteer to give information about their enemies to the police. Some informants are blackmailed into providing information—they help law enforcement officers in order to avoid publicity or prison or deportation for their own offenses.

A front-page example of the moral swamp created by the war on drugs is the case of Whitey Bulger. A crime boss in Boston, Bulger was indicted for numerous murders. He was also a confidential informant for the FBI. He escaped capture for 16 years after his FBI contacts warned him that he was about to be arrested. As the saying goes, information can be expensive.

As described in Chapter 9, the War on Terrorism also depends heavily on use of undercover agents and informants. About half of all jihadist terrorist plots between 9/11 and 2016 involved an undercover agent or informant. The War on Terrorism thus depends on the same tactics used in the war on drugs. It is useful to recall that the war on drugs was announced by President Richard Nixon in the 1970s, but it still roils the streets of America decades later. We doubt whether the tactics that have not won the war on drugs can win the War on Terrorism.

Can we understand terrorism as a form of group conflict—the warfare of the weak?

Yes.

As discussed in Chapter 2, violence is used by both state and non-state actors to control or protect some group or segment of the population. State violence is not usually called terrorism, although as examples from Mao's China, Stalin's Soviet Union, and Hussein's Iraq showed, it can have much deadlier results than terrorist violence. When terrorists use violence against the state, they engage a larger and better armed enemy in a conflict in which their only advantages are their elusiveness and the scale of the state's mistakes. Viewed this way, terrorism begins to look less like a cancer and more like an infestation of lice. They draw blood, but if we stop scratching and bludgeoning ourselves, we might find a better solution to the problem.

What can we do as individuals to build resilience against radicalization and extremism?

Radicals, extremists, and terrorists count on our emotional reaction to their attacks, including verbal attacks. What if we don't give it to them?

After 9/11, the United States recoiled in an overreaction, passing sweeping laws that gave extraordinary powers to security services, voting for wars that we are still fighting more than a decade later, and finding legal justifications to allow torture of prisoners and surveillance of citizens. The politicians who enacted those changes received a clear mandate from their constituents—us. Our anger, humiliation, and, yes, fear made us overreact to a tragic event, allowing it to define large portions of our daily lives and our national history. Keeping things in perspective is one way to build resilience to radical and terrorist challenges.

The mass media give terrorism incidents disproportionate attention, making terrorism seem far more threatening to our lives than it actually is. In fact, an individual is 4 times more likely to die of a lightning strike than of a terrorist attack.[2] Closer to our daily experience, Americans are 400,000 times more likely to die in a car accident than of terrorism. Terrorism is not among the top 10 causes of death in the United States. Instead, these include heart disease, diabetes, stroke, and Alzheimer's disease. Risk of each of these is reduced with exercise. And yet, there is an epidemic of obesity in the United States because people exercise too little and drive too much— and worry about terrorism disproportionately.

Similarly, the challenge of radical and extremist ideas is less dangerous than we think. To build resilience, we might try to come to terms with the idea that radical and extremist movements never stop. (It is useful to recall that sometimes these movements produce something good: the vote for women, desegregated schools.) A few will take up violence for their movement. Terrorist attacks will happen. No amount of Transportation Security Administration regulations will prevent terrorists from dreaming up new ways of attacking. Lone wolves will use homemade pressure-cooker bombs even if we shut down all communication and financial exchanges between suspected terrorists. Once we begin to see radicals, extremists, and even terrorists as inevitable, we can begin to try minimizing their impact rather than overreacting in trying to stomp them out.

To summarize, resilience begins with a realization: Political conflict, political grievances, political movements, and political violence are inevitable. These are less dangerous than the mass media would have us believe. Our reaction, including the mandate we give our representatives in the government, will determine how much the challengers are able to distort our way of life and our values as a society. As individuals, we have the power and the responsibility to avoid giving terrorists the jujitsu power they count on.

What can we do as a community to build resilience against radicalization, extremism, and terrorism?

Political resilience is the ability to accurately assess the damage and future risks of challenges from radicals, extremists, and terrorists and to preserve a way of life despite these risks. Radicals, extremists, and terrorists want to push us in directions that we don't want to go. Bin Laden's right-hand man, Ayman al-Zawahiri, boasted that 9/11 brought US troops into Muslim countries where they would incite jihad against the West.[3] Before he died, bin Laden boasted of putting the United States on the road to bankruptcy.[4] The lesson from our enemies is that our reactions to terrorism can be as dangerous as the terrorists. Political resilience means cultivating and preserving our cultural values.

Our enemies succeed when they divide us, inciting internal conflicts that consume our attention and resources. They succeed when we begin believing that political challengers (including our compatriots) are crazy or evil. Political resilience is building bridges across internal divides that separate Muslims from non-Muslims, rich from poor, Republicans from Democrats. A threat can break a group apart. But, as research on radicalization shows, it can also strengthen connection within the group. Political resilience is creating infrastructure that would ensure the latter. We can strengthen our ability to respond to the threat of terrorism by uniting as a nation in support of what makes us strong: freedom, opportunity, and social justice.

NOTES

Chapter 1

1. McCauley, C., & Moskalenko, S. (2008). Mechanisms of political radicalization: Pathways toward terrorism. *Terrorism and Political Violence, 20*(3), 415–433.
2. Williams, L. E., & Bargh, J. A. (2008). Experiencing physical warmth promotes interpersonal warmth. *Science, 322*(5901), 606–607.
3. https://www.start.umd.edu/gtd/search/?back=1&search=u.s.%20muslim.
4. https://www.start.umd.edu/gtd/search/?back=1&search=u.s.%20muslim.
5. Moskalenko, S. (2010). Civilians into warriors: Mechanisms of mobilization in US Army recruitment and training. *Dynamics of Asymmetric Conflict, 3*(3), 248–268.
6. Fitton, T. (2013, August 30). Weekly update: Founding Fathers extremists? *Judicial Watch.* Retrieved from https://www.judicialwatch.org/tom-fittons-weekly-update/weekly-update-founding-fathers-extremists.
7. Parkin, W. (2017, February 24). Analysis: Deadly threat from far-right extremists is overshadowed by fear of Islamic terrorism. *NPR News Hour.*
8. Lowery, W., Kindy, K., & Ba Tran, A. (2017, February 24). In the United States, right wing violence is on the rise. *Washington Post.* Retrieved from https://www.washingtonpost.com/national/in-the-united-states-right-wing-violence-is-on-the-rise/2018/11/25/61f7f24a-deb4-11e8-85df-7a6b4d25cfbb_story.html?utm_term=.11fa299633a2.

Chapter 2

1. Draft Comprehensive Convention against International Terrorism, UN Doc. A/59/894 App. II (August 12, 2005).

2. On the developments leading to the Draft Comprehensive Convention, see Rohan Perera, A. (2005). Reviewing the U.N. Conventions on Terrorism: Towards a comprehensive terrorism convention. In C. Fijnaut, J. Wouters, & F. Naert (Eds.), *Legal instruments in the fight against international terrorism* (p. 567). Boston, MA: Martinus Nijhoff.

3. The Terrorism Act 2000 (Chap. 11). Retrieved from http://www.legislation.gov.uk/ukpga/2000/11.

4. http://www.nij.gov/topics/crime/terrorism/pages/welcome.aspx#note1.

5. http://www.nij.gov/topics/crime/terrorism/pages/welcome.aspx#note1.

6. Department of Defense Dictionary of Military and Associated Terms, Joint Publication 1-02, November 8, 2002 (As amended through January 31, 2011.) Retrieved from http://www.people.mil/Portals/56/Documents/rtm/jp1_02.pdf.

7. https://www.fema.gov/media-library-data/20130726-1549-20490-0802/terrorism.pdf.

8. Edwards, L. (2010). *The legacy of Mao Zedong is mass murder*. The Heritage Foundation. Retrieved from https://www. heritage. org/asia/commentary/the-legacy-mao-zedong-mass-murder.

9. Snyder, T. (2011, January 27). Hitler vs. Stalin: Who was worse? *The New York Review of Books*. Retrieved from http://www.nybooks.com/daily/2011/01/27/hitler-vs-stalin-who-was-worse.

10. http://www.nytimes.com/2003/01/26/weekinreview/the-world-how-many-people-has-hussein-killed.html.

11. Kearns, E. M., Betus, A., & Lemieux, A. (2017). *Why do some terrorist attacks receive more media attention than others?* Retrieved from http://www.mintpressnews.com/wp-content/uploads/2017/03/SSRN-id2928138.pdf.

12. https://www.revealnews.org/article/home-is-where-the-hate-is.

13. http://abcnews.go.com/US/charleston-church-shooter-dylann-roof-sentenced-death/story?id=44674575.

14. http://www.foxnews.com/us/2017/08/12/emergency-declared-ahead-unite-right-rally-in-virginia.html.

15. http://www.independent.co.uk/news/world/politics/isis-hostage-threat-which-countries-pay-ransoms-to-release-their-citizens-9710129.html.

Chapter 3

1. https://abcnews.go.com/US/hate-groups-similar-online-recruiting-methods-isis-experts/story?id=53528932.
2. Fitton, T. (2013, August 30). Weekly update: Founding Fathers extremists? *Judicial Watch.*

Chapter 6

1. https://www.dhs.gov/countering-violent-extremism.
2. The controversy regarding Hizb as terrorist threat or anti-terrorist ally is represented at https://en.wikipedia.org/wiki/Hizb_ut-Tahrir.
3. International Association of Chiefs of Police, Office of Community Oriented Policing Services. (2014). *Online radicalization to violent extremism* [Awareness brief]. Retrieved from https://ric-zai-inc.com/Publications/cops-w0739-pub.pdf.
4. BBC News. (2005, November 7). *7 July bomber's motives examined.* Retrieved from http://news.bbc.co.uk/1/hi/uk/4444358.stm.
5. Shiffman, J. (2012, December 7). Jane's jihad. *Reuter's Special Report*, p. 6. Retrieved February 15, 2015, from http://graphics.thomsonreuters.com/12/12/JihadJaneAll.pdf.
6. Quiggin, T. (2010). Contemporary jihadist narratives: The case of Momin Khawaja. In *Countering violent extremist narratives* (pp. 84–93). The Hague, the Netherlands: National Coordinator for Counterterrorism.
7. Snow, D. A., & Benford, R. D. (1988). Ideology, frame resonance, and participant mobilization. *International Social Movement Research, 1,* 197–217.
8. McCauley, C., & Scheckter, S. (2008). What's special about U.S. Muslims? The war on terrorism as seen by Muslims in the United States, Morocco, Egypt, Pakistan, and Indonesia. *Studies in Conflict & Terrorism, 31,* 973–980.
9. Crilly, R. (2013, January 8). Stanley McChrystal criticises reliance on drones as strikes hit Pakistan. *The Telegraph.* Retrieved August 1, 2017, from http://www.telegraph.co.uk/news/worldnews/asia/pakistan/9787912/Stanley-McChrystal-criticises-reliance-on-drones-as-strikes-hit-Pakistan.html.

Chapter 7

1. Anti-Defamation League. (n.d.). *Tom Metzger/White Aryan Resistance*. Retrieved from https://web.archive.org/web/20070826114712/http://www.adl.org/learn/Ext_US/Metzger.asp.

2. Beam, L. (1992, February). Leaderless resistance. *The Seditionist*, 12. Retrieved from http://www.louisbeam.com/leaderless.htm. Beam's essay was first published in the *Inter-Klan and Survival Alert* in the early 1980s. See Durham, M. (2007). *White rage* (p. 103). Abingdon, UK: Routledge.

3. Worth, K. (2016, July 14). Lone-wolf attacks are becoming more common—and more deadly. *Frontline*. Retrieved from http://www.pbs.org/wgbh/frontline/article/lone-wolf-attacks-are-becoming-more-common-and-more-deadly.

4. CNN Security Clearance. (2011, August 16). *Obama: Biggest terror fear is the lone wolf*. Retrieved from http://security.blogs.cnn.com/2011/08/16/obama-biggest-terror-fear-is-the-lone-wolf.

5. Bjorgo, T., & Horgan, J. (Eds.). (2009). *Leaving terrorism behind: Individual and collective disengagement*. New York, NY: Routledge.

6. "Joe Stack statement: Alleged suicide note from Austin pilot posted online." (2010, April 20). *Huffington Post*. Retrieved from http://www.huffingtonpost.com/2010/02/18/joe-stack-statement-alleg_n_467539.html.

7. Yaari, E. (2017, January 10). Smart policing: How Israel catches lone wolves. *The American Interest, 12*(5). Retrieved from https://www.the-american-interest.com/2017/01/10/how-israel-catches-lone-wolves.

8. SAIR. (2017, June 10–16). The stabbing intifada: How to spot a lone wolf. *The Economist*. Retrieved from https://www.economist.com/news/international/21723113-algorithms-monitor-social-media-posts-palestinians-how-israel-spots-lone-wolf-attackers.

9. Hewitt, C. (2003). *Understanding terrorism in America: From the Klan to al Qaeda*. New York: Routledge; Chapter 5.

10. Spaaij, R. (2012). *Understanding lone wolf terrorism: Global patterns, motivations and prevention*. New York, NY: Springer.

11. Gill, P., Horgan, J., & Deckert, P. (2013). Bombing alone: Tracing the motivations and antecedent behaviors of lone-actor terrorists. *Journal of Forensic Science, 59*(2), 425–435.

12. Gruenewald, J., Chermak, S., & Freilich, J. (2013). Distinguishing "loner" attacks from other domestic extremist violence: A comparison of far-right homicide incident and offender characteristics. *Criminology and Public Policy, 12*(1), 65–91.
13. McCauley, C., Moskalenko, S., & Van Son, B. (2013). Characteristics of lone-wolf violent offenders: A comparison of school attackers and assassins. *Perspectives on Terrorism, 7*(1), 4–24.

Chapter 8

1. https://www.nimh.nih.gov/health/statistics/suicide/index.shtml; see Figures 7–9.
2. https://www.nimh.nih.gov/health/topics/suicide-prevention/index.shtml.
3. "Chicago Project on Security and Terrorism: Suicide Attack Database." Retrieved September 6, 2017, from https://cpost.uchicago.edu.
4. Hassan, R. (2011). *Life as a weapon: The global rise of suicide bombings.* New York, NY: Routledge.
5. Merari, A. (2010). *Driven to death: Psychological and social aspects of suicide terrorism.* New York, NY: Oxford University Press.
6. Lankford, A. (2013). *The myth of martyrdom: What really drives suicide bombers, rampage shooters, and other self-destructive killers.* New York, NY: Palgrave McMillan.
7. "Chicago Project on Security and Terrorism: Suicide Attack Database." Retrieved September 6, 2017, from https://cpost.uchicago.edu.

Chapter 9

1. Moskalenko, S., & McCauley, C. (2017, August). *U.S. Muslims with radical opinions feel more alienated and depressed.* Report to the Office of University Programs, Science and Technology Directorate, US Department of Homeland Security. College Park, MD: START. Retrieved from https://www.start.umd.edu/pubs/START_CSTAB_USMuslimswithRadicalOpinionsFeelMoreAlienatedDepressed_August2017.pdf.
2. Mueller, J. (2017). *Terrorism since 9/11: The American cases.* Retrieved from https://politicalscience.osu.edu/faculty/jmueller/since.html.

3. Jasko, K., LaFree, G., & Kruglanski, A. (2016). Quest for significance and violent extremism: The case of domestic radicalization. *Political Psychology, 38*(5), 815–831.
4. Koehler, D. (2017). *Understanding radicalization: Methods, tools and programs for countering violent ext*remism. New York, NY: Routledge.
5. Graham, C. (2017, May 26). What is the anti-terror Prevent programme and why is it controversial? *The Telegraph.* Retrieved from http://www.telegraph.co.uk/news/0/ anti-terror-prevent-programme-controversial.
6. Halliday, J. (2016, March 20). Almost 4,000 people referred to UK deradicalisation scheme last year. *The Guardian.* Retrieved from https://www.theguardian.com/uk-news/2016/mar/20/almost-4000-people-were-referred-to-uk-deradicalisation-scheme-channel-last-year.
7. Open Society Justice Initiative. (2016). *Eroding trust: The UK's Prevent counter-extremism strategy in health and education.* Retrieved March 4,2019, from https://www.opensocietyfoundations.org/ reports/eroding-trust-uk-s-prevent-counter-extremism-strategy-health-and-education.
8. Bertelsen, P. (2015). Danish preventive measures and de-radicalization strategies: The Aarhus model. In W. Hofmeister (Ed.), *From desert to world cities: The new terrorism* (pp. 241–254). Singapore: Konrad-Adenauer-Stiftung.
9. Williams, M. J., Horgan, J., & Evans, W. P. (2016). *Evaluation of a multi-faceted, U.S. community-based, Muslim-led CVE program.* Report to the National Institute of Justice. Retrieved from https://www.ncjrs.gov/pdffiles1/nij/grants/249936.pdf.
10. Strom, S., Hollywood, J., Pope, M., Weintraub, G., Daye, C., & Gemeinhardt, D. (2010, October). *Building on clues: Examining successes and failures in detecting U.S. terrorist plots, 1999–2009.* Institute for Homeland Security Solutions. Retrieved December 14, 2017, from https://sites.duke.edu/ihss/files/2011/12/ Building_on_Clues_Strom.pdf.
11. Kurzman, C. (2011, February 2). *Muslim-American terrorist since 9/ 11: An accounting.* Triangle Center on Terrorism and Homeland Security. Retrieved December 14, 2017, from http://kurzman. unc.edu/files/2011/06/Kurzman_Muslim-American_Terrorism_ Since_911_An_Accounting.pdf.

12. United States Department of the Army. (2007). *U.S. Army/ Marine Corps counterinsurgency field manual* (pp. 47–51). Chicago, IL: University of Chicago Press.

13. McCarthy, N. (2017, June 7). Where U.S. troops are in the Middle East. *Foreign Affairs*. Retrieved from https://www.forbes.com/ sites/niallmccarthy/2017/06/07/qatar-hosts-largest-u-s-base-in-the-middle-east-despite-allegedly-funding-extremism-infographic/#21fc02643dc7. For map, see https://www.nytimes.com/2017/10/22/opinion/americas-forever-wars.html?_r=0.

14. Shane, S. (2015, April 23). Drone strikes reveal uncomfortable truth: U.S. is often unsure about who will die. *The New York Times*. Retrieved from https://www.nytimes.com/2015/04/24/world/asia/drone-strikes-reveal-uncomfortable-truth-us-is-often-unsure-about-who-will-die.html?_r=0.

15. Fajmonova, V., Moskalenko, S., & McCauley, C. (2017). Tracking radical opinions in polls of U.S. Muslims. *Perspectives on Terrorism, 11*(2). Retrieved from http://www.terrorismanalysts.com/pt/index.php/pot/article/view/594.

16. Mueller, J. (2012). *Terrorism since 9/11: The American cases* (p. 10). Retrieved from https://politicalscience.osu.edu/faculty/jmueller/00INTR7.PDF.

Chapter 10

1. Kohler, D. (2017). *Understanding deradicalization: Methods, tools and programs for countering violent extremism*. New York, NY: Routledge; Chapter 7.

2. Durose, M. R., Cooper, A. D., & Snyder, H. N. (2014, April). *Recidivism of prisoners released in 30 states in 2005: Patterns from 2005 to 2010*. US Department of Justice Special Report. Retrieved from https://www.bjs.gov/content/pub/pdf/rprts05p0510.pdf.

3. Speckhard, A. (2011). Prison and community-based disengagement and de-radicalization programs for extremists involved in militant jihadi terrorism ideologies and activities. In L. Fenstermacher & A. Speckhard (Eds.), *Social sciences support to military personnel engaged in counter-insurgency and counter-terrorism operations: Report of the NATO Research and Technology Group 172* (NATO Science Series)..

4. Allen, G., & Dempsey, N. (2017, October 6). *Terrorism in Great Britain: The statistics* (House of Commons Library, Briefing Paper

No. CPB7613). Retrieved from researchbriefings.files.parliament. uk/documents/CBP-7613/CBP-7613.pdf.

5. Marsden, S. V. (2017). *Reintegrating extremists: Deradicalization and desistence.* London, UK: Palgrave Macmillan.

Chapter 11

1. Anderson, B. (2006). *Imagined communities: Reflections on the origin and spread of nationalism.* New York, NY: Verso.

2. Haidt, J. (2012). *The righteous mind: Why good people are divided by politics and religion* (p. 228). New York, NY: Vintage Books.

3. Moskalenko, S., McCauley, C., & Rozin, P. (2006). Group identification under conditions of threat: College students' attachment to country, family, ethnicity, religion, and university before and after September 11, 2001. *Political Psychology, 27*(1), 77–97.

4. Cialdini, R. B., & Richardson, K. D. (1980). Two indirect tactics of image management: Basking and blasting. *Journal of Personality and Social Psychology, 39*(3), 406.

5. Pennebaker, J. W. (2011). The secret life of pronouns. *New Scientist, 211*(2828), 42–45.

6. Schachter, S. (1959). *The psychology of affiliation: Experimental studies of the sources of gregariousness.* Palo Alto, CA: Stanford University Press.

7. Hatfield, E., Cacioppo, J. T., & Rapson, R. L. (1993). Emotional contagion. *Current Directions in Psychological Science, 2*(3), 96–100.

8. Coyne, J. C. (1976). Depression and the response of others. *Journal of Abnormal Psychology, 85*(2), 186.

9. Howes, M. J., Hokanson, J. E., & Loewenstein, D. A. (1985). Induction of depressive affect after prolonged exposure to a mildly depressed individual. *Journal of Personality and Social Psychology, 49*(4), 1110.

10. Rosenquist, J. N., Fowler, J. H., & Christakis, N. A. (2011). Social network determinants of depression. *Molecular Psychiatry, 16*(3), 273.

11. Ibid.

12. Hatfield, E. C., Bensman, L., Thornton, P. D., & Rapson, R. L. (2014). New perspectives on emotional contagion: A review of classic and recent research on facial mimicry and contagion. *Interpersona, 8*(2), 159–179.

13. https://www.washingtonpost.com/news/monkey-cage/ wp/2018/11/29/how-donald-trump-appeals-to-men-secretly-insecure-about-their-manhood/?utm_term=.2fae6f274b4a.
14. Ibid.
15. Krueger, A. B., & Malečková, J. (2009). Attitudes and action: Public opinion and the occurrence of international terrorism. *Science, 325*(5947), 1534–1536.
16. Murray, M. (2017, August 23). *Twelve days that stunned the nation: How Hillary lost.* NBC News. Retrieved March 31, 2017, from https://www.nbcnews.com/politics/elections/ 12-days-stunned-nation-how-hillary-clinton-lost-n794131.
17. Silver, N. (2017, May 3). The Comey letter probably cost Clinton the election so why won't the media admit as much? *FiveThirtyEight.* Retrieved March 31, 2019, from https://fivethirtyeight.com/features/ the-comey-letter-probably-cost-clinton-the-election.
18. Robb, A. (2017, November 16). Anatomy of a fake news scandal. *Rolling Stone.* Retrieved March 31, 2019, from https://www.rollingstone.com/politics/politics-news/ anatomy-of-a-fake-news-scandal-125877.
19. Ibid.
20. Ibid.
21. Gunther, R., Beck, P. A., & Nisbet, E. C. (2018). *Fake news did have a significant impact on the vote in the 2016 election: Original full-length version with methodological appendix.* Columbus, OH: The Ohio State University. Retrieved from https://u.osu.edu/cnep/ files/2015/03/Fake-News-Piecefor-The-Conversation-with-methodological-appendix-11d0ni9. pdf.
22. Murray, M. (2017, August 23). *Twelve days that stunned the nation: How Hillary lost.* NBC News. Retrieved March 31, 2019, from https://www.nbcnews.com/politics/elections/ 12-days-stunned-nation-how-hillary-clinton-lost-n794131.
23. Ibid.
24. Jewish Telegraphic Agency. (n.d.). *50,000 Jews killed in Petlura Pogroms, Paris Court Hears.* Retrieved March 31, 2019, from https://www.jta.org/1926/07/22/archive/ 50000-jews-killed-in-petlura-pogroms-paris-court-hears.
25. Sokolovskaya, E. (2014, April 23). Peace, land, bread. *Russian Life.* Retrieved March 31, 2019, from https://russianlife.com/stories/ online/peace-land-bread.

26. Romano, A. (2008, July 30). McCain's crafty* ad strategy. *Newsweek.* Retrieved March 31, 2019, from https://www. newsweek.com/mccains-crafty-ad-strategy-219642.

27. Moskalenko, S., & McCauley, C. (2018). *The marvel of martyrdom: The power of self-sacrifice in a selfish world.* New York, NY: Oxford University Press.

28. Miller, N. K. (2004). The girl in the photograph: The Vietnam War and the making of national memory. *JAC,* 261–290.

29. Nasaw, D. (2009, September 14). US military action in Somalia: Black Hawk Down to today's attack. *The Guardian.* Retrieved March 31, 2019, from https://www.theguardian.com/ world/2009/sep/14/black-hawk-down-us-somalia.

30. Slovic, P., Västfjäll, D., Erlandsson, A., & Gregory, R. (2017). Iconic photographs and the ebb and flow of empathic response to humanitarian disasters. *Proceedings of the National Academy of Sciences of the USA, 114*(4), 640–644.

31. Ibid.

32. https://www.google.com/search?q=iconic+photo+viet+cong+sh ot+by+soldier&ie=utf-8&oe=utf-8&client=firefox-b-1-ab.

33. Speltz, M. (2016, September 22). How photographs define the civil rights and Black Lives Matter movements. *Time Magazine.* Retrieved March 31, 2019, from http://time.com/4429096/ black-lives-matter-civil-rights-photography.

34. Bytes Daily. (2011, November 23). *Iconic photographs: Kent State University.* Retrieved March 31, 2019, from http://bytesdaily. blogspot.com/2011/11/iconic-photographs-kent-state.html.

35. https://www.cnn.com/2013/09/01/world/gallery/iconic-images/index.html.

36. A boy's body on the beach radicalizes for the refugees and against nationalist efforts to keep them out. Nazi images of golden Germans in the hands of diseased communists and Jews radicalized against communists and Jews. A helpless Viet Cong executed by a South Vietnamese general radicalizes for the Viet Cong and against the South Vietnamese army. A young woman screaming over the body of a student protester shot by the National Guard radicalizes for the protesters and against the government. Police dogs attacking an unarmed protester radicalizes for the protesters and against the police. The "bags man" confronting a tank radicalizes for the protesters and against Chinese state power in Tiananmen Square. Bodies of US

soldiers dragged through the streets of Mogadishu radicalized against their "peacekeeping" mission.

37. Gorman, E. B. (2006). *Perspective by incongruity in visual advertising: Applying Kenneth Burke's theory to the Adbusters anti-consumerism campaign.* Thesis, Rochester Institute of Technology, Rochester, NY. Retrieved from https://scholarworks.rit.edu/theses/8041.

38. Stangor, C., & McMillan, D. (1992). Memory for expectancy-congruent and expectancy-incongruent information: A review of the social and social developmental literatures. *Psychological Bulletin, 111*(1), 42.

39. Maheswaran, D., & Chaiken, S. (1991). Promoting systematic processing in low-motivation settings: Effect of incongruent information on processing and judgment. *Journal of Personality and Social Psychology, 61*(1), 13.

40. Marshall, A. (2015, November 17). *Why La Marseillaise is the only song that matters right now.* BBC. Retrieved March 31, 2019, from http://www.bbc.com/culture/story/20151117-why-la-marseillaise-is-the-only-song-that-matters-right-now.

41. Ibid.

42. Spalding, N. J. (2003). Reducing anxiety by pre-operative education: Make the future familiar. *Occupational Therapy International, 10*(4), 278–293.

43. Gebauer, L., Kringelbach, M. L., & Vuust, P. (2012). Ever-changing cycles of musical pleasure: The role of dopamine and anticipation. *Psychomusicology: Music, Mind, and Brain, 22*(2), 152.

44. Pereira, C. S., Teixeira, J., Figueiredo, P., Xavier, J., Castro, S. L., & Brattico, E. (2011). Music and emotions in the brain: Familiarity matters. *PLoS One, 6*(11), e27241.

45. Heingartner, A., & Hall, J. V. (1974). Affective consequences in adults and children of repeated exposure to auditory stimuli. *Journal of Personality and Social Psychology, 29,* 719–723.

46. Orr, M. G., & Ohlsson, S. (2001). The relationship between musical complexity and liking in jazz and bluegrass. *Psychology of Music, 29,* 108–127.

47. Trost, W., Ethofer, T., Zentner, M., & Vuilleumier, P. (2011). Mapping aesthetic musical emotions in the brain. *Cerebral Cortex, 22*(12), 2769–2783.

48. https://www.youtube.com/watch?v=FN7r0Rr1Qyc.

49. Molloy, P. (2014, November 11, 2006). Are politicians too dumb to understand the lyrics to "Born in the USA"? *The Daily Beast.* Retrieved April 2, 2019, from https://www.thedailybeast.com/are-politicians-too-dumb-to-understand-the-lyrics-to-born-in-the-usa.

50. York-Wooten, K. (2008, August 1). John Mellencamp and campaign music. *Newsweek.* Retrieved April 2, 2019, from https://www.newsweek.com/john-mellencamp-and-campaign-music-87671.

51. Baer, D. (2017, January 31). People naturally sync their bodies, breathing—and skin. *The Cut.* https://www.thecut.com/2017/01/how-interpersonal-synchrony-works.html

52. Goldstein, P., Weissman-Fogel, I., Dumas, G., & Shamay-Tsoory, S. G. (2018). Brain-to-brain coupling during handholding is associated with pain reduction. *Proceedings of the National Academy of Sciences of the USA, 115*(11), E2528–E2537.

53. Liu, S., Zhou, Y., Palumbo, R., & Wang, J. L. (2016). Dynamical correlation: A new method for quantifying synchrony with multivariate intensive longitudinal data. *Psychological Methods, 21*(3), 291.

54. Cialdini, R. (2016). *Pre-suasion: A revolutionary way to influence and persuade.* New York, NY: Simon & Schuster.

55. Vickhoff, B., Malmgren, H., Åström, R., Nyberg, G., Engvall, M., Snygg, J., . . . Jörnsten, R. (2013). Music structure determines heart rate variability of singers. *Frontiers in Psychology, 4,* 334.

56. Saavedra, S., Hagerty, K., & Uzzi, B. (2011). Synchronicity, instant messaging, and performance among financial traders. *Proceedings of the National Academy of Sciences of the USA, 108*(13), 5296–5301.

57. Ibid.

58. Goldstein, P., Weissman-Fogel, I., Dumas, G., & Shamay-Tsoory, S. G. (2018). Brain-to-brain coupling during handholding is associated with pain reduction. *Proceedings of the National Academy of Sciences of the USA, 115*(11), E2528–E2537.

59. Rao, H., & Dutta, S. (2012). Free spaces as organizational weapons of the weak: Religious festivals and regimental mutinies in the 1857 Bengal Native Army. *Administrative Science Quarterly, 57*(4), 625–668.

60. Ibid.

61. Knapp, R. (1944). A psychology of rumor. *Public Opinion Quarterly, 8*(1), 22–37. Retrieved from http://www.jstor.org/stable/2745686.

62. Rosnow, R. L., Yost, J. H., & Esposito, J. L. (1986). Belief in rumor and likelihood of rumor transmission. *Language & Communication, 6*(3), 189–194.

63. Bordia, P., & Difonzo, N. (2004). Problem solving in social interactions on the internet: Rumor as a contagion. *Social Psychology Quarterly, 67*(1), 33.

64. Nasi, J. O., & Sweatland, J. (2015). *Cultivating the grapevine: An analysis of rumor principles and concepts.* Doctoral dissertation, Naval Postgraduate School, Monterey, CA.

65. Rao, H., & Dutta, S. (2012). Free spaces as organizational weapons of the weak: Religious festivals and regimental mutinies in the 1857 Bengal Native Army. *Administrative Science Quarterly, 57*(4), 625–668.

66. Moskalenko, S., & McCauley, C. (2018). *The marvel of martyrdom: The power of self-sacrifice in a selfish world.* New York, NY: Oxford University Press.

67. StopFake.org. (2014, July 15). *Fake: Crucifixion in Slavyansk.* Retrieved April 2, 2019, from https://www.stopfake.org/en/lies-crucifixion-on-channel-one.

68. Warrick, A., & Troianovski, A. (2018, December 10). Agents of doubt: How a powerful Russian propaganda machine chips away at Western notions of truth. *Washington Post.*

69. Mak, A. (2017, November 1). Here are some of the social media posts that Russia used to meddle in the 2016 election. *Slate Magazine.*

70. Meyer, J. (2018, October 1). How Russia helped swing the election for Trump. *The New Yorker.*

71. Ibid.

72. https://en.wikipedia.org/wiki/War_dance.

73. Chun, S., Gentry, J. W., & McGinnis, L. P. (2005). Ritual aspects of sports consumption: How do sports fans become ritualized? *ACR Asia-Pacific Advances, 6,* 331–336.

74. A *hopak* is an athletic Ukrainian dance, originating from the Ukrainian military, the Cossacks.

75. Vacharkulksemsuk, T., & Fredrickson, B. L. (2012). Strangers in sync: Achieving embodied rapport through shared movements. *Journal of Experimental Social Psychology, 48*(1), 399–402.

76. Reddish, P., Fischer, R., & Bulbulia, J. (2013). Let's dance together: Synchrony, shared intentionality and cooperation. *PLoS One, 8*(8), e71182.

77. Cialdini, R. (2016). *Pre-suasion: A revolutionary way to influence and persuade.* New York, NY: Simon & Schuster.
78. Wiltermuth, S. S., & Heath, C. (2009). Synchrony and cooperation. *Psychological Science, 20*(1), 1–5.
79. Ibid.
80. Belluck, P. (2011, May 2). Hearts beat as one in a daring ritual. *The New York Times.*
81. Bernhardt, P. C., Dabbs, J. M., Jr., Fielden, J. A., & Lutter, C. D. (1998). Testosterone changes during vicarious experiences of winning and losing among fans at sporting events. *Physiology & Behavior, 65*(1), 59–62.
82. Cialdini, R. B., Borden, R. J., Thorne, A., Walker, M. R., Freeman, S., & Sloan, L. R. (1976). Basking in reflected glory: Three (football) field studies. *Journal of Personality and Social Psychology, 34,* 366–375.
83. Ibid.
84. McCauley, C. (2001). The psychology of group identification and the power of ethnic nationalism. In D. Chirot & M. Seligman (Eds.), *Ethnopolitical warfare: Causes, consequences, and possible solutions* (pp. 343–362). Washington, DC: APA Books.
85. Rosenberg, E., & Ohiheiser, A. (2018, September 4). Zena Bash moved her hand, and the #Resistance saw a White power signal. Then she did it again. *Washington Post.*
86. Tajfel, H. (1970). Experiments in intergroup discrimination [Abstract]. *Scientific American, 223,* 96–102.
87. Drutman, L. (2008, December 17). Does old glory have a dark side? *Pacific Standard.*
88. Becker, J. C., Enders-Comberg, A., Wagner, U., Christ, O., & Butz, D. A. (2012). Beware of national symbols. *Social Psychology, 43*(1).
89. Hassin, R. R., Ferguson, M. J., Shidlovski, D., & Gross, T. (2007). Subliminal exposure to national flags affects political thought and behavior. *Proceedings of the National Academy of Sciences of the USA, 104*(50), 19757–19761.
90. Sibley, C. G., Hoverd, W. J., & Duckitt, J. (2011). What's in a flag? Subliminal exposure to New Zealand national symbols and the automatic activation of egalitarian versus dominance values. *Journal of Social Psychology, 151*(4), 494–516.
91. Guéguen, N., Bougeard-Delfosse, C., & Jacob, C. (2015). The positive effect of the mere presence of a religious symbol on compliance with an organ donation request. *Social Marketing Quarterly, 21*(2), 92–99.

92. Ahmed, A., & Salas, O. (2013). Religious context and prosociality: An experimental study from Valparaíso, Chile. *Journal for the Scientific Study of Religion, 52*(3), 627–637.

93. Razpurker-Apfeld, I., & Shamoa-Nir, L. (2015). The influence of exposure to religious symbols on outgroup stereotypes. *Psychology, 6*(5), 650.

94. Prentice, D. A., & Miller, D. T. (1993). Pluralistic ignorance and alcohol use on campus: Some consequences of misperceiving the social norm. *Journal of Personality and Social Psychology, 64*(2), 243–256.

95. Ibid.

96. Callahan, S. P., & Ledgerwood, A. (2016). On the psychological function of flags and logos: Group identity symbols increase perceived entitativity. *Journal of Personality and Social Psychology, 110*(4), 528.

97. Skitka, L. J. (2005). Patriotism or nationalism? Understanding post-September 11, 2001, flag-display behavior 1. *Journal of Applied Social Psychology, 35*(10), 1995–2011.

98. Allert, T. (2009). *The Hitler salute: On the meaning of a gesture.* New York, NY: Picador.

99. Benford, R. D., & Snow, D. A. (2000). Framing processes and social movements: An overview and assessment. *Annual Review of Sociology, 26*(1), 611–639.

100. Petty, R. E., & Cacioppo, J. T. (1984). The effects of involvement on responses to argument quantity and quality: Central and peripheral routes to persuasion. *Journal of Personality and Social Psychology, 46*, 69–81.

101. As mentioned previously, self-sacrifice for a mass identity defies rational choice.

102. Walsh, K. (2008, January 17). The battle cry that backfired on Howard "The Scream" Dean. *USA News and World Report.*

103. Lyons, K., & Walters, J. (2019, January 4). Ocasio-Cortez's response to jibes about college dance video? A congressional dance video. *The Guardian.*

104. This problem seems to plague the USA Democrats more than Republicans (https://www.brookings.edu/blog/order-from-chaos/2015/10/29/republicans-are-from-the-heart-democrats-are-from-the-head).

105. Williams, L. E., & Bargh, J. A. (2008). Experiencing physical warmth promotes interpersonal warmth. *Science, 322*(5901), 606–607.

106. Milgram, S. (1963). Behavioral study of obedience. *Journal of Abnormal and Social Psychology, 67*(4), 371.
107. Elliot, A. J., & Devine, P. G. (1994). On the motivational nature of cognitive dissonance: Dissonance as psychological discomfort. *Journal of Personality and Social Psychology, 67*(3), 382.
108. https://www.youtube.com/watch?v=24adApYh0yc.

Chapter 12

1. McCauley, C., & Moskalenko, S. (2011). *Friction: How conflict radicalizes us and them.* New York, NY: Oxford University Press.
2. https://www.washingtonpost.com/world/national-security/hate-crimes-rose-17-percent-last-year-according-to-new-fbi-data/2018/11/13/e0dcf13e-e754-11e8-b8dc-66cca409c180_story.html?utm_term=.ee821581e045.
3. Follman, M., Aronsen, G., & Pan, D. (2019, February 15). *US mass shootings, 1982–2019: Data from Mother Jones' investigation.* Mother Jones. Retrieved April 2, 2019, from https://www.motherjones.com/politics/2012/12/mass-shootings-mother-jones-full-data.
4. https://en.wikipedia.org/wiki/List_of_incidents_of_civil_unrest_in_the_United_States#2010–2018.
5. Barrouquere, B. (2018, November 4). *Florida man who killed two women at yoga studio spoke of "incel" hero Elliot Rodger in online video.* Southern Poverty Law Center. Retrieved from https://www.splcenter.org/hatewatch/2018/11/03/florida-man-who-killed-two-women-yoga-studio-spoke-incel-hero-elliot-rodger-online-video.
6. Hetherington, M., & Weiler, J. (2018). *Prius or pickup? How the answers to four simple questions explain America's great divide* (p. 129). Boston, MA: Houghton Mifflin.
7. League, A. D. (2016, October 19). *Anti-Semitic targeting of journalists during the 2016 presidential campaign.* Retrieved from https://www.adl.org/sites/default/files/documents/assets/pdf/press-center/CR_4862_Journalism-Task-Force_v2.pdf?_ga=1.32908478.1822026016.1481832255.
8. Romo, V. (2018, August 3). *Police end Las Vegas shooting investigation: No motive found.* NPR. Retrieved April 2, 2019, from https://www.npr.org/2018/08/03/635507299/las-vegas-shooting-investigation-closed-no-motive-found.
9. Barrouquere, B. (2018, November 4). *Florida man who killed two women at yoga studio spoke of "incel" hero Elliot Rodger in online*

video. Southern Poverty Law Center. Retrieved from https://
www.splcenter.org/hatewatch/2018/11/03/florida-man-who-
killed-two-women-yoga-studio-spoke-incel-hero-elliot-rodger-
online-video.

10. https://www.nytimes.com/2018/10/28/us/gab-robert-bowers-
pittsburgh-synagogue-shootings.html.

11. https://www.nytimes.com/2017/01/31/upshot/are-you-
married-to-your-party.html.

12. McKew, M. (2018, February 12). Did Russia affect the 2016
election? It's now undeniable. *Wired*.

13. Sidahmed, M. (2017, November 8). The night they can't
forget: Hillary Clinton supporters recall the election. *The
Guardian*. Retrieved April 2, 2019, from https://www.
theguardian.com/us-news/2017/nov/07/the-night-they-cant-
forget-hillary-clinton-supporters-recall-the-election.

14. Cillizza, C. (2018, November 2). *Donald Trump didn't tell the truth
83 times in 1 day*. CNN. Retrieved April 2, 2019, from https://
www.cnn.com/2018/11/02/politics/donald-trump-lies/index.
html.

15. Cillizza, C. (2018, August 28). *Donald Trump thinks 52% of
Americans approve of the job he's doing: They don't*. CNN. Retrieved
April 2, 2019, from https://www.cnn.com/2018/08/27/politics/
donald-trump-poll-fake/index.html.

16. Watson, E. C. (2018, November 5). *Trump cites fake poll claiming
African-American approval rating increase*. OkayPlayer. Retrieved
April 2, 2019, from https://www.okayplayer.com/news/trump-
fake-poll-fox-black-approval-rating.html.

17. https://www.nytimes.com/2019/01/25/us/politics/trump-
shutdown-border-wall-fact-check.html.

18. Borick, C., Rabe, B., Fitzpatrick, N., & Mills, S. (2018). *Issues in
energy and environmental policy*. University of Michigan. Retrieved
from http://closup.umich.edu/files/ieep-nsee-2018-spring-
climate-belief.pdf.

19. Leviston, Z., Walker, I., & Morwinski, S. (2013). Your opinion on
climate change might not be as common as you think. *Nature
Climate Change, 3*(4), 334.

20. Bennetts, M. (2016, August 21). 25th anniversary of
Soviet coup met with hostility, indifference in Russia. *The
Washington Times*. Retrieved April 2, 2019, from https://

www.washingtontimes.com/news/2016/aug/21/
1991-soviet-coup-25th-anniversary-met-with-hostili.

21. Brown, R. (1965). *Social psychology*. New York, NY: Free Press.

22. Rothschild, D., & Malhotra, N. (2014, September 22). Are public opinion polls self-fulfilling prophecies? *Research & Politics*.

23. Henshel, R. L., & Johnston, W. (1987). The emergence of bandwagon effects: A theory. *Sociological Quarterly, 28*(4), 493–511.

24. Broida, R. (2019, March 4). *How to spot fake reviews on Amazon, Best Buy, Walmart and other sites.* CNet.com. Retrieved April 2, 2019, from https://www.cnet.com/how-to/spot-fake-amazon-reviews-with-fakespot.

25. Egebark, J., & Ekstrom, M. (2011, October 14). *Like what you like or like what others like? Conformity and peer effects on Facebook.* Retrieved from http://www2.ne.su.se/paper/wp11_27.pdf.

26. McCauley, T. (2015). The war of ideas on the internet: An asymmetric conflict in which the strong become weak, *Dynamics of Asymmetric Conflict, 8*(1), 79–90.

27. Romm, T., & Wagner, K. (2017, October 30). *Facebook says 126 million people in the U.S. may have seen posts produced by Russian-government-backed agents.* Vox. Accessed April 3, 2019, from https://www.recode.net/2017/10/30/16571598/read-full-testimony-facebook-twitter-google-congress-russia-election-fake-news.

28. https://www.washingtonpost.com/technology/2018/12/16/new-report-russian-disinformation-prepared-senate-shows-operations-scale-sweep.

29. Ibid.

30. NBC News. (2018, November 5). *NBC News Signal presents factory of lies: Democracy under attack.* Retrieved April 2, 2019, from https://www.nbcnews.com/video/nbc-news-signal-presents-factory-of-lies-democracy-under-attack-1362496579619?v=raila&.

31. Glenza, J. (2018, August 23). Russian trolls "spreading discord" over vaccine safety online. *The Guardian.* Retrieved April 2, 2019, from https://www.google.com/amp/s/amp.theguardian.com/society/2018/aug/23/russian-trolls-spread-vaccine-misinformation-on-twitter.

32. Roeder, O. (2018, July 31). *Why we're sharing 3 million Russian troll tweets.* FiveThirtyEight. Retrieved April 3, 2019, from https://fivethirtyeight.com/features/why-were-sharing-3-million-russian-troll-tweets/?ex_cid=538twitter.

33. Poulsen, K. (2018, October 31). *Americans are easy Marks for Russian trolls, according to new data*. The Daily Beast. Retrieved April 3, 2019, from https://www.thedailybeast.com/americans-are-easy-marks-for-russian-trolls-new-data-prove.

34. Prigg, M. (2017, December 22). Did YOU fall for a Russian propaganda post? Facebook releases tool to tell people if they engaged with controversial "internet research agency" accounts. *The Daily Mail*. Retrieved April 3, 2019, from https://www.dailymail.co.uk/sciencetech/article-5207017/Did-fall-Russian-propaganda-Facebook-tell-you.html.

35. Volkov, D. (2015). *Supporting a war that isn't: Russian public opinion and the Ukraine conflict*. Carnegie Moscow Center. Retrieved from https://carnegie.ru/commentary/61236.

36. Haidt, J., Seder, P. J., & Kesebir, S. (2008). Hive psychology, happiness, and public policy. *Journal of Legal Studies, 37*(S2), S133–S156.

37. Statista. (2017). *Population density of the United States from 1790 to 2017 in residents per square mile of land area*. Retrieved April 3, 2019, from https://www.statista.com/statistics/183475/united-states-population-density.

38. World Atlas. (2017). *European countries by population density*. Retrieved April 3, 2019, from https://www.worldatlas.com/articles/european-countries-by-population-density.html.

39. Russonello, B., & Stewart, L. L. C. (2011). *The 2011 Community Preference Survey: What Americans are looking for when deciding where to live*. Opinion Research Strategic Communication. http://www.trb.org/Main/Blurbs/165146.aspx

40. Cox, W. (2008). America is more small town than we think. *New Geography, 9*.

41. https://en.wikipedia.org/wiki/Housing_in_Europe.

42. Buehler, R. (2014). *9 Reasons the US ended up so much more car-dependent than Europe*. City Lab. Retrieved July 12, 2016, from https://www.citylab.com/transportation/2014/02/9-reasons-us-ended-so-much-more-car-dependent-europe/8226.

43. Isidore, C., & Luhby, T. (2015, July 9). Turns out Americans work really hard . . . but some want to work harder. *CNN Money*. Retrieved from https://money.cnn.com/2015/07/09/news/economy/americans-work-bush/index.html.

44. DeAngelis, T. (2007). America: A toxic lifestyle. *Monitor on Psychology, 38*(4), 51.

45. Cigna. (2018). *Cigna 2018 U.S. loneliness index*. Retrieved April 3, 2019, from https://www.cigna.com/assets/docs/newsroom/loneliness-survey-2018-fact-sheet.pdf.

46. Euronews. (2017). *Which is Europe's loneliest country?* Retrieved April 3, 2019, from https://www.euronews.com/2017/06/29/what-is-europes-loneliest-country.

47. McPherson, M., Smith-Lovin, L., & Brashears, M. E. (2006). Social isolation in America: Changes in core discussion networks over two decades. *American Sociological Review, 71*(3), 353–375.

48. Ibid.

49. Latane, B., Liu, J. H., Nowak, A., Bonevento, M., & Zheng, L. (1995). Distance matters: Physical space and social impact. *Personality and Social Psychology Bulletin, 21*(8), 795–805.

50. McPherson, M., Smith-Lovin, L., & Brashears, M. E. (2006). Social isolation in America: Changes in core discussion networks over two decades. *American Sociological Review, 71*(3), 353–375.

51. Whaite, E. O., Shensa, A., Sidani, J. E., Colditz, J. B., & Primack, B. A. (2018). Social media use, personality characteristics, and social isolation among young adults in the United States. *Personality and Individual Differences, 124*, 45–50.

52. Morin, A. (2018, June 18). Loneliness is as lethal as smoking 15 cigarettes per day. *Inc.* Retrieved April 3, 2019, from https://www.inc.com/amy-morin/americas-loneliness-epidemic-is-more-lethal-than-smoking-heres-what-you-can-do-to-combat-isolation.html.

53. The Conversation. (2014, June 25). *Suicide rates and World Cup results: beyond the numbers game*. Retrieved April 3, 2019, from https://theconversation.com/suicide-rates-and-world-cup-results-beyond-the-numbers-game-28114.

54. Andriessen, K., & Krysinska, K. (2009). Can sports events affect suicidal behavior? A review of the literature and implications for prevention. *Crisis, 30*(3), 144–152.

55. Keenan, A. (2018, December 18). Facebook refused to hand over location data on users who engaged with Russian trolls: Study author. *Yahoo! Finance*. Retrieved April 3, 2019, from https://finance.yahoo.com/news/facebook-refused-hand-over-data-145644301.html.

56. Business Insider. (2019). *People in Chengdu, China will be able to walk anywhere in 15 minutes or less*. Retrieved April 3, 2019, from https://www.businessinsider.com/cities-going-car-free-ban-2017-8#people-in-chengdu-china-will-be-able-to-walk-anywhere-in-15-minutes-or-less-3.

Chapter 13

1. Gade, E. K., Hafez, M. M., & Gabbay, M. (2019). Fratricide in rebel movements: A network analysis of Syrian militant infighting. *Journal of Peace Research*. Retrieved from https://journals. sagepub.com/doi/abs/10.1177/0022343318806940.

2. Mosher, D., & Gould, S. (2017, January 31). How likely are foreign terrorists to kill Americans? The odds may surprise you. *Business Insider*. Retrieved April 3, 2019, from http://www.businessinsider.com/ death-risk-statistics-terrorism-disease-accidents-2017-1.

3. Reuters. (2007, May 5). *Qaeda's Zawahiri says Iraq bill shows U.S. defeat*. Retrieved from http://www.reuters.com/article/ 2007/05/06/us-qaeda-zawahri-idUSN0529849520070506.

4. CNN. (2004). *Bin Laden tape*. Retrieved April 3, 2019, from https://www.cnn.com/2010/US/01/24/bin.laden.terror.tape/ index.html

FURTHER READING

Chapter 1

Horgan, J. (2008). From profiles to pathways and roots to routes: Perspectives from psychology on radicalization into terrorism. *Annals of the American Academy of Political and Social Science, 618*(1), 80–94.

McCauley, C., & Moskalenko, S. (2011). *Friction: How radicalization happens to them and us.* New York, NY: Oxford University Press.

Chapter 2

Horgan, J. G., & Horgan, J. (2004). *The psychology of terrorism.* New York, NY: Routledge.

Merari, A. (2010). *Driven to death: Psychological and social aspects of suicide terrorism.* New York, NY: Oxford University Press.

Sageman, M. (2004). *Understanding terror networks.* Philadelphia, PA: University of Pennsylvania Press.

Chapter 3

Hoffman, B. (2006). *Inside terrorism* (2nd ed.). New York, NY: Columbia University Press.

McCauley, C., & Moskalenko, S. (2016). *Friction: How conflict radicalizes them and us* (Rev. ed.). New York, NY: Oxford University Press. (Chapters 2–4)

Shaffer, R. (2017). *Joby Warrick. Black flags: The rise of ISIS.* New York, NY: Doubleday.

Chapter 4

Carson, J. V. (2016). Left-wing terrorism: From anarchists to the radical environmental movement and back. In G. LaFree & J. D. Freilich (Eds.), *The handbook of the criminology of terrorism* (pp. 310–322). Malden, MA: Wiley-Blackwell.

McCauley, C., & Moskalenko, S. (2016). *Friction: How conflict radicalizes them and us* (Rev. ed.). New York, NY: Oxford University Press. (Chapters 4–6)

Sageman, M. (2004). *Understanding terror networks*. Philadelphia, PA: University of Pennsylvania Press.

Chapter 5

Chirot, D., & McCauley, C. (2006). *Why not kill them all? The logic and prevention of mass political murder*. Princeton, NJ: Princeton University Press.

Leuprecht, C., Hataley, T., Moskalenko, S., & McCauley, C. (2010a). Containing the narrative: Strategy and tactics in countering the storyline of global jihad. *Journal of Policing, Intelligence and Counter Terrorism, 5*(1), 42–57.

Leuprecht, C., Hataley, T., Moskalenko, S., & McCauley, C. (2010b). Winning the battle but losing the war? Narrative and counter-narratives strategy. *Perspectives on Terrorism, 3*(2), 25–35.

McCauley, C. (2017). Toward a psychology of humiliation in asymmetric conflict. *American Psychologist, 72*(3), 255.

McCauley, C., & Moskalenko, S. (2011). *Friction: How radicalization happens to them and us*. New York, NY: Oxford University Press.

Chapter 7

Gill, P., Horgan, J., & Deckert, P. (2014). Bombing alone: Tracing the motivations and antecedent behaviors of lone-actor terrorists. *Journal of Forensic Sciences, 59*(2), 425–435.

McCauley, C., & Moskalenko, S. (2014). Toward a profile of lone wolf terrorists: What moves an individual from radical opinion to radical action? *Terrorism and Political Violence, 26*(1), 69–85.

McCauley, C., Moskalenko, S., & Van Son, B. (2013). Characteristics of lone-wolf violent offenders: A comparison of assassins and school attackers. *Perspectives on Terrorism, 7*(1), 4–24.

Moskalenko, C., & McCauley, C. (2011). The psychology of lone-wolf terrorism. *Counseling Psychology Quarterly, 24*(2), 115–126.

Chapter 8

Bloom, M. (2005). *Dying to kill: The allure of suicide terror*. New York, NY: Columbia University Press.

McCauley, C. (2014). How many suicide terrorists are suicidal? *Behavioral and Brain Sciences, 37*(4), 373–374.

McCauley, C., Moskalenko, S., & Van Son, B. (2013). Characteristics of lone-wolf violent offenders: A comparison of assassins and school attackers. *Perspectives on Terrorism, 7*(1), 4–24.

McCauley, C., & Segal, M. (1987). Social psychology of terrorist groups. In C. Hendrick (Ed.), *Review of personality and social psychology* (Vol. 9, pp. 231–256). Beverly Hills, CA: Sage.

Moskalenko, S. (2013). Review of Adam Lankford: The myth of martyrdom. *Terrorism and Political Violence, 9*, 840–843.

Seifert, K., & McCauley, C. (2014). Suicide bombers in Iraq, 2003–2010: Disaggregating targets can reveal insurgent motives and priorities. *Terrorism and Political Violence, 26*(5), 803–820.

Chapter 9

Coolsaet, R. (2017). *Anticipating the post-Daesh landscape* (Paper No. 97). Brussels, Belgium: Egmont: Royal Institute for International Relations. Retrieved from https://biblio.ugent.be/publication/8532931

McCauley, C. (2017). Constructing terrorism: From fear and coercion to anger and jujitsu politics. In M. Stohl, R. Burchill, & S. Englund (Eds.), *Constructions of terrorism: An interdisciplinary approach to research and policy* (pp. 79–90). Oakland, CA: University of California Press.

McCauley, C., & Moskalenko, S. (2015). Western Muslims volunteering to fight in Syria and Iraq: Why do they go, and what should we do? *Freedom from Fear Magazine*, Issue 11. Retrieved from http://f3magazine.unicri.it/?p=1073

Chapter 10

Hwang, J. C. (2018). *Why terrorists quit: The disengagement of Indonesian jihadists*. Ithaca, NY: Cornell University Press.

Kohler, D. (2017). *Understanding deradicalization: Methods, tools and programs for countering violent extremism*. New York, NY: Routledge.

Marsden, S. V. (2017). *Reintegrating extremists: Deradicalization and desistence*. London, UK: Palgrave Macmillan.

McCauley, C. (2011). Group desistence from terrorism: The dynamics of actors, actions, and outcomes. In R. Coolsaet (Ed.), *Jihadi terrorism and the radicalisation challenge: European and American experiences* (2nd ed., pp. 187–204). Burlington, VT: Ashgate.

Chapter 11

Allert, T. (2009). *The Hitler salute: On the meaning of a gesture.* New York, NY: Picador.

Cialdini, R. (2016). *Pre-suasion: A revolutionary way to influence and persuade.* New York, NY: Simon & Schuster.

Petty, R. E., & Cacioppo, J. T. (1984). The effects of involvement on responses to argument quantity and quality: Central and peripheral routes to persuasion. *Journal of Personality and Social Psychology, 46,* 69–81.

von Scheve, C., & Salmella, M. (Eds.). (2014). *Collective emotions.* New York, NY: Oxford University Press.

Chapter 12

Jamieson, K. H. (2018). *Cyberwar: How Russian hackers and trolls helped elect a president—What we don't, can't, and do know.* New York, NY: Oxford University Press.

Putnam, R. D. (2001). *Bowling alone: The collapse and revival of American community.* New York, NY: Simon & Schuster.

Chapter 13

Aly, A., Taylor, E., & Karnovsky, S. (2014). Moral disengagement and building resilience to violent extremism: An education intervention. *Studies in Conflict & Terrorism, 37*(4), 369–385.

Awan, A. N., Hoskins, A., & O'Loughlin, B. (2011). *Radicalization and media: Connectivity and terrorism in the new media ecology.* London, UK: Routledge.

Huey, L. (2015). This is not your mother's terrorism: Social media, online radicalization and the practice of political jamming. *Journal of Terrorism Research, 6*(2), 1–16.

Rohan, G., & Salim, M. N. (2013). *Countering extremism: Building social resilience through community engagement* (Vol. 1). Singapore: World Scientific.

INDEX

Page references to tables are indicated by *t's*.
For the benefit of digital users, indexed terms that span two pages (e.g., 52–53) may, on occasion, appear on only one of those pages.